GOD
loves YOU

And There's Nothing You Can Do About It!

PHILLIP TREAT

Phillip and his grandson, Jordan, heading into worship services.

"The greatest gift we can give this world is to plant the seed of faith in future generations."

PHILLIP TREAT

CONTENTS

SECTION TWO: OUR LOVE FOR GOD

SECTION THREE: OUR LOVE FOR OTHERS

FOREWORD

Phillip Treat is faithful and resilient. His words in this book do not represent an idea of faith, but a lived faith, one that has walked through storms, valleys, and seasons that would have tempted many to give up. As his son, I've had a front-row seat to a man who chooses God not just in the high moments but in the quiet, hidden ones.

I have been in ministry for my entire adult life, and that calling was shaped directly by the way I watched my father follow Jesus with conviction and humility. Many of the moments he describes in this book are ones I witnessed firsthand, times when he stood at a crossroads and once again chose to trust God. His faith has never been perfect, and he would be the first to admit that. But I learned as much from his questions and struggles as from his victories, because he walked through them with honesty and courage.

I remember the day I found out I had been cut from the basketball team in tryouts in sixth grade. My father had played basketball all the way through college, and I knew how excited he was for me to follow in his footsteps. A part of the feeling I had about being cut that day was that I had let him down. However, I remember so vividly my dad taking me to get ice cream, buying me a gift, and continually telling me how proud of me he was and how much God loved me. He was and is a good dad to me, because he is continually learning from the Father of all mankind.

What has always marked my father is a unique blend of wisdom and humility. He disciplined me when I needed it, encouraged me when I doubted myself, and listened (truly listened) even when I was the one who still had so much to learn. He cares about people deeply, and he's genuinely curious about the insights and experiences others carry.

This is not a linear book with a tidy beginning and end. It is a book of reflections full of moments, memories, and insights that reveal the heart of a man who has tried, day after day, to walk faithfully with

God. These pages capture the same wisdom that has shaped me, and I believe they will bless you in the same way they have blessed so many who have crossed his path.

My prayer is that as you read, you will sense the sincerity of his faith, the depth of his journey, and the hope he continually finds in the Lord.

~Brandyn Treat

PREFACE

In 1772, John Newton wrote the poem "Amazing Grace" for his New Year's Day sermon. Well over 250 years later, as we sing the song, it still penetrates our hearts as if it were written yesterday. Why? Because the message is true. Grace is amazing. Grace is the greatest gift from God. It is something we cannot purchase or earn. It is something we are so undeserving of, yet God continues to offer it to all people.

David was an adulterer and a murderer. But we know him as a man after God's own heart. How can this be? Grace!

A woman, who was caught in the act of adultery, was thrown at the feet of Jesus. A mob had gathered around with rocks in their hands, ready to end her life. Yet she walked away forgiven. How can this be? Grace!

Peter had just told Jesus that he would die for Him. Yet when pressed, Peter denied even knowing Jesus. Later, Peter stood and preached the first gospel sermon, and the church was born that day. How can this be? Grace!

Paul was a man who stood opposed to Jesus and punished anyone who believed in Him. Yet Paul became the greatest missionary and writer this world has ever seen. How can this be? Grace!

And now, what about you? What sins have you committed? How have you hurt God? Yet there is absolutely nothing you have done that will exclude you from the gift of grace being extended to you.

"He has saved us and called us to a holy life—not because of anything we have done but because of his own purpose and grace. This grace was given us in Christ Jesus before the beginning of time" (2 Timothy 1:9).

God loves you! And there is nothing you can do about that.

INTRODUCTION

Every Thursday morning I sit at my desk and type some words of encouragement to be given to the congregation when they arrive for worship on Sunday. This book is a compilation of seven years of those writings. As I revisited each of these articles I found four distinct themes: God's great love for us, our love for God, our love for others and our love for ourselves. These are the basic principles of Christianity. It begins with God's love for us. God loves each of us individually before we were even born. His love never wavers as we stumble through our lives. We should respond to God's love by loving Him. God's love is then made complete in us when we love others. But we can't truly love others if we do not love ourselves.

Here is the undeniable truth that I hope to express to you through this book, God loves you and there is nothing you can do about that. We have given God every reason to stop loving us, but He continues to love us anyway.

Adam and Eve learned this in the Garden of Eden. They broke the one and only rule that God gave them. Yes, they had to face consequences for their disobedience. But God continued to love them and bless them.

Abraham and Sarah learned this when they doubted the promise of God. Not only did God keep His promise, He continued to walk with them throughout the rest of their lives.

Moses learned this after he murdered a man and went into hiding for forty years. God not only continued to love him, Moses became the spokesperson for God and the leader of God's people.

David learned this after he was guilty of adultery and murder. David would later say that not only does the Lord delight in him, but the Lord turned his darkness into light.

Peter learned this after denying knowing Jesus three times on the morning of His crucifixion. Peter would be restored and become a key player in the beginning of the church.

The apostle Paul learned this after persecuting believers in Jesus. Paul received forgiveness for his past and became the greatest missionary this world has ever seen.

And I have learned that God loves me and there is nothing I can do about that. After living in rebellion to God for nearly four years He saved me and called me into ministry. Many times since then I have failed as a husband, father, minister, and friend and in my personal life. But God's love is constantly there. When I turn to Him I find forgiveness and strength.

That same love is there for you as well. No matter how much you have rebelled against God, no matter how far you have wandered away from God, no matter how much you have hurt others, no matter how heinous your sins have been, God continues to love you. There is nothing you can do that will change that fact.

I hope you will be blessed by the short devotionals in this book as I share some biblical stories, some moments in my personal life and some happenings in this world. God loves you and there is nothing you can do about that.

SECTION ONE:

GOD'S *love* FOR US

1. GRACE IS A BEAUTIFUL THING

Our first granddaughter entered this world early Tuesday morning. Mom and baby are doing great and went home Wednesday. Baby Joanna was greeted by her two big brothers, who were so excited. Her oldest brother, Judah (five years old), told her, "You're going to be a beautiful girl when you grow up." And Jordan (three years old) told his baby sister, "When you grow up as a kid, we will love you." If that doesn't warm your heart, you may need to check to make sure you have a pulse.

Our daughter Tori and her husband Ross chose the name Joanna Grace. The name Joanna means "God is gracious." Tori told us that her full name means "grace upon grace." I must admit that I had to go back to the book of Luke to remind myself who Joanna was in the Bible. Joanna was the wife of Chuza, who was the manager of Herod Antipas's household estate. She was healed by Jesus and along with some other women, traveled with Jesus and His disciples from town to town, supporting them from their own means. Joanna was also one of the women who was at the empty tomb early on Sunday morning. She was one of the women who first reported the empty tomb to the disciples. That means she was one of the first people ever to share the message of the risen Savior!

We are blessed to have Joanna in our lives. Yes, I am talking about my granddaughter. But we are all blessed to have the grace of God extended to each of us. Now, more than ever, I am convinced that grace is a beautiful thing.

"All this is for your benefit, so that the grace that is reaching more and more people may cause thanksgiving to overflow to the glory of God" (2 Corinthians 4:15).

2. LESSONS FROM 2020

If you are reading this, you have made it through 2020. It was a year full of challenges and surprises. We have all had our lives and our plans altered in some way. We had to adjust and adapt to the ever-changing conditions. Here are three lessons that 2020 reminded me of that I need to take with me into the year 2021.

First lesson: This life is difficult. This is true for everyone, from the richest to the poorest, from the smartest to the simplest, from the strongest to the weakest, and from the righteous to the unrighteous. Jesus let us know that this world would have challenges for all of us.

"I have told you these things, so that in me you may have peace. In this world you will have trouble. But take heart! I have overcome the world" (John 16:33).

"Therefore do not worry about tomorrow, for tomorrow will worry about itself. Each day has enough trouble of its own" (Matthew 6:34).

Second lesson: We need each other. This year, we were told to quarantine at home and practice social distancing. Our gathering places, including church buildings, had to close their doors. We now hesitate to give handshakes or hugs. This isolation has hurt what it means to be a member of the Lord's church.

"And let us consider how we may spur one another on toward love and good deeds, not giving up meeting together, as some are in the habit of doing, but encouraging one another—and all the more as you see the Day approaching" (Hebrews 10:24-25).

Third lesson: God is with us. We may have to spend some time isolated from each other, but we are never isolated from God. He is with us at all times.

Yet I am always with you; you hold me by my right hand. You guide me with your counsel, and afterward you will take me into glory. Psalm 73:23-24

What will the upcoming year hold in store for us? If history tells us anything, this next year will be full of good times, bad times, challenges, and victories. Keep God with you every step of the way.

3. SEEING OTHERS THROUGH THE EYES OF GOD

I am an Okie from Muskogee. Literally! I was born at the Muskogee General Hospital. And as Merle Haggard said, "I'm proud to be an Okie from Muskogee." However, being an Okie comes with several stereotypes. Let me clear up a few. No, not everyone from Oklahoma is from a Native American tribe. Yes, most of us will stand on the porch and watch for tornadoes rather than taking shelter. No, we don't all live in trailer parks. Yes, most of us think the Oklahoma Sooners are the greatest, regardless of how many wins and losses they have. And no, we don't want to hear that the name "Sooner" basically means "criminal."

But Oklahoma is not the only place that suffers from stereotypes. People from New York are all rude. Alaskans all live in igloos. People from the West Coast are all liberal hippies. People from Boston have worse accents than people from Texas. There actually may be a little truth to that one. We know these are not true, but they shape how some people think. And the church is not immune to stereotypes. We put labels on people like liberal, conservative, progressive, or traditional. We stereotype people by the clothes they wear, the hair on their head or their face, the amount of makeup they apply, or if they have tattoos. I'm thankful that God sees us differently than we see each other.

"For God does not show favoritism" (Romans 2:11).

God sees each of us as individuals. We are not judged or loved because of where we are from, our heritage, or our outward appearance. God created each of us to look different and have our own unique likes, dislikes, and personalities. But God created each of us with a heart that has the potential to love Him and love others. We are all created in the image of God. May we all see ourselves and others through the eyes of our creator.

4. HINGE POINTS

At fifty-eight years of age, I can look back on my life and see two undeniable points where my life dramatically changed direction. The first one was my sixteenth birthday. Turning sixteen is supposed to be one of those big birthdays in life. Not only can you drive, but you also start to feel like an adult. My sixteenth birthday started with me going to school to take a test during first period. Then my sister picked me up to take me to the Oklahoma City courthouse for my parents' divorce hearing. The judge took me back into his chambers and asked me who I preferred to live with, my mother or my father. My sister and I left the courthouse and got some lunch. She took me to the DMV, and I got my driver's license. Then she took me back to school for basketball practice. After practice, a friend gave me a ride to my newly broken home. It was then that my life began to spiral out of control. I became a person who I am ashamed of today.

Fast forward four years to my second hinge point. I was sitting in the Dean's office at a Christian college, waiting to find out if I was being kicked out of school and sent back home. By their rules, my actions were completely deserving of expulsion. Before the Dean entered, I had a heart-to-heart moment with God. I confessed to God that I had driven my life off the road and into the ditch by my actions and my attitude. Then I committed to God that, regardless of the Dean's decision, I was truly going to make Him the Lord of my life. Fortunately, I was able to stay in school. Since that day, I have not lived perfectly, but I have lived committed.

What I now realize is that these two hinge points were not about the events that occurred in my life. They were about the decisions that I freely chose to make.

"But if serving the Lord seems undesirable to you, then choose for yourselves this day whom you will serve, whether the gods your ancestors served beyond the Euphrates, or the gods of the

Amorites, in whose land you are living. But as for me and my household, we will serve the Lord" (Joshua 24:15).

We can use events in our lives as excuses for our mistakes. The truth is that it all comes down to the choices we make. We can choose to follow God, or we can choose to live for ourselves, playing the victim card. God has done all He can to save you. Now the choice is yours.

5. THE GOSPEL MESSAGE

Close your eyes for a second and picture a peacock. Did you do it? I believe I can safely guess that everyone pictured a beautiful plumage of iridescent colors. If that guess is true, then everyone pictured a male peacock. Have you ever seen a female peacock? (Actually, they are called peahens.) They are either brown or gray, with no other coloration. Why the big difference? The peacock (male) uses his outward appearance to attract females.

When it comes to religion, most people have the same mindset as the peacock. We feel our outward appearance is the most important. That what most really matters is our appearance, our attendance, our good deeds, our contribution, etc. That is the peacock mindset. My plumage is my value.

In all honesty, that is true about religion. But what God wants from us is a relationship. How we look, going to worship services, serving others, and giving to the church are all great things. But they are all the externals. God wants to connect with us on a heart level.

In the time that Jesus lived among us, who were the peacocks? They were the religious leaders. They dressed the part, they prayed so others could see them, they blew trumpets when they made their contributions to the Temple so everyone could see how much they were putting into the offering plate. Who were the peahens? They were the shepherds, the tax collectors, the widows, the lepers, the blind, the lame, and the sinners. Who was Jesus attracted to? Jesus was unimpressed with the plumage of the religious leaders. But Jesus was drawn to those who were downtrodden, overlooked, or forgotten.

The simple message of the gospel is that our best isn't good enough and our worst doesn't disqualify us. Jesus gave His life so we wouldn't have to prove ourselves anymore. Yesterday's successes aren't enough to get us in, and today's failures aren't enough to keep us out.

"For it is by grace you have been saved, through faith—and this is not from yourselves, it is the gift of God—not by works, so that no one can boast" (Ephesians 2:8-9).

6. BAD NEWS SANDWICH

One of my favorite titles given to Jesus is "Prince of Peace." The title was given by the prophet Isaiah. The name seems to make sense. God is love, and He sent His Son into the world to bring eternal salvation. It sure sounds like a mission of peace. That is, until you read the gospels. As Jesus entered the world as an infant, Herod sought to kill Him. At one time in His life, the people took Jesus to the edge of a cliff, planning to throw Him off. His disciples would argue over which one of them was the greatest, and they never really understood when Jesus spoke about his death and resurrection. You could also say that Jesus was estranged from His family. Add to all of that, the religious leaders of the day constantly tried to trap Him. They accused Him of awful things, they lied about Him and persuaded the Romans to sentence Him to death. Then there was the mocking, spitting, beating, and the crucifixion. Does that sound like the life of the Prince of Peace?

"I have told you these things, so that in me you may have peace. In this world you will have trouble. But take heart! I have overcome the world" (John 16:33).

These are the words Jesus spoke to His disciples. It's what I call a "bad news sandwich." That is bad news sandwiched between good news. The bad news: You will have trouble in this world. The good news: You can have peace because Jesus has overcome the world. This message is true for us as well. During our lifetime, we will all have troubles. Sometimes it seems like that is all we have. But listen to the words of Jesus. In the midst of our troubles, we can still have peace. How? Because Jesus has overcome the world.

So, when trouble comes, remember that this world is only temporary. Look to Jesus. Then sit down and have a sandwich.

7. YOU WANNA HAVE A CATCH?

One of my all-time favorite movies is "Field of Dreams." SPOILER ALERT! I feel like I have to say this, even though the movie is over thirty years old: The movie centers around a struggling Iowa corn farmer named Ray Kinsella. Not only is he struggling financially, but he is also struggling mentally because of his troubled relationship with his father. As a teenager, Ray did not get along with his father. The only thing they had in common was their love for baseball. Their relationship ended when Ray refused to play catch with his father. They exchanged harsh words and never spoke again. Ray's father died before they could make amends.

One day in the cornfield, Ray hears a voice that says, "If you build it, he will come." He goes from confused, to scared, to angry before he decides to plow under his corn crop and build a baseball field. The movie takes several twists and turns, including deceased baseball players walking out of the corn to play baseball on the field, a trip to Boston to attend a Red Sox game with a recluse author name Terrence Mann, a trip to Minnesota, where he has an encounter with deceased doctor who played one inning of professional baseball, Ray's daughter almost choking to death, and through it all, the bank begins the foreclosure process to take his farm.

The first time I watched the movie, I knew nothing about the plot or the outcome. I was wrapped up in every moment, not sure what would happen next. That is what makes a great movie—the unpredictability of each scene that leaves the viewer on edge. One person who is never on edge about the outcome is the director. The director sees each scene in light of the whole story. When God looks at our lives, it's like He is sitting in the director's chair. He is never nervous about our future or our past because He knows how the story will end. We get stressed and troubled at every problem we face, but the director knows these events are only setting up the best part.

"Do not let your hearts be troubled. You believe in God; believe also in me. My Father's house has many rooms; if that were not so, would I have told you that I am going there to prepare a place for you? And if I go and prepare a place for you, I will come back and take you to be with me that you also may be where I am"
(John 14:1-3).

At the end of "Field of Dreams," we see Ray Kinsella playing a game of catch with his father and healing all the hurt that was in his heart. As a Christian, that is how our eternity will end—just spending time with our Heavenly Father. We may not understand every scene in our lives. All we can do is trust the director. THE END

8. WHAT'S MY NAME?

As I was growing up, I was confused about my middle name. My full name is Phillip Scott Treat. The reason I was confused was because of what I heard more often than Phillip Scott. I thought my middle name was "STOP." If I was bouncing a ball in the house, my mom would say, "Phillip, stop." If I was playing music too loud, I would hear, "Phillip, stop." If I was asking too many questions, I was told, "Phillip, stop." Rarely did hearing "Phillip, stop" ever actually make me stop. However, if I heard my mom say, "Phillip Scott," that would stop me in my tracks. When you hear an authority figure call you by name, it gets your attention. This is not true just of mothers. When a teacher, a coach, or a police officer calls you by name, you tend to stop and listen. Why? Because it means not only do they know you, but they also have something to say.

"Now this is what the Lord says. He created you, people of Jacob; he formed you, people of Israel. He says, "Don't be afraid, because I have saved you. I have called you by name, and you are mine" (Isaiah 43:1).

What an awesome thought that the creator of all things knows my name. Out of the billions of people that have ever lived, God knows me. Not only does God know our proper names, He has some other names that He calls us by:

- Child of God (John 1:12)
- Friend (John 15:15)
- Justified (Romans 3:24)
- Accepted (Romans 15:7)
- Heir (Galatians 4:7)
- Righteousness (2 Corinthians 5:21)
- Free (Galatians 5:1)

- Blessed (Ephesians 1:3)
- New creation (2 Corinthians 5:17)
- Chosen (Ephesians 1:4)
- Redeemed (Ephesians 1:7)
- God's handiwork (Ephesians 2:10)
- Citizen in heaven (Philippians 3:20)
- Temple of the Holy Spirit (1 Corinthians 6:19)

Those are some names that will definitely make Phillip stop and listen.

9. TRUST THE BUILDER

When I turn on my TV, it can be both overwhelming and underwhelming at the same time. I have no idea exactly how many channels we have at home. (I stopped counting when I got to 400.) It's overwhelming because there are so many. It's underwhelming because so little of the content interests me. But one thing I notice when I scan through the guide is the number of shows about renovating and flipping houses. These shows will take an old, dilapidated house and turn it into something that looks new and beautiful. They will take an old-style house and repurpose the space by breaking down a wall or two. They will completely gut the house by stripping it down to the bare bones, then rebuild it in such a way that it is barely recognizable. They bring new life into an old space.

Keith Green wrote a confessional song titled, "My Eyes are Dry," that reminds me of those old houses.

This world will sometimes make us feel old and dilapidated. Sometimes we will feel gutted and stripped down to our bare bones. But take heart. That just may be the exact moment when God is about to do something new. Our God is the master of taking a mess and turning it into a mansion. As painful as it may be, we just need to trust the builder.

"Therefore, if anyone is in Christ, the new creation has come: The old has gone, the new is here!" (2 Corinthians 5:17).

10. JACK IS IN TROUBLE AGAIN!

As a father, I am always trying to find something that myself and my children can enjoy together. When my son became a teenager, we found a television show we both enjoyed. The show was called *24*. The lead character, played by Kiefer Sutherland, was named Jack Bauer. Jack was the head of the Los Angeles Counter Terrorist Unit. The series ran for nine seasons. Each season, Jack would have to stop a terrorist plot that was going to destroy America as we know it. Every season had twenty-four episodes, and they all ended the same way. Right before the credits rolled, Jack would find himself in a situation where there was no way out. Show over! We would have to wait a whole week to see how Jack was going to get out of this jam. My wife and daughter refused to watch the show with us. It was just too intense for them. But each week when the show ended, Krista would ask the same question, "How was it?" And each week, I would answer with the truth, "Jack is in trouble again. I don't know how he is going to get out of this one."

Obviously, Jack somehow survived week after week. Do you want to know Jack's secret to survival? It's actually simpler than you think. Jack had a deal with the writers. Whatever mess Jack got into, they would always write a plot twist that would get him out. And at the end of every season, the terrorist lost while America and Jack survived.

We have a lot in common with Jack Bauer. This world and our sin will put us in some helpless situations. We will find ourselves at the brink of destruction. We say to ourselves, "There is no hope." If you find yourself there, just remember we have some promises given to us by "The Writer."

"If we confess our sins, he is faithful and just and will forgive us our sins and purify us from all unrighteousness" (1 John 1:9).

"But thanks be to God! He gives us the victory through our Lord Jesus Christ" (1 Corinthians 15:57).

As a child of God, we have the promise of victory in the end. Even if and when this world claims our physical life, we will still find victory. So put your life in the trustworthy hands of the writer. He loves you. And He is willing to die so that you may find victory.

11. FORE!

I love to play golf. I started playing when I was in the seventh-grade. Oddly enough, my score hasn't improved much over the past 40 plus years. Shooting par for the average golf course is seventy-two. I have occasionally finished a round of golf in the mid-eighties. I usually shoot in the nineties. But I have had a few bad days where I hit triple digits. For me, a typical round of golf will include a couple of great shots, a bunch of average shots, and a few absolutely stupid mistakes. It always makes me smile when I am watching the professional golfers on TV and one of them hits their ball in the water. It reminds me that even the best golfers make mistakes.

The game of golf parallels our spiritual life in so many ways. A standard is set (par). Sometimes you make it, but often you fail. To be a good golfer, you need to practice every day. To improve your game, you need to read about golf and learn from others who are better than you. Golf is more of a mental game than a physical game. If you fail to concentrate on every shot, you will find yourself in trouble. Alice Cooper, who is not only a rock and roll icon from the '70s but also an avid golfer, said, "Mistakes are a part of the game. It's how well you recover from them—that's the mark of a great player."

Golf gives me a little glimpse of how God sees us. He is not surprised when we fail. Life is pretty tough. Jesus didn't come just to offer guidance to us to help us get it right. He is with us, even when we blow it.

"See what great love the Father has lavished on us, that we should be called children of God! And that is what we are!" (1 John 3:1).

As children of God, we are not defined by our success or our failures. We are defined by God, who calls us His beloved children. So, tee the ball up and do your best. FORE!

12. LEAD ME HOME

My youth group decided they wanted to go on Wilderness Trek. That meant we would spend one week sleeping in tents and hiking through the mountains of Colorado. One of my jobs would be to prepare them physically for the challenge. One spring Monday morning, I woke up early to check out a trail at the Elk City State Park, near Independence, Kansas. I learned a few things that day. First, hiking by yourself is not a great idea. Especially when you are unfamiliar with the trail. Second, being first on the trail in the morning means you have to deal with a lot of spider webs. I eventually found a big stick that I held in front of me to catch the webs. Third, if you get lost, you are in big trouble. (Remember when I said hiking by yourself is not a good idea?) I accidentally got off the trail and spent several panic-stricken hours trying to find my way back. What should have been a leisurely 3-hour hike became a 6-hour adventure.

Losing your way on a trail is not good. Losing your way in life can be devastating. That moment when you look up and realize you are nowhere near where you meant to be. Maybe circumstances led you down the wrong path. Maybe bad decisions and their consequences landed you in a bad place. Regardless of the reasons or the excuses, you find yourself far from your desired path. As I said, losing your way on a trail is not good, and losing your way in life can be devastating, but losing your way spiritually will have eternal consequences. If you examine your heart and realize that you are not in a right relationship with God, you have a decision to make. You can give up and accept your eternal destiny. Or you can reach out to God and renew your relationship with Him.

"Show me your ways, Lord, teach me your paths. Guide me in your truth and teach me, for you are God my Savior, and my hope is in you all day long" (Psalm 25:4-5).

You may have wandered away from God, but He has not wandered away from you. You have not strayed beyond the reach of God's grace. God is not punishing you for your mistakes. He is just waiting for you to turn your eyes to him. He will show you the trail that will lead you home.

13. THE GREATEST

"For God so loved the world that he gave his one and only Son, that whoever believes in him shall not perish but have eternal life" (John 3:16).

This verse is probably the most famous verse in the Bible. I would say that it is the absolute greatest verse in the Bible. Why is it the greatest? Because it tells the entire gospel in one sentence.

FOR GOD—the greatest lover. SO LOVED—the greatest degree. THE WORLD—the greatest company. THAT HE GAVE—the greatest action. HIS ONE AND ONLY SON—the greatest gift. THAT WHOEVER—the greatest opportunity. BELIEVES—the greatest simplicity. IN HIM—the greatest attraction. SHALL NOT PERISH—the greatest assurance. BUT—the greatest difference. HAVE—the greatest promise. ETERNAL LIFE—the greatest blessing.

Yes, I believe it is the greatest verse in the Bible. However, just knowing that means very little. The verse must be lived and not just known. Many people who don't know Jesus may know this verse. And many people who don't know Jesus may know you. If we, as Christians, do not show the love of Christ to others by what we say and what we do, this verse becomes nothing more than a bumper sticker or a sign held up at football games.

God sent His Son so that you may be saved. Accept this gift of grace. Then live every day as a reflection of the love that God has given to you. Don't just know the verse, live it!

14. GOD HAS A NAME FOR YOU

Did you have a nickname growing up? Sometimes nicknames are given to us in jest and bear no resemblance to us. Like when the center on the basketball team is called "Shorty" or the big defensive tackle is called "Tiny." Other times, nicknames can be spot-on. I was fortunate. I have a catchy, easy-to-remember last name, so people just called me "Treat." I'm not sure how they meant it, but I took it as a compliment.

When we are trying to figure out who we are in life, those nicknames or labels can stick with us. When a kid gets a nickname that refers to their weight, intelligence, or how poor they are, it can define them the rest of their life. It's strange how the negative ones seem to stick.

In my study of David and Goliath, I came across a potential nickname for David. Goliath refers to David as just a stick. David could have taken that as an insult and been intimidated. But instead, he let it roll off him and showed Goliath what God could do with just a stick. The first time Simon Peter met Jesus, he was given a nickname. Jesus called Peter the rock. To the other disciples, and Peter to some extent, this was a name mocking Peter because of his proclivity to indecisiveness. But Jesus saw something in Peter that said that this man is solid. In the end, Jesus was right. Peter became as solid as a rock in defense of his faith in God.

The world may give you names or labels to define you and hold you down. Don't let them do it. The only opinion that matters is what God thinks of you. God has a name for you, "His Beloved!" That is who you are, and that is what you are. Don't ever forget it.

"I no longer call you servants, because a servant does not know his master's business. Instead, I have called you friends, for everything that I learned from my Father I have made known to you"
(John 15:15).

15. SOMETIMES YOU'RE THE NINETY-NINE; SOMETIMES YOU'RE THE ONE

I have always admired those people who seem to go through life confidently, knowing who they are, where they are, and where they are going. Like the kid in seventh-grade biology class who said, "I'm going to go to medical school and become a doctor." Then they did exactly that. I suppose I admire that because I'm the guy who changed my major between my junior and senior year of college. (By the way, I don't recommend that.)

Have you ever had that moment as an adult when you look in the mirror and ask yourself, "Who am I really? What am I doing with my life? Where am I heading?" There is a word that describes that feeling: LOST.

When Jesus told the parable of the lost sheep in Luke 15, I believe the application can be made of not just being spiritually lost but also being emotionally and physically lost. Yes, if I do not know the Lord or have rejected Him in my life, He will seek me to bring me under His care. But also, if I find myself in life with no sense of direction as to where I am or where I am heading, God will seek me out. He will not leave me just blowing in the wind.

"For this is what the Sovereign Lord says: I myself will search for my sheep and look after them" (Ezekiel 34:11).

God knows your name. God knows where you are. You were created for a purpose. You are not an accident. You are not disposable. The loving protection and guidance of God is there for you. He is waiting for you to reach out to Him. He will find you, joyfully put you on His shoulders, and put you on the right path.

16. THAT'S JUST GOOD PARENTING

Try to picture a mother standing in the doorway of her toddler's room. The room is a mess, and it's time to clean it up. Some of you don't have to imagine this scenario; you live it every day. All you need is for the toys to be picked up and the bed to be made. You have two choices. First, you could just do it yourself. It would only take five minutes, and the job would be done right. Second choice, you could have your toddler do it. If your child does it, the job could take an hour, and it wouldn't be done perfectly. What do you do? I know what a good mom does: She calls her toddler into the room and instructs them every step of the way. Yes, the child will complain. Yes, the child will get distracted. But how else are they going to learn?

I wonder if this is how God feels when He watches us fumble our way through a problem. Yes, God could fix it with a single word spoken. But if He did, we would have learned nothing. Instead, He guides us through our problems. He listens as we complain about the situation. He watches as we get distracted, and He is patient when we take a few missteps along the way. God's goal is not to make us miserable or suffer. His goal is to make us stronger. So, He patiently walks with us towards a mission accomplished or a lesson learned.

"But do not forget this one thing, dear friends: With the Lord a day is like a thousand years, and a thousand years are like a day. The Lord is not slow in keeping his promise, as some understand slowness. Instead he is patient with you, not wanting anyone to perish, but everyone to come to repentance" (2 Peter 3:8-9).

Our heavenly Father is patiently leading us down a road that will bring us to Him. The road is going to be full of roadblocks and distractions. But just listen to Him and follow. The struggle will be worth it!

17. GOD'S GOT THIS

On Thursday, I attended the funeral of a friend of mine from Tulsa named Jeff Deys, who passed away suddenly. Jeff was a few years younger than me. He is the only chiropractor I have ever visited. I think he was literally trying to break my back! He is also the only person who has ever talked me into trying sushi. Never again! You never had to wonder what Jeff was thinking. He was honest and blunt. Jeff was a good man, a good husband, and a good father. Jeff's passing is difficult for me to understand for a number of reasons. Just two years ago, Jeff lost his wife Lisa to cancer. Jeff and Lisa had two daughters. Their oldest, Kayden Joy, has special needs and will need constant care for the rest of her life. After the passing of his wife, Jeff was there for Kayden to meet her every need.

I love and worship God, who I believe is all-powerful. That is what makes Jeff's passing difficult for me to understand. How could an omnipotent God allow this to happen? Why would God allow Jeff to have a heart problem that would take him away from caring for his daughters, who had just recently lost their mother? Maybe you have asked similar questions. We have all experienced times when our faith in God clashes with the pains of this world. It makes us want to follow in the footsteps of Job and demand that God give us an explanation. Job lost his children, his riches, and then his health. He asked God for an explanation of what had happened in his life. God responded and spoke to Job for four chapters (Job 38-41). Job did not get the answers he was looking for, but he did receive the answer that he needed. That answer is that our loving God has got this, even when we don't understand.

"For now we see only a reflection as in a mirror; then we shall see face to face. Now I know in part; then I shall know fully, even as I am fully known" (1 Corinthians 13:12).

Someday we will understand. But for now, we just have to hang on to our faith. Please pray for Kayden Joy and Alexa, the daughters of Jeff and Lisa Deys. Pray also for the family and friends who are struggling to find answers in the midst of this tragedy. And pray for yourselves to hold on to your faith when life seems so unfair. God's got this, even when we don't understand.

18. ONLY A STEP

When I was a youth minister, I had the thrill of taking my group on Wilderness Trek. On Monday morning we were taken to a cliff and told that we were all going to rappel down to the bottom. After a short instruction period, I found myself harnessed up and standing on the edge of this mountain. With my back to the cliff and my eyes on the instructor, I heard the instructor say, "Now just lean back and start walking." In my mind I was thinking, "How do I get myself in these situations? I could just make some excuse about letting the teens do this activity and just walk away." The instructor could sense my fear, so he locked eyes with me and said, "Trust me. It will be okay." The next thing I know, I have my back to the ground, and I'm looking straight up to the sky as I scale down the edge of this mountain. When I got to the bottom, I was asked if I would ever do that again. Once I caught my breath, I responded, "Absolutely!"

Peter is one of my favorite characters in the Bible to talk about. One night, Peter and the disciples were in a boat trying to cross the lake when a storm rolled in. They were fighting the wind, waves, and rain when they saw Jesus walking on the water. What should have been comforting only terrified them even more.

> *"But Jesus immediately said to them: 'Take courage! It is I. Don't be afraid.' 'Lord, if it's you,' Peter replied, 'tell me to come to you on the water.' 'Come,' he said. Then Peter got down out of the boat, walked on the water and came toward Jesus"*
> *(Matthew 14:27-29).*

Have you ever thought about the courage it took for Peter to shift his weight from the boat to the water? He must have had butterflies in his stomach like I did on the edge of that cliff. For Peter, I believe it was a step of faith that was motivated by fear. His thought process must have been, "I'd rather be over there with Jesus than in this boat that is about to sink."

When the difficulties of life have you feeling petrified and powerless, don't curl up and quit. Just look to Jesus and take a step of faith toward Him. Jesus is bigger than our fears. Jesus is bigger than our logic. Jesus is bigger than any storm we will ever face. Muster up the courage and take that first step of faith. You may get a little wet along the way, but He will never let you sink.

19. CALL ON HIS NAME

The first time it happened I was just an innocent child. My mom and I were at the store when I wandered away from her. When I realized I was lost, I just sat down and started crying. A store employee found me in the aisle. She held my hand and walked me to the front of the store. I told her that my name was Phillip and I couldn't find my mother. She grabbed a microphone and announced to the entire store, "We have a little lost boy up here named Phillip. Would his mother please come to the front of the store?" I was relieved to see my mom, and she was glad to find me. But from that moment on, I was hooked on hearing my name. Any time I could slip away from my mom in the store, I would run to the front of the store to tell them that I was lost and my name was Phillip. They would announce my name over the intercom. I was elated, and my mom was furious. But as mad as she would get at me, she would eventually forgive me. However, the next store we went into, I would attempt a repeat performance.

Looking back, she was giving me a good example of the way we sin and how God responds. Our first sins happen because we fall to temptation or we simply make a mistake. But much like little Phillip, we tend to do the same things over and over. God has every reason to write us off. He could say, "That's it! I forgave you, and you just keep on sinning. I'm through with you." But somehow God continues to forgive His children when we sincerely repent.

"My dear children, I write this to you so that you will not sin. But if anybody does sin, we have an advocate with the Father—Jesus Christ, the Righteous One. He is the atoning sacrifice for our sins, and not only for ours but also for the sins of the whole world" (1 John 2:1-2).

You'll be glad to know that I do not run to the front of the store just to hear my name announced anymore. I'm not sure how my wife would react if she heard, "We have a little lost man up here named Phillip. Would his wife please come to the front of the store?" She may just leave and never come back. The good news is that God has not run out of forgiveness for me yet. When I call on His name I will find forgiveness.

20. OH, THOSE BOYS ...

"Children's children are a crown to the aged ..." (Proverbs 17:6).

Last week, Krista and I got to keep our grandboys for four days. Jordan just turned two, and Judah is about to have his fourth birthday. Krista and I are ... well, let's just say we are older than that. The weekend was filled with reading books, playing with cars, shooting off Nerf rockets in the backyard, eating hot dogs and pancakes on a stick, changing diapers, evening bath time, a few tears, along with lots of giggles and snuggles. Every day, Jordan would bless us with a short nap. But Judah was non-stop from sunup to sundown. On Monday, the boys returned home. Monday evening, Krista and I were sitting in the living room looking at the mess that was left behind. Then we looked at each other. I'm not sure what was a bigger mess—us or the living room.

My project for the weekend was to build the boys a swing set. Saturday, after lunch, I told the boys I had a surprise for them, but they would have to wait for a while. I went out to the back porch and opened up the box. To my surprise, there were more than 3,000 boards, screws, hooks, and brackets. Needless to say, seven hours later, I had completed nine of twenty-four steps in my construction project. Sunday night at 11 p.m., I had completed sixteen of the twenty-four steps. The swing set was finally completed about thirty minutes before they had to leave on Monday. But that thirty minutes was worth it! Their smiles and their laughter were worth every minute I spent working.

It made me wonder if that is how God feels when He sees us enjoying the creation He made for us. Our smiles and laughter must fill Him with joy. As they were leaving, Judah gave me a big hug and said, "Thank you, Pop Pop, for the swing set." I didn't need that, but it sure felt good.

Can we all stop this week and thank God for the blessings that He has lavished on us?

"Every good and perfect gift is from above, coming down from the Father of the heavenly lights, who does not change like shifting shadows" (James 1:17).

21. WHERE IS GOD IN THE FACE OF TRAGEDY?

On Wednesday morning, April 19, 1995, a tragedy happened in my hometown. A man chose to put a bomb weighing more than 2 tons in a truck and park it in front of a federal building in downtown Oklahoma City. At 9:02 a.m., he detonated the bomb, killing 168 people, including nineteen children. Many of my classmates were directly and indirectly affected by this act of terrorism. Exactly five years later, the Oklahoma City National Memorial Museum was opened on the bombing site. I was there that day to see the memorial and hear President Bill Clinton speak. I encourage everyone to spend an afternoon at this museum. It is heartbreaking and sad while also being inspirational. There is a beautiful reflecting pool, a survivor wall, a tree that withstood the blast, and 168 empty chairs memorializing those who were killed that day.

Only one thing that disappoints me about the memorial. Across the street, they erected a statue of Jesus. That seems appropriate, but the statue of Jesus has His back turned to the bombing site. His head is turned downward, and His hands are covering His face. That is not an accurate reflection of how our God faces tragedy. Our God will never turn away from our human tragedy, and He will never cover His eyes when evil abounds.

"The Lord himself goes before you and will be with you; he will never leave you nor forsake you. Do not be afraid; do not be discouraged" (Deuteronomy 31:8).

These words were delivered from Moses to the Israelites as they were about to go to battle to claim the promise land. I hope you hear these words today. If you have been a victim of evil or if tragedy has taken place in your life, know that God is with you. He will never cover His eyes and turn away from you. He will walk with you through the most difficult times you face.

If you are in the Oklahoma City area, it would be well worth your time to visit this memorial. Just stay on the right side of the street.

22. THE LOVE OF GOD

All parents try to do their best. I've never known or heard of a parent who intentionally tried to fail. But at the same time, there are no perfect parents. All parents have made mistakes in one form or another. I can remember as a child being rewarded with a special bump in my allowance or a special meal of my choosing when I brought home a good report card. I can remember getting to stop for ice cream when I scored the winning run or made the winning shot. I also remember getting a spanking or being grounded for being disobedient or because of the numerous mistakes I made. That seems like good parenting. So good, in fact, that I did the same thing as a parent. Our kids were rewarded for good behavior and achievements and punished for failures or disobedience. Here's the problem with that parenting method; it seems like your parents' love waivers with successes and failures. From a child's perspective, it seemed like my parents loved me more when I did good and less when I fell short.

That same thinking is easily transferred to our relationship with God. He is our Heavenly Father, right? Then His love must work in the same way. If I do what is right and I am successful, then His love for me is strong, and I will be blessed. On the other hand, if I am sinful and have no achievements, then He must be disappointed, and I will incur His punishment. That is not the way the love of God works!

God's response to our success is LOVE. God's response to our failures is LOVE. Money, big houses, status, and health are not God's blessings for being good. Poverty, financial struggles and poor health are not God's punishment for failures. The love of God is consistent. Our God is more concerned with our character than our accomplishments. Our God is more concerned with our heart than our performance. There is absolutely nothing that can separate us from the love of God.

"For I am convinced that neither death nor life, neither angels nor demons, neither the present nor the future, nor any powers, neither height nor depth, nor anything else in all creation, will be able to separate us from the love of God that is in Christ Jesus our Lord" *(Romans 8:38-39).*

23. STOP HIDING AND START LIVING

Hide-and-Seek is a game that has stood the test of time. I remember playing it as a child, I remember playing it with my kids, and I look forward to playing hide and seek with my grandson. Because he is not even a year old yet, we play a variation of hide-and-seek called "peekaboo." Peekaboo relies on the concept that if I can't see you then you can't see me. Eventually we will graduate to a time when I have to count to ten while he goes and hides. And let's be honest, I WILL WIN! Why? Because children are not that good at hiding.

As fun and silly as those games are, adults continue to play peekaboo and hide-and-seek. The only difference is that we play it spiritually. Satan tries to convince us that peekaboo really works. If I can't see God (or at least I'm not thinking about God), then He can't see me. Or I can hide in the darkness because God can only see me when I am in the light. If you are guilty of playing those games with God take heart, you are not the first one to try this. Long ago, a couple named Adam and Eve tried to play this game. After sinning, the only two people on Earth tried to hide from their Creator. It didn't work then, and it doesn't work now.

"Nothing in all creation is hidden from God's sight. Everything is uncovered and laid bare before the eyes of him to whom we must give account" (Hebrews 4:13).

Playing hide-and-seek with God demonstrates a faith struggle. Not only does our God see everything, nothing we do "in the dark" will ever put us out of reach of God's grace. Our misguided thinking leads us to believe that God would never forgive us if He knew everything about us. So, we hide. This is the very reason that God sent His Son to live among us. By His death, burial, and resurrection we can find forgiveness and the hope of eternal life.

We are all familiar with John 3:16, but the verse that follows is just as important.

> *"For God did not send his Son into the world to condemn the world, but to save the world through him" (John 3:17).*

Let's stop hiding, and let's start living.

24. FIVE SMOOTH STONES

"Goliath stood and shouted to the ranks of Israel, "Why do you come out and line up for battle? Am I not a Philistine, and are you not the servants of Saul? Choose a man and have him come down to me. If he is able to fight and kill me, we will become your subjects; but if I overcome him and kill him, you will become our subjects and serve us." Then the Philistine said, "This day I defy the armies of Israel! Give me a man and let us fight each other." On hearing the Philistine's words, Saul and all the Israelites were dismayed and terrified" (1 Samuel 17:8-11).

Don't you just hate bullies? Goliath was nothing but a bully. He stood before the army of Israel and taunted them. Then he took it one step further and defied them. But, to give Goliath the benefit of the doubt, by human standards, he had every right to do so. He was bigger and stronger than any one man in the entire Israelite army, especially David. David was a little scrawny shepherd boy who had no business fighting a giant. But we all know how it ended. David stood victorious over the giant, having knocked him out and then decapitating him. How did that happen? David wasn't fighting a physical battle. He was fighting a spiritual battle. When you have faith in God, He will use His power through you to defeat the enemy.

Evil is a bully! Whether it comes in the form of a person or just the world in which we live. If we try to face evil on our own, we will either be defeated or we will act like the rest of the Israelite army and run to cower in our tents. Goliath wanted to keep the battle on a physical level where he had the advantage. David took it to a spiritual level where Goliath didn't stand a chance.

When you face evil in our world, you have a choice to make. You can make it a physical battle and stand to fight on your own. Odds are you will be defeated. Or you can make it a spiritual battle by turning it over to God and tapping into His strength. In doing so, the odds shift dramatically in your favor. If you are facing a bully right now that seems impossible to overcome, just turn it over to God and check your pockets. God will slip you a few stones that will bring your enemy to his knees.

25. TAPES

Have you ever had the opportunity to do something that could be great? But there is a voice in your head that says, "Why even try? You know you are going to fail." That's happened to all of us. Have you ever had the opportunity to pursue a relationship with someone? But that voice in your head tells you, "Why even try? You know they are only going to hurt you." That's happened to all of us. Have you ever been at the point of making a commitment to God or deepening your commitment to God? Then that voice in your head speaks up and says, "Why even try? You know you are not worthy to be a child of God." We've all been there. Where do you think those voices come from?

I call those voices "tapes." (Let me clarify something for the young folks. Tapes are what we older people used to listen to and record things on before the digital age.) We all have tapes in our heads that play daily. Some are encouraging and confidence-building. But most are destructive and keep us from living boldly or feeling good about ourselves. These tapes get embedded in our brains at an early age. They are put there by parents, siblings, friends, teachers, coaches, and anybody's opinion we value. They are on permanent playback, and they guide our decision-making and our self-esteem. They are hard to remove. But the good news is that they can be replaced. They can be replaced when you start to value the opinion of God over the opinion of others.

"See what great love the Father has lavished on us, that we should be called children of God! And that is what we are!" (1 John 3:1).

Our enemy will use whoever and whatever to put those negative tapes in our heads. We cannot let that voice be the one that guides our lives. Replace those tapes with the voice of God. God loves you. You are His child.

26. LET IT RAIN

As I sit in my office to write this article, it is pouring rain outside. Rain is one of those things we have a love/hate relationship with. We absolutely need the rain for vegetation. The spring showers make the grass grow, and the flowers bloom. So, rain is good, right? Well, too much rain can flood the land and wash out some of our outdoor activities. The rain today caused our church men's league softball game to be called off. Thus, the love/hate relationship with rain. I hate that I don't get to spend the evening with the men on our team. But this softball season has been a struggle for me physically, so I'm not too upset.

When you think of rain in the Bible, the first thing that probably comes to mind is Noah and the ark. Wickedness ruled the land to the point that God regretted even making man. God could have chosen any number of ways to remove this evil from the Earth. But He chose rain. Rain would do the trick, while at the same time God would preserve mankind through the rain by saving Noah and his family. Many times in the Bible, God withheld rain from the land, causing famines. When Elijah the prophet prayed for the rain to stop, it did not rain for three and a half years. Then he prayed, and the Lord sent rain down on the land. Today, the weathermen can predict it, but God controls it.

There is another type of rain that God sends down to us. It's not water, it's righteousness.

"Sow righteousness for yourselves, reap the fruit of unfailing love,
and break up your unplowed ground; for it is time to seek the Lord,
until he comes and showers his righteousness on you"
(Hosea 10:12)

"You heavens above, rain down my righteousness; let the clouds shower it down. Let the earth open wide, let salvation spring up, let righteousness flourish with it; I, the Lord, have created it"
(Isaiah 45:8).

Let the floodgates open!

27. BABY STEPS

This is a big week for the Treat family. Our grandson, baby Judah, is turning one! One year ago, we got the call that our daughter was in labor. Because of the pandemic, we could not be there with her. So, we were in the parking lot having worship outside when we received word that everyone was okay, and we got our first picture. Now we are anticipating his first solo steps. He can pull himself up. He can take a few assisted steps. But then, plop—he falls right on his bottom. And we all clap and cheer. All parents have been there. We help, we watch, we hope, we encourage, and then one day, it happens. An unbalanced and wobbly step followed by a plop. Have any of us ever chastised or punished our child because of the plop? No. We are so proud of the step or two that was taken.

I have come to believe that this is how God sees us. He's not disappointed that we are not walking, jogging, or running yet. He is our proud Father who is either holding our hands, or He is in front of us holding out His arms, just willing our steps to happen. He is waiting to see if we are as courageous as He made us to be. When we take a step, He isn't surprised when we stumble or angry when we fall. He simply helps us up, praises our baby steps, and gives us the opportunity to walk again.

"For it is by grace you have been saved, through faith—and this is not from yourselves, it is the gift of God—not by works, so that no one can boast. For we are God's handiwork, created in Christ Jesus to do good works, which God prepared in advance for us to do" (Ephesians 2:8-10).

Our God is not an angry dad who punishes us for our plops. He is the proud Father who celebrates the steps we take. Our Father has big plans for our future. There will be plopping, but just get up and keep walking.

28. NOT JUST ONE OF THE FLOCK

When you drive by a field and see a herd of cattle, what do you see? If you are like me, you just see cows. Nameless, faceless cows. But ask the rancher what he sees. He sees them as individuals. He was there at their birth. He knows their tendencies. He knows their personalities.

The same thing could be said about a shepherd. If you see a flock of sheep, what do you see? Exactly that—sheep. But what does a shepherd see? To him, every little lamb is different. Every lamb has a story. And every lamb has a name. The shepherd knows his sheep. He calls them by name.

*"I am the good shepherd; I know my sheep and my sheep know me
—just as the Father knows me and I know the Father—and I lay
down my life for the sheep" (John 10:14-15).*

When you see a crowd of people, what do you see? Imagine yourself at a big conference or a sporting event where there are thousands of people. What do you see? My guess is that you see people. Not so with our God. He sees *person*. He sees each person as an individual. He was there at their birth. He knows their tendencies. He knows their personalities. He knows every cell in their body and the number of hairs on their head. And He was willing to lay down His life for every one of them.

God knows you. You are not just one of the masses. You are known. You are loved. And you are worth dying for.

29. SCARRED HOPE

This week, I am away at Soul Quest. It is a camp for middle school and high school students on the campus of York University in York, Nebraska. Six of our students from Eastern Hills are here with me. Our theme for camp this week is "Scarred Hope." We are studying different people in the Bible who held on to their hope in God through the toughest of circumstances. What I have come to realize is that everyone's hope is scarred in some way, even Jesus. While Jesus was here He was lied about, criticized, discouraged, falsely accused, beaten, and eventually killed. Yet, through it all, He held on to the hope of His Father in heaven and His mission.

The person I have been teaching about every day is Simon Peter. In the latter part of Peter's life, he held on to his hope in God. But earlier in Peter's life, he could best be described as a mess. He left everything to follow Jesus. But he could not stop talking when he needed to be quiet. Peter walked on water. But he also sank because he lost his faith. Peter made a bold commitment to Jesus at the last supper. But he denied even knowing Jesus three times that very night. Yes, Peter was a mess. But God used him greatly in His Kingdom.

"Above all, love each other deeply, because love covers over a multitude of sins" (1 Peter 4:8).

Peter wrote these words because Peter lived these words. Peter loved Jesus. Peter also failed Jesus. But Peter received grace and mercy because Jesus loved Peter. In the same way, our lives can get really messy at times. But never forget that God loves you, and His love covers a multitude of sins. We are His beloved children—not because we are perfect, but because of His great love for us. All hope comes with scars on it. Just never let go of your hope in Him.

30. LONGING FOR HOME

It's vacation season! As reflected in our attendance through the summer, many families leave home, searching for fun and relaxation. When our kids were young, we tried to give them some good memories by taking them on vacation. We took them to the beautiful mountains of Colorado to do some hiking and white-water rafting. We took them to Sandusky, Ohio. Why? So, we could go to Cedar Point Amusement Park (the roller coaster capital of the world). We took them to Canada to see Niagara Falls. We took them to Destin, Florida, to spend a week on the white sand. We even took them to Graceland in Memphis, Tennessee. However, I might have been the only one who enjoyed that trip.

Vacations are great. Sometimes you get to stay in a nice hotel. Other times, you get to stay in the homes of relatives. When I was a kid, we went to Washington, DC. We may be the only family in history that went to our nation's capital and stayed in a tent. That is probably why I don't enjoy camping to this day.

The only problem I have with vacation is this: It's not home. That may sound stupid, but it's true. I never really feel comfortable on vacation. I'm not sleeping in my bed in my house with all of my stuff around. I don't know the streets and where all the stores and restaurants are located. And all the people around me are strangers. It may be tons of fun. But it's not home.

"Dear friends, I urge you, as foreigners and exiles, to abstain from sinful desires, which wage war against your soul" (1 Peter 2:11).

Peter describes Christians as foreigners or exiles in this life. Another translation uses the words strangers and aliens. So, what does that mean? You never get too comfortable on vacation because you know soon, you will be going home. As a Christian, I should never get too comfortable in my earthly life because I am not really at home.

Even when life is good and I am having fun, it's not really home. The Bible tells us that God is preparing for us a heavenly home. That is what we were made for, that is where we will be most comfortable. So, let's enjoy our vacation here on Earth. Because before long, we will be heading home.

31. FINDING LOVE AND ACCEPTANCE

I know I'm going to date myself with this reference, but do you remember the TV character named Eddie Haskell? He was a recurring character on the show, "Leave it to Beaver." Eddie was the best friend of Wally Cleaver, who was the older brother of Beaver Cleaver. For the record, I was not around when the show aired in the late 1950s and early 1960s. But as a child, I did watch the show on reruns. Eddie Haskell was portrayed by Ken Osmond, who passed away during the pandemic in 2020. Eddie was supposed to be on only one episode, but his role was so convincing that they wrote him into almost 100 episodes. Eddie Haskell was the neighbor kid who kissed up to all the adults. When the adults weren't present, he was a real scoundrel. Eddie knew how to play the game. He looked good and sounded good when he needed to, but when the grownups' eyes were off of him, he let his true character come out. I believe the reason he was so beloved as a character is because we all have a little Eddie Haskell inside of us.

We want people to see us in our best light. So, when certain eyes are on us, we put our best foot forward. We "perform" so we can receive love and acceptance. We attempt to play the same game with God. On Sundays, we put on our best clothes and our best face because we have been taught that Sunday is "the Lord's Day." We try to perform so we will receive love and acceptance from God.

God doesn't want us to just behave better. He wants us to be His. He knows all of our behind-the-scenes antics, and He still loves us. Love and acceptance from God are not performance-based—they are heart-based.

"See what great love the Father has lavished on us, that we should be called children of God! And that is what we are!" (1 John 3:1).

Do your best to be loved and accepted because of who you are. KNOW that you are loved and accepted because of whose you are.

32. LOVE IS ...

On Wednesday nights, we have been studying the definition of love that Paul writes in 1 Corinthians 13.

"Love is patient, love is kind. It does not envy, it does not boast, it is not proud. It does not dishonor others, it is not self-seeking, it is not easily angered, it keeps no record of wrongs. Love does not delight in evil but rejoices with the truth. It always protects, always trusts, always hopes, always perseveres. Love never fails"
(1 Corinthians 13:4-8).

I have said throughout this study that this definition of love is really beating me up. The reason it is so difficult is because when you boil it all down, we are simply told to love God and love others. That seems easy enough until you really dig into this definition. It's as if my love for God and others is challenged every moment of every day. If I may be so bold as to add some thoughts to Paul's definition of love. This has helped me, and maybe it will help you.

LOVE IS a verb. Love is not just something you feel or something you are in; love is something you *do*. Love is only love when you act on it. What good is it if I say, "I love you," and do nothing? Simply put, love takes effort.

LOVE IS a choice. This is why love is more than a feeling. I may say, "I love you," but I don't really feel like doing anything. If it is real love, I will decide to act on it regardless of how I may be feeling at the moment.

LOVE IS the measuring stick of our relationship with God. We are not judged only by our actions or the results of our actions. We are judged by what is going on in our hearts.

"Therefore, as God's chosen people, holy and dearly loved, clothe yourselves with compassion, kindness, humility, gentleness and

patience. Bear with each other and forgive one another if any of you has a grievance against someone. Forgive as the Lord forgave you. And over all these virtues put on love, which binds them all together in perfect unity" (Colossians 3:12-14)

The Bible is really nothing more than a love story. It tells us about our God who created us in His image. By page 5 in my Bible, God has lost His relationship with the ones He loves the most. The rest of the Bible tells us all that God has done to get us back. And the Bible closes with God's family being reunited. It is the greatest love story of all time.

33. ONE MOMENT IN TIME

It was exactly one year ago that one moment altered my life. I was in York, Nebraska, at a camp called Soul Quest. We were doing a service project, cleaning out the city's bus barn. They wanted a bank of lockers removed. I took a dolly and tried to move the lockers so the teens could sweep and clean up around them. The lockers fell and landed on my leg. I spent the rest of the day at the hospital and the rest of the week in a boot. I suffered a lot of soft tissue damage, but fortunately, no broken bones. But I could still relate to these words penned by David.

"Have mercy on me, Lord, for I am faint; heal me, Lord, for my bones are in agony" (Psalm 6:2).

I spent the next several weeks walking on crutches. I spent the next couple of months preaching while sitting on a stool. I spent the next five months going to the wound care doctor every week. And to this day, I have to spend some time every morning taking care of my leg. That seems like a pretty steep price to pay for one moment in time.

I'm still trying to reflect and understand just what lesson I was supposed to learn from all of this. Here are two that I was thinking about this morning: the devastation of sin and the love of God. Just one lapse in judgment or just one bad decision can affect the rest of your life. Just one sin can hobble you. However, we have a God who loves us. And our God is greater than our sin.

"He heals the brokenhearted and binds up their wounds" (Psalm 147:3).

We have all made mistakes in the past. But God offers us forgiveness and healing. It may take a while, and we may have to live with some consequences. But God will be with you every step of the way. I'm looking forward to the day when I can walk down the streets of gold with no scars on my leg.

34. WE HAVE ALL MADE TYPOS; LET IT GO

My first preaching job was at the Clark Avenue Church of Christ in Granite City, Illinois. I served there for a little over nine years. On a good Sunday, we would have ninety people attend our worship service. At the office, I was a staff of one. That meant I was alone every day I went to the office. For some, that may sound like torture. As an introvert, I had no problem with that.

Being alone gave me the quiet time that would calm my soul. But being alone meant that all the office work landed on my desk. The only thing I really dreaded each week was the bulletin. I was the writer, editor, printer, and folder. I didn't mind the writing, printing, and folding so much. But the editing part was a real struggle. I made my fair share of mistakes. Most notably was the announcement I printed when our food pantry was running low. I challenged everyone to "stuff the pantry." But I left the *R* out of the word pantry. The congregation had a good laugh about that one.

Also, I wrote an announcement about our upcoming youth lock-in. My editing skills failed me once again, and it was advertised as "our upcoming youth lick-in." Spell check will catch misspelled words. But it will not catch correctly spelled words that have no business being in the sentence. I needed an editor to point out my obvious mistakes. The church in Granite City has invited me to come back several times to visit and to preach. While visiting, no one reminded me of my editing mistakes in the bulletin. We just laughed, cried, and loved on each other as we reminisced about our time together.

Many people live their lives seeing God only as an editor with a red pen who does nothing more than highlight our mistakes. They fail to see the loving God who is our creator. His joy is not found in pointing out our mistakes. His joy is found in the heart of His creation. Is there is a typo or two in the pages of your life? Don't obsess over it. He's not! He will help you make the changes you need to make. His purpose for your life is much bigger than giving you a failing grade.

"For I will forgive their wickedness and will remember their sins no more" (Hebrews 8:12).

35. THE BEAUTY OF GOD

The first time that I ever spoke through an interpreter was in Haiti. I was a young youth minister, and our congregation sponsored an orphanage in Cap-Haitien. Along with a few of our elders, I went over for a weekend visit. While there, I was asked to speak at the Sunday morning worship service. That morning, I spoke on the power and love of God that can connect us from different parts of the world. One of the examples I used was the rainbow.

Following services, the head of the orphanage took me aside and told me that they don't have rainbows in Haiti. I naively believed him, and everyone had a good laugh at my expense. He then smiled and told me that they have the most beautiful rainbows in Haiti. The rainbow is just one example of God's beauty on display. As much as I talk bad about my two years spent in West Texas, they have the most beautiful sunsets I have ever seen. The beauty of God can be seen all around us every day if we are looking for it.

"He has made everything beautiful in its time. He has also set eternity in the human heart; yet no one can fathom what God has done from beginning to end" (Ecclesiastes 3:11).

Another example of God's beauty can be seen when we look at each other. Remember that we were all made in the image of God. There is a piece of God's beauty in each of us. Too often, we look at the negative in one another. We see someone, point out their flaws, and make judgments about them. What would happen if, instead of judging others, we looked for the uniquely beautiful part of them that was made in the image of God? Not only would that brighten our day, it would be a great step in unifying us rather than dividing us.

The verse in Ecclesiastes goes on to mention eternity. If we think we have seen something beautiful here on Earth, just imagine what we will see in heaven.

36. VALUE FAITH OVER PERFECTION

Several years ago, while on vacation, Krista and I went to see *Hamilton* on Broadway. To say that this is an award-winning musical would be a huge understatement. At the 70th Tony Awards, *Hamilton* received a record-breaking sixteen nominations and won eleven awards, including Best Musical. It also received a Pulitzer Prize for Drama. During the performance, Krista was on the edge of her seat. I'm a little embarrassed to say that I was not nearly as overwhelmed as she was. I would prefer seeing children doing the Nativity scene at Christmastime. Don't get me wrong, *Hamilton* was amazing. Every singer was a professional, hitting every note and step to perfection. While at the typical kids' Nativity play, there will be forgotten lines, mistimed entrances, shepherds fighting, Mary waving at her parents, and Joseph's beard falling off. And those are the plays that don't include live animals!

Which of these looks more like real life to you? We would love for our lives to be as perfect as a Broadway performance. But most of our lives look more like the children muddling our way through life while trying to tell the greatest story ever told.

"For it is by grace you have been saved, through faith—and this is not from yourselves, it is the gift of God—not by works, so that no one can boast" (Ephesians 2:8-9).

So, don't get bent out of shape when you fall short of perfection. We will all take some missteps along the way. We will say and do some things that we will later regret. Value faith over perfection. Faith allows us to accept the grace of God. Faith allows us to recover from our failings and keep trying. Faith allows us to move on when others hurt us. And faith will allow us imperfect people to share the message of our perfect God.

37. STREAMS OF MERCY NEVER CEASING

Does the name Robert Robinson ring a bell? I can safely say that you have not run into him lately. He died on June 9, 1790. You have never met him, but I would guess that you have sung a song he wrote in 1757. He wrote one of my all-time favorite hymns, "Come, Thou Fount of Every Blessing."

Let me remind you of the first verse of his song:

Come, thou fount of every blessing, tune my heart to sing Thy grace.
Streams of mercy, never ceasing, call for songs of loudest praise
Teach me some melodious sonnet, sung by flaming tongues above
Praise the mount, I'm fixed upon it, mount of Thy redeeming love

For years, Robert Robinson served as a Methodist preacher. But later in life, he drifted away from the Lord. On one occasion, he was riding on a stagecoach. A lady sitting next to him struck up a conversation with him. She asked, "What do you think of this hymn I have been reading?" The hymn was "Come, Thou Fount of Every Blessing." He confessed to her that he was the author of that hymn and that his relationship with the Lord had faded. She responded by saying, "But these streams of mercy are still flowing." Her words (his own words) pierced his heart, and he was restored to the Lord.

I love this story for two reasons. First, the words that Mr. Robinson felt and wrote were true when he was close to God and true when he had drifted away from God. The second reason I love this story is the lady who dared to share what was on her heart with a stranger. Her loving words helped bring a lost sheep back into the fold.

"But because of his great love for us, God, who is rich in mercy, made us alive with Christ even when we were dead in transgressions—it is by grace you have been saved"
(Ephesians 2:4-5).

38. JESUS DOES

"The Word became flesh and made his dwelling among us. We have seen his glory, the glory of the one and only Son, who came from the Father, full of grace and truth" (John 1:14).

For only a little over 30 years, the Son of God walked among us. Precious years. Precious days. Precious moments. With only that amount of time, Jesus made the most out of every second of every day. But as we read the gospels, we find something interesting. Jesus didn't spend every moment preaching and spending time with influencers. Jesus took some of His precious moments to spend with people who many would have just passed by. Here are a few of them:

Jesus spoke to, touched, and healed a man with leprosy. A man who others would not dare to go near.

Jesus took the time to speak to a Canaanite woman who was crying out and bothering everyone around her. He commended her faith and healed her daughter.

Jesus met a man one day who was cast aside by society and made to live in a graveyard. Jesus spoke with him, cast the demons out of His life, and made him a missionary.

Jesus took time out of a very busy day to speak to a woman who had been sick for twelve years and isolated from society. Jesus healed her and called her a precious name: "daughter."

Jesus stopped when He saw a widow who was on her way to the cemetery to bury her only son. Jesus had compassion for her. Not only did they talk, Jesus raised her son.

Jesus had a long conversation with a four-time-divorced Samaritan woman. He gave her life hope and purpose.

While others are enjoying a festival, Jesus went to a pool that is surrounded by blind, lame, and paralyzed people. Jesus talked with a man who had been paralyzed for thirty-eight years. Jesus healed him and sent him on to his new life.

If you ever feel unlovable, just read through the gospels. Jesus loves all people. Especially those that the world may ignore. Others may not love you, but Jesus does!

39. YOU HAVE BEEN CHOSEN

Have you ever been a part of a "schoolyard pick-em"? Most of us have. The genesis of that term is when you are in school, and you go to recess. Teams need to be picked for a game that requires you to kick, hit, or throw a ball. The two most talented kids are designated captains. The rest of the kids line up and begin to look at their shoes while they kick around in the dirt. You are just hoping to hear your name called early. It is humiliating when you are the last one standing. It is even more humiliating when the captain who is getting stuck with you says to the other captain, "You can have him."

We often say, "Kids can be so cruel." But schoolyard pick-em doesn't end with childhood. As you get a little older, you may apply to a college and wait to hear if you are accepted. Filling out a resume for a job is a form of schoolyard pick-em. Also waiting to hear your name called for a promotion at work. Even sending a friend request on Facebook and waiting for a response. It's not that kids are cruel or adults are cruel—we live in a cruel world.

With God, it is different. We get to hear those words we longed to hear on the playground. He reaches out to every one of us and says, "I want you on my team!" God not only picks us for His team, He gave His Son as a sacrifice so we could have the honor of being chosen by Him. All we have to do is accept His invitation.

"Then Peter began to speak: 'I now realize how true it is that God does not show favoritism but accepts from every nation the one who fears him and does what is right'" (Acts 10:34-35).

The decision is yours. Stop looking at your shoes and kicking the dirt. Accept the invitation and join God's team. By the way, God's team wins in the end!

40. MY FAVORITE WEDDING

Through my years as a minister, I have had the privilege of officiated at least fifty weddings. Each wedding was special in its own way. But three in particular stand out. The first one, obviously, was my own wedding. I will never forget that moment when the doors opened and Krista walked down the aisle toward me. She looked so beautiful. She was a gift that I did not deserve. At the second very special wedding, I had a different view of that moment. The doors opened and I walked my daughter Tori down the aisle. At the third very special wedding, I was standing on a stage with my son as the doors opened and his bride Emily walked down the aisle. Each of those moments has been burned into my memory. It is that moment when the past, as important as it was, is now left behind. The only thing that matters is the future. Commitments are made, vows and rings are exchanged, followed by a kiss. Then the bride and groom walk arm in arm into a new relationship.

"Husbands, love your wives, just as Christ loved the church and gave himself up for her to make her holy, cleansing her by the washing with water through the word, and to present her to himself as a radiant church, without stain or wrinkle or any other blemish, but holy and blameless" (Ephesians 5:25-27).

There is a wedding in our future that will be even greater. Except it won't be doors that will open—it will be the clouds. And on that day we, the church, will be presented to the groom, who is Jesus. As He looks at us, He will not see the scars that sin has left on us. He will only see His beautiful bride. Then we will walk arm in arm with our groom into a new eternal relationship. This is a wedding that you don't want to miss!

41. THE DECISION IS YOURS

On August 29, 2005, Hurricane Katrina made landfall in the city of New Orleans. The hurricane devastated the city, causing major flooding due to breaches in the levees. An estimated 1,500 people lost their lives, and almost 2 billion dollars' worth of damage was reported. In response, NBC aired a fundraising show that brought in more than 50 million dollars for relief for those who were affected. Many celebrities donated their time and talent as their hearts went out to the people of New Orleans and the surrounding area. But one particular celebrity stood out to me. I had always liked Harry Connick Jr. as an actor and a musician. But his actions after the storm made me a devoted fan. While everyone else stood at a distance singing and giving speeches, Harry Connick Jr. was waist-deep in the floodwater helping those in need. At the benefit concert, he barely had a voice left to sing because he had spent the previous days talking and praying with the people of New Orleans. Why was he different from all of the other celebrities? Harry is from New Orleans. Those were his people. Because of his love for them, he could not stand at a distance. He entered their "mess" and did everything he could to see them through this tragedy.

"The Word became flesh and made his dwelling among us. We have seen his glory, the glory of the one and only Son, who came from the Father, full of grace and truth" (John 1:14).

We live in a fallen world that is, quite frankly, a big mess. We are waist deep in sin and we are not able to find relief on our own. God refused to stand at a distance while we struggle. He sent His one and only Son into our mess. Jesus lived, breathed, and walked among us. And He gave up His own life to be the only sacrifice that can save us. God has given us a lifeline. So, each of us has a decision. Will we drown in the devastation of this world, or will we embrace the Savior who entered our world to save us? The decision is yours.

42. A SHAMEFUL MOMENT CAN LEAD TO A NEW REVELATION

Last week, Krista and I were blessed to spend our thirty-third anniversary on vacation in Mexico. There are a million great things I could tell you about our trip, and I will if you ask. But I do want to tell you about one moment that I had while there that no one else knows about (not even Krista). While at the resort, I had the single most stupid thought that has ever entered my brain. It's not only stupid, it's borderline racist. While at the resort, there was a Spanish family of four who had brought their little dog with them. They were yelling, trying to get their dog to come sit by their chairs. As I watched this happen, this stupid thought went through my head, "What are they doing? Don't they know dogs don't speak Spanish?"

I'm not proud of my ignorance and stupidity that allowed that thought to enter my brain. But it did lead me to some thoughts on a deeper level. I have always wanted to learn Spanish, but I have never taken the time to learn. I am not bilingual. At times, I feel as though I am barely uni-lingual. Spanish was not the only other language I heard while on vacation. I heard many languages spoken that I couldn't even identify. It made me wonder, "How are we all going to communicate with each other in heaven? How are we going to sing praises to God together when we don't speak the same language? So, I searched the Bible. Here is the best answer I could find:

"However, as it is written: 'What no eye has seen, what no ear has heard, and what no human mind has conceived'—the things God has prepared for those who love him" (1 Corinthians 2:9).

I guess in heaven we will all have a new language that we can all speak and understand. What we lost at the tower of Babel, we will regain in heaven. I'm looking forward to learning a new language and new songs. But the question still remains, will dogs be able to understand us then?

43. HOLD ME, JESUS

Do you ever just have one of those days when the world seems to be against you? I believe we all do at times. I was having one of those days a couple of weeks ago. I jumped in my truck to run another useless errand. I hit shuffle on my iPod and just let Apple choose from nearly 3,000 songs what would serenade me down the road. I think God overrode Apple and said, "Let me get this one." The chosen song was one that I forgot was even on my iPod called "Hold Me Jesus" by Rich Mullins. It was just what I needed that day.

Music has always touched me deeply. I thank God that He inspired others to write songs that speak truth to my heart. I also thank God that He can work through my IPOD to remind me that He has not forgotten about me.

"Praise be to the God and Father of our Lord Jesus Christ, the Father of compassion and the God of all comfort, who comforts us in all our troubles, so that we can comfort those in any trouble with the comfort we ourselves receive from God"
(2 Corinthians 1:3-4).

44. KEEP ON LOVING YOU

I did a lot of dumb things as I was growing up, and yet somehow my mom continued to love me. Here is just a sampling of a very long list:

I once spilled an entire bottle of syrup on our carpet. That was not an easy spill to clean up.

My mom caught me stealing quarters from her change purse because a friend and I were going to the arcade. For any younger people reading this that are confused by part of that sentence, go ask someone who grew up in the '80s.

When I had my driver's permit, I borrowed my mom's car without her knowledge to go to the church to play volleyball. On the way home I ran into a parked car.

Again, this is just a short sample of a much longer list. The most amazing thing about all of my childhood mess-ups is that my mom continued to love me. This made no sense until I had children of my own. I will not take this opportunity to list their stupid mistakes. But needless to say, there were plenty. As frustrating as they were, I continued to love them.

We have all made our fair share of mistakes that go against the will of our heavenly Father. But there is no mistake you have made that can make God stop loving you. Do you remember the parable of the prodigal son? The father loved him while he was at home. The father loved him when he left home. The father loved him while he was in the faraway land, wasting his money. And the father loved him when he returned home. The father's love was consistent when the son shined or when the son was messing up.

"For I am convinced that neither death nor life, neither angels nor demons, neither the present nor the future, nor any powers, neither height nor depth, nor anything else in all creation, will be able to separate us from the love of God that is in Christ Jesus our Lord" (Romans 8:38-39).

God doesn't like your mistakes, but He loves you. And there is nothing you can do about that!

45. THE BEAUTIFUL DIVERSE FAMILY OF GOD

What is your favorite parable of Jesus? Most people answer that with a parable that either encourages them or backs up a belief they already have. Rarely does someone answer with a parable of Jesus that challenges them or goes against a belief they have held onto for years. In Luke 14, Jesus tells a parable that we have come to know as the Parable of the Great Banquet. With this parable, Jesus, the master teacher, challenges every one of His listeners. In the parable, a man was preparing a great banquet. The man in the parable is God and the great banquet is His Kingdom. When the time for the banquet came, few guests decided to attend. Many of the invited guests made excuses as to why they could not attend. So, the man extended the invitation to those who were downtrodden. Some came, but there were still seats available. Then the invitation was extended to any and everyone.

The main point of the parable is that everyone is invited to be a member of God's Kingdom. Everyone includes those who were raised in believing families, those who have been beat up by life, and everyone else, regardless of their situation. EVERYONE! There is absolutely nothing you have done in life that disqualifies you from the invitation of God. The underlying point of the parable is aimed at those who are already members of God's Kingdom. It may sound like the same thing: Everyone is invited to be a part of the Kingdom of God. That means whoever God accepts we all must accept. Regardless of their race, their background, their economic standing, their education, their political party, their social standing, their social awkwardness, their hygiene, their talents … If God calls them, they are as much a part of His Kingdom as anyone else.

"For the grace of God has appeared that offers salvation to all people" (Titus 2:11).

You are invited to be a member of God's church family. And every family member is just as important as any other.

46. I LOVE YOU JUST THE WAY YOU ARE!

Recently, while we were on vacation with the entire family, we hired a photographer to take some family pictures. My wife, daughter, and daughter-in-law picked out our clothing. If I could be so bold to speak for all of the boys, we would have preferred shorts and T-shirts, but we really didn't have a say in the matter. We met the photographer down by the river and took about a thousand pictures. Literally, a thousand pictures. As we finished up, the photographer told us to pick our favorite 20, and she would use AI (artificial intelligence) to fix any imperfections. That sounded good until we got the results back. There was a picture of our little grandson Judah that was just beautiful. But upon closer inspection she had altered his face just a bit. The picture looked like it should be in a magazine advertising the perfect child. But none of us were happy with it. It just wasn't Judah.

"My frame was not hidden from you when I was made in the secret place, when I was woven together in the depths of the earth"
(Psalm 139:15).

It is amazing to think that the God who made the entire universe made you specifically. The God who created the depths of the ocean and every creature that inhabits it also created every detail of you, right down to the smallest cell in your body. And here is the best part: that same God absolutely loves everything about you. God made you! There has never been another like you, and there never will be. We don't need artificial intelligence to make us better. We just need to thank our Creator and embrace who we are. Don't spin your wheels trying to change the things that God created. Just live in a way that brings you closer to the One who loves you the most. And to the photographer who tried to "fix" our grandson's face, BACK OFF! He's perfect just the way he is.

47. ANCHOR POINTS

For the record, I have spent very little time sailing on the ocean (six days to be exact). In all honesty, I have spent very little time in a boat on a lake. But I have watched movies, watched the news, and heard personal stories of what can happen to a vessel on the water during a storm. The most devastating story that comes to mind is attending the funeral of a seven-year-old boy who lost his life on Lake Oologah in Oklahoma. This boy was a friend and baseball teammate of my son. During the funeral, the dad stood before us and told their story. They were fishing when a storm came up and capsized their boat. Their boat went down, and the two of them were left floating in the middle of the lake with only an ice chest to keep them afloat. They began paddling for the nearest shore, but the wind was against them. So, they turned and began paddling for the far shore. When his son became too tired and too cold to paddle anymore, the father held him in his arms. As night fell, his son died in his arms before they could reach dry land.

Storms can be deadly when you are caught in the middle of one, especially when you are on the water being tossed to and fro. What you need is an anchor point. If you drop your anchor deep in the water, it will latch on to something solid that is immune from the storm. Yes, you will have to endure the wind and the waves, but your anchor point will keep you stable.

"We have this hope as an anchor for the soul, firm and secure. It enters the inner sanctuary behind the curtain, where our forerunner, Jesus, has entered on our behalf" (Hebrews 6:19-20).

As we have to endure the storms of life that come our way, I want to give you three anchor points that can keep you stable. The first anchor point is "My life matters." You are not just one of billions of people who have lived. You are a creation of God. He knows you, and He loves you. The second anchor point is "My sins have been paid for." My failures have not doomed me. God sent his Son to save me. And the final anchor point is "My death is not eternal." We all face the same fate, the end of our earthly lives. But through Jesus we have eternal life in the presence of God. I hope these anchor points will give you something to hold tight when life gets rough.

48. THE REAL GIFT

My family always loved going to Nana's house for Christmas. Her home was warm and inviting. She would cook enough food to last us through the New Year. And what can I say about the decorations? Macy's Christmas department would be jealous if they ever set foot in Nana's house in December. But the centerpiece was always the Christmas tree. It was a large, beautifully decorated tree that could not contain the presents underneath. Just like the food, Nana would go overboard with presents. And it seemed like every one of the presents were professionally wrapped by Santa's elves. It was beautiful and also sad. It was sad because the wrapping paper, ribbons and bows were going to be torn up and tossed to the side because the real gift was on the inside.

That's a lot like us. God took the time to make each of us unique. He gave us eyes to see, ears to hear, mouths to speak, legs to take us places and hands to work and help others. But all of that is just wrapping paper, ribbons and bows. The real gift is what is on the inside.

"Do you not know that your bodies are temples of the Holy Spirit,
who is in you, whom you have received from God?"
(1 Corinthians 6:19).

I thank God for the wrapping paper that is my exterior. But I love God for the gift of the Holy Spirit that dwells within me. In time the wrapping paper, ribbons and bows will all be discarded. But the gift inside will endure forever. We are all special to God. But remember that we are just packages carrying the real gift.

49. BY THE GRACE OF GOD

Just a little while back, we received a phone call from our daughter. She was very excited to tell us our new grandbaby had rolled over. My daughter and my wife were both very excited. My thought was, "Uh-oh, he's getting mobile." From the time children start crawling until they turn eighteen, parents save their lives about once a week.

"Don't put that in your mouth."
"Please don't poke that in the light socket."
"Put the knife down."
"You have to eat something green."
"Look both ways before you cross the street."
"If you are riding your bike, please put your helmet on."
"Yes, you do need to take driver's education."
"Please don't hang around him. He will get you killed."

It is amazing that most children even see their eighteenth birthday. Most kids are completely oblivious how many times we parents have actually saved their lives. Where would they be without us?

Do you think God may feel the same way about His children? Yes, God has given us the instructions to keep us from walking into certain death. But our God takes it even one step further: He protects and sustains us. Just like our children have no idea all what all we actually do for them, we cannot comprehend what all God does for us. We live believing that we protect and provide for ourselves. But it is our Heavenly Father who constantly provides for us and guides us away from certain dangers.

After having children, I remember multiple times calling my mom just to say, "Thank you. I never realized how much you did for me." I'm anxiously awaiting those calls from my children. In the meantime, let's all stop and thank our Creator for all He has done for us.

"He is before all things, and in him all things hold together"
(Colossians 1:17).

50. THERE'S A CHAIR WAITING FOR YOU

Some of my favorite Thanksgiving memories are from going to my grandparents' house in Muskogee, Oklahoma, to spend the holiday with our family. My Grandpa and Grandma Brown's house was so small, but that didn't matter. Ten adults and thirteen grandchildren would all gather there for Thanksgiving dinner. In one room was the adult table. As they ate, they would discuss politics, church, the school system, and world affairs. I remember the conversation getting pretty heated. How could it not with five strong-willed women and five stubborn men?

In the other room, the thirteen grandchildren all gathered with our paper plates. Sadly, we didn't have a "kiddie table." We all had to sit on the floor. What I remember about the meal was good food, lots of laughs, and pure chaos. I have a vivid memory of one of my cousins stepping on my mashed potatoes with his farm boots. I just scraped off the top layer and continued eating. In my memory it was pure joy.

If Jesus had been at our Thanksgiving meal back then, where do you suppose He would have chosen to eat? We often see Jesus in a crowd, spending time with the children. When questioned about it, Jesus would pick up a child, place them on His lap, and tell the adults that kids should be our model of faith.

"He called a little child to him, and placed the child among them. And he said: "Truly I tell you, unless you change and become like little children, you will never enter the kingdom of heaven"
(Matthew 18:2-3).

Let's face the facts. The world's problems will not be solved sitting around the Thanksgiving table. As persuasive as you may be, you will most likely not change anyone's political views while eating turkey and dressing. Before you say something that may hurt someone's feelings, stop and look at the kiddie table. It may look a little chaotic, but that is where pure joy is found. So, pull up a small chair and enjoy your time together. Even if someone steps on your mashed potatoes.

51. LEFTOVERS

I'm not a real big fan of leftovers. They rarely taste as good when they are reheated on the second day. Except for Thanksgiving. I will keep eating Thanksgiving leftovers till they are gone. Here is my secret go-to with Thanksgiving leftovers: a turkey and dressing sandwich. That is a piece of white meat, a layer of dressing, and a splash of gravy between two slices of bread. YUMMY!

There is another group of people who did not enjoy leftovers the next day—the Israelites in the desert. Every morning for forty years, they would wake up and the ground would be covered with a layer of manna. Many scholars have debated whether manna was more like a saltine or a pancake. My stance is, who really cares? What we do know about manna is that if you tried to store some away for the next day, it would go sour. It was literally "use it or lose it." God made manna to be eaten, not stored. But God was faithful. The next morning there would be a fresh layer of manna on the ground.

"Then the Lord said to Moses, "I will rain down bread from heaven for you. The people are to go out each day and gather enough for that day" (Exodus 16:4).

The love of God is very similar to manna. Every morning, we wake up to a fresh new batch of love from God. And God is faithful. Tomorrow morning, we will wake up to more love from God. But that love is not meant to be stored up. We are to go out and share the love of God with others. If we try to hoard that love and not share it, just like manna, it will sour. Go out today and share the love of God with others. And trust God that more will be given to you tomorrow.

52. IT'S YOUR CHOICE

In Luke 15, Jesus tells the parable of a man who made a number of choices. The first choice we see him make is the choice to leave home. Even though his father loves him and has provided for him, the young man believes there is something better out there for him beyond the confines of home. So, he decides to leave. The next choice he makes is to take in all the pleasures of being away from home. But after this point, the choice is no longer his. He is out of money, and there is a famine in the land. He must take a job feeding pigs in order to survive. He can't even choose to eat the pig's food for fear of losing his job. He has only one more choice. He can choose to stay and live in the mess he has made of his life. Or he can choose to go back home. He must choose. No one can make this choice for him.

Jesus tells this story to clearly illustrate what we have all done with our lives. According to Romans 3:23, we have all made the choice to leave the loving care of our Father. Whether we find ourselves at rock bottom and out of choices or we are enjoying the pleasures of this world, we are still in the same condition as the man in Luke 15. We are lost. The man then makes the choice to go back home, unsure of what he would find. Would he even be allowed to step on the property? Would he be chastised by his father? Would he forever be treated like a second-class citizen for his bad choices? What he found back home was the same father he had left, a loving provider.

"So he got up and went to his father. "But while he was still a long way off, his father saw him and was filled with compassion for him; he ran to his son, threw his arms around him and kissed him"
(Luke 15:20).

That is the same choice that each of us has to make. Will we decide to keep a distance from our Heavenly Father? Or will we decide to come back home? Jesus tells us what is waiting for us at home. We will be greeted by our Father, we will be called His child, and He will provide for us exactly what we need: forgiveness! The choice is yours.

53. FRIDAY AFTERNOON

What would have been going through your mind if you had been there on that Friday afternoon? That Friday afternoon when Jesus was dead on the cross and the world went dark. If you were a believer in Jesus, you would have felt lost and hopeless. It would have been logical to conclude that good had been defeated. Not only did the world go dark, the Earth shook, and the temple veil had been torn in two. The beaten, lifeless body of Jesus had been placed in a sealed tomb. All hope was lost.

There was only one who was not worried about the current situation. That was God. Not only is God the creator of this world, but He also had a plan to save His children. His plan would require some dark times. Even though He shared His plan to all the people through His prophets, they still could not comprehend. But through the darkness and chaos, God's plan was still on track and moving forward. By sunrise on Sunday morning, the next step of God's plan occurred. The grave was no longer sealed, and Jesus was alive and well. Jesus was breathing, walking, talking, and eating with the very people who thought all hope was lost.

As we live our lives, there will undoubtedly be some dark times. There will be times of chaos and confusion. There will be times that all hope seems lost. There will be times that it will seem like God and His children are defeated. Do not lose hope. God has a plan, and it is right on track. We may not fully understand it until Jesus comes again. But hang in there. God's got this!

"In a flash, in the twinkling of an eye, at the last trumpet. For the trumpet will sound, the dead will be raised imperishable, and we will be changed. But thanks be to God! He gives us the victory through our Lord Jesus Christ. Therefore, my dear brothers and sisters, stand firm. Let nothing move you. Always give yourselves

*fully to the work of the Lord, because you know that your labor in
the Lord is not in vain" (1 Corinthians 15:52, 57-58).*

54. THE FINISH LINE

On an April morning in 2006, I ran the Oklahoma City Bombing Memorial Marathon. I ran the 26.2 miles without stopping. The only time I walked was through the water stations because I was not coordinated enough to run and drink at the same time. That morning there was a cruel irony. As we were standing at the starting line, we could see the finish line just a block away. It was just right there. But in order to get to that finish line I knew it would take a lot of sweat, pain, and determination. During the run, there were times I wanted to quit, times when my body ached, and times when I was not sure if I would ever make it to the end. But I overcame, and I finished!

Did you know that the distance between Bethlehem and Jerusalem is only six short miles? Bethlehem was the place of Jesus's birth, and only six miles away is where they would crucify Jesus and lay His lifeless body in a tomb. The starting line and the finish line were not that far away from each other. However, the journey between them was a long and winding road. Jesus was mocked, falsely accused, hindered by others, and discouraged along the way. But Jesus never quit. He was focused on completing His mission.

In our lives, we will face numerous obstacles along the way. We will face discouragement, temptations, health issues, relationship problems, addictions, and the desire to just quit. Don't give up! The finish line is not that far away. Stay focused on the goal and just keep putting one foot in front of the other.

"Therefore we do not lose heart. Though outwardly we are wasting away, yet inwardly we are being renewed day by day. For our light and momentary troubles are achieving for us an eternal glory that far outweighs them all. So we fix our eyes not on what is seen, but on what is unseen, since what is seen is temporary, but what is unseen is eternal" (2 Corinthians 4:16-18).

If the road gets too hard, here is a secret that will help you. The finish line is not really the finish line. It is actually the starting line. The tomb was not the end for Jesus, and the tomb is not the end for us. It is only the beginning of eternity.

55. A HOLIDAY REMINDER

This time of year can often bring out the worst of people. You can see it when you are driving. You can see it when you are shopping. You can see it when you are eating at a restaurant. Kindness and patience are gone. Selfishness and rudeness rule the day. But this time of year can also bring out the best of people. Some will take this opportunity to serve others, give gifts, and do random acts of kindness.

This time of year can also expose the best and the worst of us internally. For some, this time of year can be filled with nothing but joy. We get a few days off of work. We get to spend time with family. We take the time to eat, play games, and just enjoy each other's company. But at the same time, the holiday season can be a reminder of the pain in your life. A reminder of a loved one who is no longer with us. A reminder of a relationship that is broken. A reminder of lost health.

If you find yourself struggling to find joy this time of year, remember that God has not forgotten you.

His love for you is so great that He sent His Son just for you.

"For there is born to you this day in the city of David a Savior, who is Christ the Lord" (Luke 2:11).

He is with you in your pain.

"The Lord is near to those who have a broken heart" (Psalm 34:18).

He is with you in your sorrow.

"Blessed are those who mourn, for they shall be comforted" (Matthew 5:4).

He is busy preparing your eternal dwelling place.

"My Father's house has many rooms; if that were not so, would I have told you that I am going there to prepare a place for you?" (John 14:2).

And He will comfort you personally when you get there.

"He will wipe every tear from their eyes. There will be no more death or mourning or crying or pain, for the old order of things has passed away" (Revelation 21:4).

Have a blessed holiday season. And remember, God loves you, and there is nothing you can do about that.

56. DON'T MISS THE WHOLE STORY

This is the time of year that I (and about every other preacher) talk about the name Immanuel. Immanuel means "God with us." We talk about God stepping down from heaven and taking the form of a human. We talk about Him walking among us and breathing our air. We talk about Him healing, weeping, teaching, praying, and connecting with humanity. All of that is good, but it is not the whole story. In a few short months, we will be focusing on the sacrificial Lamb of God. Immanuel came into this world not just to live among us; He came to save us. He suffered pain and agony as He willingly gave His life as a sacrifice for our sins. When Jesus took His last breath, it wasn't really His last breath. On the third day, He rose from the grave with the keys to death and hell in His hand. The full manger points to the empty tomb. All of that is good, but it is not the whole story.

The whole story is this: Because of Immanuel, because of the crucifixion of Jesus, because of the empty tomb, we now have the opportunity of eternal life. This life for us is just the opening act. Our death is not the final curtain. There is an encore. And that encore goes on and on and on for all of eternity. What we do in Act 1 determines our encore. God has done all He can do. The decision is now ours!

"For God so loved the world that he gave his one and only Son, that whoever believes in him shall not perish but have eternal life. For God did not send his Son into the world to condemn the world, but to save the world through him" (John 3:16-17).

57. TRUST YOUR GUIDE

One of the years when I used to take the youth group to Colorado to go on Wilderness Trek, we decided to go up a day early to go white-water rafting. The word "rafting" is incredibly misleading. When I think of rafting, I picture lazily letting the currents gently move me downstream while I float on a raft, trying to get a suntan. The reality of white-water rafting on the Arkansas River in Colorado was much different.

First of all, the water was freezing cold. Add to that the currents constantly twisting and turning you. And if the currents didn't flip your raft over, the random rocks in the middle of the river would. At one particularly peaceful spot, our guide had us paddle the boats to the shore and get out. He walked us down the river a few hundred yards to show us what we were about to encounter. It was a part of the river that was very difficult. We watched for about 30 minutes as raft after raft failed to negotiate that part of the river. Many people got flipped out of their rafts and were just swimming for survival. He then looked at us and said, "All right, let's go!" We were terrified.

We got into our rafts and began to paddle. It was at that moment that I began to understand how the disciples must have felt while they were in a fishing boat fighting the storm, thinking they were about to die. As we made our way through that section of the river, I desperately wanted Mark 4:39 to happen in my life.

"He got up, rebuked the wind and said to the waves, 'Quiet! Be still!' Then the wind died down and it was completely calm"
(Mark 4:39).

I'm happy to tell you that our entire youth group made it through the rapids, and not one of us was flipped out of the raft. The key lesson I learned that day was the importance of having an experienced guide in the raft and trusting everything he said. It was a Bible lesson that I will never forget. Roaring rapids will come to you in life. So, make sure you have Jesus in the boat with you. Listen to Him, trust Him, and do exactly what He tells you to do. And eventually, you will make it to peaceful waters.

58. THE FULL MANGER AND THE EMPTY TOMB

"Therefore the Lord himself will give you a sign: The virgin will conceive and give birth to a son, and will call him Immanuel"
(Isaiah 7:14).

This time of year, there is a lot of focus on the baby in the manger. The name Immanuel means "God with us." The disciple John words it this way:

"The Word became flesh and made his dwelling among us. We have seen his glory, the glory of the one and only Son, who came from the Father, full of grace and truth" (John 1:14).

The manger was not only filled with the baby Jesus, but it was also full of grace and truth. That full manger serves to fill us as well. Jesus says in John 10:10 that He came to give us a fullness of life. Paul has several things to say about the fullness Jesus brought into this world. In Romans 14:14, Paul says he is fully persuaded in the Lord Jesus. In 1 Corinthians 15:58, he says we are to give ourselves fully to the work of the Lord. In 2 Corinthians 13:9, he prays that we may be fully restored. In Colossians 1:28, he says that through teaching we may become fully matured in Christ.

The full manger points us to the empty tomb. The empty tomb not only shows the power of God, but it teaches us that death is defeated. The empty tomb gives us the hope of eternal life in the presence of the One who filled the manger. The pessimist says the cup is half empty. The optimist says the cup is half full. The Christian knows that as we empty ourselves, God will fill us with His blessings.

59. REAL WORLD PROBLEMS

Recently, I was talking to my daughter, who told me she has a children's Bible that she reads to her son. One thing she realized is that all the stories in the children's Bible have been "cleaned up" a bit. For instance, you can read all about Noah and the ark and the animals and the flood. But you will not read about the time he got drunk and fell asleep naked in his tent. You can read all about David being a shepherd and slaying the evil giant. But you will find no mention of his moral failure with Bathsheba and the arranged murder of her husband Uriah. Omitting those parts of the story in a children's Bible is a wise move. We want our babies to learn about God without giving them information that their young minds aren't ready to handle.

But as we grow, we need to graduate from the children's Bible. This is why I love to do textual sermon series and studies of biblical characters. The Bible pulls no punches. It tells us the good, the bad, and the ugly. I'm glad it does because that more accurately describes my life. There is some good, some bad, and some ugly. And reading the stories of Noah, Abraham, David, Paul, and others lets me know God can handle all of life.

Sometimes you hear Christians say that following Jesus will make you more successful. Just listen to their sermons, podcasts, or read some of their books, and you will hear it. They say God wants to bless you. And by "bless," they mean make you rich. Sometimes it sounds like God is a short-order cook and will make us whatever we ask Him. But Jesus never said anything like that. He clearly said He didn't come to make life easier for us. He came to rescue us and make our lives more purposeful by making us more like Him.

Jesus never promised to eliminate all the chaos from our lives. He said He'd bring meaning to the chaos. If you wonder why you still face some of the same struggles you brought into your relationship with God, you are in good company. He promises to be with us while we reach toward Him to find more meaning in our circumstances. That's the real blessing.

"In this world you will have trouble. But take heart! I have overcome the world" (John 16:33b).

60. LET'S CLEAN THIS MESS UP

It's amazing what passes for entertainment on television. You turn on one channel, and you find people living on an island for thirty-nine days, trying to survive and make a million dollars. If you don't want to watch that, you can change over to the 600-pound people trying to lose enough weight so they have to have their extra skin removed. No? Well then, you can watch someone who is addicted to eating couch cushions. Yuk! Let's watch some housewives screaming at each other. Not your thing? How about some working people? You can watch some people driving trucks down an icy road or watch high school dropouts trying to catch crabs in the Bering Sea. This is what we call reality TV.

There is another show out there that is awful enough that it will make you do something good. The show is called "Hoarders." Just one episode will make you get off the sofa and clean out your closets. This show features people who live in houses stacked wall-to-wall and floor-to-ceiling with clutter. Clutter is actually a nice word for useless stuff or trash. These people live in houses they can barely walk through, and it has become normal to them. If you are like me, you watch and just shake your head, wondering how it could ever get so bad.

Before we all stand in judgment, let's stop and take inventory of our lives. We may not live in a house full of junk, but we live with hearts and heads full of junk. We cling to bad memories and past failures like they were treasures. There is a reason Jesus said that to enter the kingdom of God, we must become like little children. Little children don't have a bunch of junk lying around. On "Hoarders," they send a crew into the house to clean up the mess. The hoarders resist at first, but eventually the house gets clean, and they have a whole new lease on life.

"'Come now, let us settle the matter,' says the Lord. 'Though your sins are like scarlet, they shall be as white as snow; though they are red as crimson, they shall be like wool.'" (Isaiah 1:18).

Are you holding on to memories, past failures, and sins that are cluttering up your life? Have they been there for so long that you have just gotten used to living with them? God doesn't send in a crew; He sent His Son. The cleanup happens when we accept the grace He offers. Isn't it about time that we clean this mess up and start living?

61. GOD LOVES YOU

God loves you, and there is nothing you can do about it. Yes, you! God loves us each individually. God knows you better than you even know yourself. He knows everything you have done. He knows everything you have ever said. He knows every thought you have ever had. And yet He loves you with a love that can never be broken.

"For I am convinced that neither death nor life, neither angels nor demons, neither the present nor the future, nor any powers, neither height nor depth, nor anything else in all creation, will be able to separate us from the love of God that is in Christ Jesus our Lord" *(Romans 8:38-39).*

It's true. God loves you when you are at your best, and God loves you when you are at your worst. His love never wavers. God continued to love Adam and Eve when they ate the forbidden fruit. They had to face consequences, but God's love for them continued. God continued to love Abraham when he doubted that God would fulfill His promise. God continued to love and provide for the Israelite people when they grumbled against Him in the desert. God's love for David never ceased, even when he committed horrible sins. Peter was still loved by God when he denied even knowing Jesus. God's loving patience was shown to Thomas when he doubted the resurrection. Paul was loved by God when his life was committed to persecuting Christians. And God loves you. Even in your deepest and darkest moments, there is nothing that can separate you from the love of God. The only question that remains is how will you respond? Will you return His love? Even if you doubt, disobey, deny, betray, or stand against God, He will never cease to love you. God loves you, and there is nothing you can do about it!

OUR
love
FOR GOD

62. LET IT SHINE

Last summer our two-year-old grandson was staying with us and got to attend Vacation Bible School for a couple of days. To this day he will still ask me to sing the "This Little Light of Mine" song. He loves to scream "NO!" in the verse that talks about hiding it under a bushel. He also loves to blow (spit) in the verse that talks about not letting the devil put out your light. I wanted to know the history of this song, so I Googled it. Two things surprised me: First, the author of this song is unknown. It just seemed to show up. Second, Bruce Springsteen performed this song live in concert. His enthusiasm matched any kid I have ever seen at VBS. While the author of the song is unknown, the origin of the song is not.

"You are the light of the world. A town built on a hill cannot be hidden. Neither do people light a lamp and put it under a bowl. Instead, they put it on its stand, and it gives light to everyone in the house. In the same way, let your light shine before others, that they may see your good deeds and glorify your Father in heaven" (Matthew 5:14-16).

Jesus did not say these words to the politicians or the religious leaders of the day. He said them to the common people like you and me. Jesus knew the darkness of this world and that the cure for darkness is light. He reminded us of our mission to go out and let the light of the love of God shine through us wherever we go. We are not to hide our relationship with God. We are called to live it every day and everywhere we go. Don't miss the last few words in Matthew 5:16. Being the light means glorifying God, not ourselves. So, let's let it shine, all the time, let it shine!

63. BEST YEAR EVER!

It's already that time of year. That time of year when we start failing on our New Year's resolutions. Yes, it's only the first week of January, but that shows how committed, or non-committed, we are to our new goals. According to the latest Statista poll, this year's most popular New Year's resolutions are really no different than any other year. The top three are: save money, exercise more, and eat healthier. No big surprise. Maybe you have some other resolutions you are trying to keep. Let me, and Solomon, suggest a New Year's resolution that is not only attainable, but will significantly make your life better.

"Commit to the Lord whatever you do, and he will establish your plans" (Proverbs 16:3).

To accomplish our goals, we usually start with a plan. Next, we put steps in place to accomplish our plan. Then we make every effort to take those steps. The problem with that is we often take the wrong first step. As a matter of fact, every step in that plan is wrong. Far too often we make plans then pray and ask God to bless them. Not only does that plan have an element of selfishness, but it also has an element or arrogance. It is saying to God that what I want is the most important thing, and I know better than You. Try this instead—the first step we need to take is to commit our lives to the Lord. After that, we allow God to establish our plans and direct our steps.

This year, make a resolution to commit your life fully to the Lord. Then you and God together can dream big. God's got a really, really good success rate of accomplishing His purpose. Actually, He's perfect. Become a part of God's purpose instead of asking God to become a part of your purpose. Make this year the greatest year of your life.

64. FINAL REQUEST

Have you ever watched a movie where someone, with their last breath, makes a dying request? It is usually taken very seriously by those who hear their words. If the movie is a love story, a spouse may hear the dying request and learn to love again. If the movie is an inspirational story, a child may hear the request and go on to live a productive life. If the movie is a horror story, the final request had better be honored or the dead person will come back to haunt you! What a final request represents is the deepest desire of the person who knows that their time on Earth is drawing to a close. In 2020, Krista and I sat and listened to the final request of her older sister. Susan, Krista's older sister, passed away early in 2021. Since then, we have done our best to honor the request she shared with us. We do that because of the depth of our love for Susan.

When Jesus knew that His earthly life was coming to an end, He shared the Passover meal with the disciples. Just moments before His arrest, trial, and crucifixion, Jesus spent a few hours in the garden in prayer. As Jesus prayed, He made a final request to His Father that includes each of us.

> *"My prayer is not for them alone. I pray also for those who will believe in me through their message, that all of them may be one, Father, just as you are in me and I am in you. May they also be in us so that the world may believe that you have sent me. I have given them the glory that you gave me, that they may be one as we are one—I in them and you in me—so that they may be brought to complete unity. Then the world will know that you sent me and have loved them even as you have loved me"* (John 17:20-23).

Jesus's final request was that those who believe in Him will be unified. Then He adds that the unity of believers will point the rest of the world to the truth. Will we honor the final request of our Savior? The decision is up to each of us.

65. MOVING MOLEHILLS

I can remember the Bible class in great detail. I was in the second-grade and our teacher had us read the following verse:

"He replied, 'Because you have so little faith. Truly I tell you, if you have faith as small as a mustard seed, you can say to this mountain, "Move from here to there," and it will move. Nothing will be impossible for you'" (Matthew 17:20).

Probably the reason I remember it so clearly is that the teacher passed out mustard seeds. As I held that small seed in my hand, I thought, "Surely I have at least this much faith." So, armed with that information and remembering some other words of Jesus when He said, *"Let the little children come to me, and do not hinder them, for the kingdom of heaven belongs to such as these,"* I set off to move some mountains. Keep in mind that I grew up in Del City, Oklahoma. There are no mountains in Del City. So, in reality, I set off to move a few molehills. Needless to say, I became discouraged after several unsuccessful tries to move red dirt from one place to another.

With a few years behind me, I now realize I was being too literal with Jesus's words from Matthew 17. They are not about actually moving mountains. What Jesus was saying was that with the power of God in your life, you are able to do things that are beyond your own capabilities. As we begin this New Year, let me challenge you to dream big. Set some lofty goals. Goals are different from resolutions. Resolutions are things you know you can do if you only apply a measure of self-discipline. It is easy to set resolutions that you know you have the ability to reach. Go bigger! Set some goals that only God can reach. Then pray hard, stay diligent, and see what God can do.

"Jesus replied, 'What is impossible with man is possible with God'"
(Luke 18:27).

66. HOW TO GROW YOUR FAITH

How do I grow my faith? Well, I guess we have to start with the meaning of the word faith.

"Now faith is confidence in what we hope for and assurance about what we do not see" (Hebrews 11:1).

So, how do I grow my faith? I probably need to do an extensive Hebrew or Greek word study of the word faith to truly understand it. Maybe we need to have a few sermons or Bible classes on how we can grow our faith. Or even better yet, a seminar! A whole weekend dedicated to making our faith stronger. Those are all great things, but none of them will help you reach your stated goal of growing your faith. There is one sure-fire way to grow your faith. Get your nose out of the Bible and your body out of the church building and start doing stuff. In Hebrews 11, we see a listing of people of great faith. One thing they all have in common is a verb—they all *did* stuff.

- Able BROUGHT God an offering
- Noah BUILT an ark
- Abraham OBEYED and WENT and later OFFERED his son
- Isaac BLESSED Esau and Jacob
- Jacob WORSHIPED
- Moses LEFT Egypt and KEPT the Passover
- Rahab WELCOMED the spies

"The world and its desires pass away, but whoever does the will of God lives forever" (1 John 2:17).

To understand faith, you will need to study and pray. But there is only one way to grow faith: The only way to grow faith is to get out there and *do*. Find your own verb that God has uniquely equipped you to fulfill. Then get out there and do it!

67. ON THE OTHER HAND

Typically, when I sit down to write an article, I am filled with joy and enthusiasm to share some thoughts on God's Word. Today is different. Two weeks ago, as we were worshiping in our building, just a couple hours from here, a man entered a worship service with evil in his heart. At the beginning of their communion time, he stood up and began shooting at members of the church, killing two. Before he could do any more harm, a member of the church's security team fired a shot and killed the gunman. So many things are wrong with that situation. First, that anyone would enter a worship service with evil in their heart and then act on it. Secondly, that the time of the incident was during our most sacred time of worship. A time when we remember the sacrifice that Jesus made for our eternal salvation. Thirdly, that a church needs a security team that is trained for such a situation.

I found myself saying, "Well, these are the times we are living in." But that statement is incorrect. Since humans have existed, evil has existed. Good has always had an enemy. Is it wrong or showing a lack of faith for a church to be prepared? Let me remind you of scripture from the book of Nehemiah. The book of Nehemiah is about God's people rebuilding the walls around Jerusalem. As these good people were doing the Lord's work, enemies tried to deter them.

"From that day on, half of my men did the work, while the other half were equipped with spears, shields, bows, and armor. The officers posted themselves behind all the people of Judah who were building the wall. Those who carried materials did their work with one hand and held a weapon in the other" (Nehemiah 4:16-17).

Evil wins when the work of the Lord stops. It's sad that we must live with one hand on our weapon because the enemy is near. But don't forget that the other hand continues the work.

68. GET IN THE GAME

Are you a game show watcher? Do you watch shows like Jeopardy and get frustrated at the contestants because they can't come up with the right answers (or questions)? Meanwhile, you are sitting in your La-Z-Boy with all the knowledge. As you watch *Wheel of Fortune*, do you want to pull your hair out because the contestants cannot figure out the phrase that is so painfully obvious? In sports, we call that being an armchair quarterback. That is someone who knows it all and thinks they can do it all, but they are not on the field. What good is it if you have all the right answers but you are not in the game? The same could be said about faith.

"What good is it, my brothers and sisters, if someone claims to have faith but has no deeds? Can such faith save them?"
(James 2:14).

Faith alone is much like sitting on the couch with all the right answers. But if your faith is not accompanied by actions, it is useless. Read through Hebrews 11. It contains a list of people who are acknowledged for their great faith. The one thing they all have in common is that their faith was shown by their actions. Abel *offered*. Noah *built* the ark. Abraham obeyed and *went*. Isaac *blessed* his sons. Jacob *worshiped*. Joseph *spoke*. Moses *left* Egypt. The Israelites *passed through* the Red Sea. Rahab *welcomed* the spies.

You cannot be saved by works alone. And you cannot be saved without faith. True faith is always shown by actions. Following Jesus is not just about learning the right ideas, saying the right words, memorizing a couple of verses, and singing the right songs. Following Jesus is about getting off the pew and *living* your faith.

"As the body without the spirit is dead, so faith without deeds is dead" (James 2:26).

Let's get off the couch, get in the game and make a difference in our world!

69. ONE FOOT IN FRONT OF THE OTHER

When I was twelve years old, my older brother ran his first marathon. He was eighteen at the time. When he got home, I had a million questions. Did you really run twenty-six miles? Did you take a shortcut? Did you ever stop? Did you win? How long did it take? Did you have to go to the bathroom? Some of my questions showed my preteen ignorance. But one thing I knew for sure, some day I wanted to run a marathon. I made a commitment that day, I will run a marathon!

Fast forward ten years. My brother was twenty-eight years old and I was twenty-two when he ran his second marathon. As he told me about running his second marathon, it reminded me of my commitment. In my heart I still wanted to run a marathon but with my life I had done absolutely nothing about it. I renewed my commitment: I will run a marathon! Fast forward another ten years. My brother now had three marathons under his belt. I still had zero. The desire was still there, but there was no action to back it up. The task seemed overwhelming. I knew it was possible for a human to complete a marathon. But I never got off the couch to actually do it myself.

When I was thirty-eight years old, I finally found the motivation. I went to the track at the high school to see what I could do. I could almost complete one lap before I had to stop and walk. It took more than a year of dedicated training, but one April morning in 2006, at the age of thirty-nine I found myself at the starting line of the Oklahoma City Bombing Memorial Marathon. Just a little over four hours later, I crossed the finish line and completed a commitment I had made twenty-seven years earlier.

Just wanting something will not make it happen. Just committing to something will not make it happen. It can only happen when you put one foot in front of the other and totally commit. Knowing you should make a commitment to Christ is a good start, but it means nothing. The only thing that matters is when you go all in and make a total commitment.

"So they pulled their boats up on shore, left everything and followed him" (Luke 5:11).

When Peter, James, and John were called by Jesus to follow Him, they left everything behind. They show us what it means to go all in. There's an old saying, "The longest journey begins with a single step." Don't just consider making a commitment to Jesus. Get off the couch and just put one foot in front of the other.

70. GIANTS WILL FALL

One of the first Bible stories we learn as children is the battle between David and Goliath. Two armies stood facing each other with a valley between them. The Israelite army looked across the valley at the Philistine army. Their army was not so intimidating, but one man was. Goliath could bump his head on a basketball goal if he stood on his tiptoes. His armor and equipment alone would outweigh the average soldier. His bark was so intimidating that no one dared to see if he had the bite to back it up. It is no surprise that the Israelite army would tuck tail and run when challenged by Goliath. Wouldn't you?

We do it every day. Satan stops us in our tracks by putting a Goliath in our path. That Goliath steals our joy, our progress, our dignity, our faith, and our victory. The soldiers were right to believe they were unable to defeat their enemy. It took David to remind them what they were fighting for, who they were fighting for, and by whose power they could overcome their enemy. David knew the secret; it's God's power, not ours. David confidently spoke these words to Goliath.

"All those gathered here will know that it is not by sword or spear that the Lord saves; for the battle is the Lord's, and he will give all of you into our hands" (1 Samuel 17:47).

Those words were not spoken to only inform the Philistine army; they were spoken to remind the Israelite army of the power of their God. When Goliath blocks your path, don't tuck tail and run. Step forward confidently with the assurance that no enemy is greater than the power of God.

71. THE DESTINATION IS WORTH THE STRUGGLE

I spent part of last week with my mom in the hospital and in a skilled nursing facility. She was able to walk into the hospital. But after spending 12 days on her back in bed, she was unable to stand on her own. Her desire is to get back to her independent living apartment and to be able to drive to the store. I told her that the decision to do that was in her hands. In physical therapy, they would ask her to do things that would be hard to do. If she wants to reach her goal, she will have to do the little things today that will lead her to the bigger things for tomorrow.

That's a lot like life for all of us. "I want to lose weight and get in shape." Are you willing to start exercising and eating right today and make that a habit? "I want to have a beautiful garden that we can eat from." Are you willing to till the ground, plant the seeds, water, and pull weeds? "I want a strong marriage." Are you willing to do the little things each day for the rest of your life? I believe that we all would like to spend eternity in heaven. But just wanting it doesn't make it happen. It's the little daily decisions that will lead us to our destination. One day Jesus was asked, "Of all the commandments, which is the most important?"

"'The most important one,' answered Jesus, 'is this: "Hear, O Israel: The Lord our God, the Lord is one. Love the Lord your God with all your heart and with all your soul and with all your mind and with all your strength." The second is this: "Love your neighbor as yourself." There is no commandment greater than these'"
(Mark 12:29-31).

To love God with everything you have and to love others is not a one-time thing. It is something that you have to do on a moment-to-moment basis. Yes, it will be hard at times. But the destination will be worth the struggle.

72. KEEP RUNNING

As I have studied the battle between David and Goliath in 1 Samuel 17, one of my favorite phrases is found in verse 48. "David ran quickly toward the battle line to meet him." Do you wonder if, as David was running toward Goliath, he had the thought in the back of his mind, "This is not a good idea"? I don't know how anyone in his shoes could help but think that. But David had two things that would override any doubts: courage and passion. He had a passion for God that fueled his courage to try. Passion and courage are two qualities every great leader possesses.

I will never forget the first time I was asked to preach at a church on Sunday morning. I was only 14 years old. My brother and his college friends were going to Colorado to lead a Saturday youth rally at a small church. With hindsight, I think my mom told my brother to take me with them. They were also asked to lead the worship on Sunday morning. I was honored when they asked me to preach. Again, with hindsight, I think the truth is that none of them wanted to prepare a lesson. I was so nervous, but the group of college guys filled me with passion and courage. So, I stood up that Sunday morning and knocked it out of the park (in my mind). I can only hope that no one recorded my sermon.

When it comes to our commitment to God and our work in His kingdom, let me encourage you to be like David. Run forward with passion and courage. Don't let fear of failure keep you on the sidelines. In basketball, there is an old saying, "You miss every shot you don't take." No one in the history of the sport has ever made every shot they have taken. The mindset of a champion tells them that the next shot is going in, just keep shooting.

"… being confident of this, that he who began a good work in you will carry it on to completion until the day of Christ Jesus"
(Philippians 1:6).

The road a Christian travels is not a straight and easy path. It is filled with giants, failures, challenges, and discouragement. Just keep running. Don't give up on God. He will never give up on you.

123

73. STRUGGLING WITH A DECISION?

Yogi Berra was a man who was credited with some great quotes. Some of my favorites are, "No one goes there nowadays, it's too crowded," "A nickel ain't worth a dime anymore," "You can observe a lot of just by watching," and "Always go to other people's funerals, otherwise they won't come to yours." But my favorite "Yogi-ism" is "When you come to a fork in the road, take it." I love that quote because we have all been there.

We have all come to a point in life where we have to make a decision. We stress about it, we weigh the pros and the cons, and if we are a Christian, we need to spend time in prayer. But eventually, the moment will come when a decision needs to be made. That's what happened to me years ago. I was at a fork in the road and had to make a big life decision. I prayed, I fasted, and I waited for God to give me an answer. But the answer did not come. So, I went to a friend who had been at a similar crossroads in life. He told me something that was hard to understand, but I have never forgotten it. He said, "Some decisions are not a matter of right and wrong. God is not concerned with which way you go. His only concern is that you take Him with you."

"And whatever you do, whether in word or deed, do it all in the name of the Lord Jesus, giving thanks to God the Father through him" (Colossians 3:17).

Some decisions we make in life are the choice to be sinful or holy. Those are obvious decisions for a Christian. But there are some decisions we have to make that are just decisions. Don't get stuck at a crossroads. Pray about it. Then take God with you down the road you choose. Maybe Yogi was right, when you come to a fork in the road, take it!

74. WILL YOU PLAY THE GAME?

Our "Empowering Subjects" seminar last weekend started with a game. We were given little information but lots of rules. One of the rules we had to obey was that decisions had to be made. First, a leader of the group had to be chosen. Then officers had to be assigned. A name for the group had to be selected, and a banner had to be drawn. We then had to choose various actions for our group and how to face a few tragedies. While doing all of this, we were never really sure what the purpose of the game truly was. Except …

There was a scoreboard on the screen. The scoreboard kept track of each team's score in three different fields: treasury, prestige, and happiness. With each decision we made, our score changed. Most of us have a competitive nature, so we could not keep ourselves from watching our score and comparing it with the other teams. Obviously the team with the highest scores wins the game, right? As we learned what boosted our score, we focused our attention and decisions on climbing up the scoreboard. Once the game was over, everything was explained. The scores that everyone was focused on were irrelevant to the game. The instructor compared them to secular values, others' opinions, and social media. We got so focused on what everyone else thought that we miss the entire point of the game.

"Listen, my dear brothers and sisters: Has not God chosen those who are poor in the eyes of the world to be rich in faith and to inherit the kingdom he promised those who love him?" (James 2:5).

Years ago, I learned a phrase, and I try to live by it every day: "Live for an audience of One." It is so tempting to live to please others, to try to meet their expectations, and to seek favor in their eyes, that we forget that only one opinion really matters. So, here is the question, will you play the game, or will you live to please God?

75. JUST DO IT!

I think I'm missing out on something that is big money. I don't want to pay big money; I want to make big money. The big money-maker sweeping the nation right now is home workout equipment. Do you remember when home workout equipment consisted of a step that you just stepped on and stepped off? Maybe you wanted to spend a little more money so you invested in a treadmill (which eventually became a place to hang laundry). Now they are selling products like the Peloton bike. It connects to your Wi-Fi, and you compete live with people all around the world. I saw a commercial the other day for a product called "The Mirror." This is a mirror you hang in your home, and a holographic ghost instructor shows up to lead you through a workout. I don't know for sure if they can actually see you, but it would still creep me out.

You would think with all of these big money products that people were just craving to work out. For most of us, the desire to work out and actually working out are two completely different things. Sure, I would like to be in great shape. And according to some people in my life who choose not to filter their words, I need to work out—often! But all the money spent on equipment and all the desire in the world really doesn't matter if you don't have the obedience to actually get off the couch and do it.

Talking about obedience is a lot like spending money on workout equipment. It doesn't mean anything unless you actually do it. Sure, many of us want the end result of obedience—an eternal home in heaven. But what good does it do to sit on the pew and talk about it if no one actually does it?

Obedience is something that no one can do for you. It is a decision that you make that must be put into action. So, let's not just spend time sitting in our church buildings and talking about obedience; let's get off the pew and JUST DO IT!

"Jesus replied, 'Anyone who loves me will obey my teaching. My Father will love them, and we will come to them and make our home with them. Anyone who does not love me will not obey my teaching. These words you hear are not my own; they belong to the Father who sent me'" *(John 14:23-24).*

76. MAKING THE GRADE

Have you ever heard the expression "God grades on the curve"? You may have, but I can promise you this: You didn't read it in the Bible. God grading on the curve means if I am better than most people, I must be okay. So many people try to justify their "rightness" with God this way. Things are said like, "Well, at least I have never killed anyone," or "I have never spent any time in prison," or "I have never prostituted my body for money," or "I have never gotten so drunk that I passed out." We say these things to lower others and therefore elevate ourselves.

But here is the problem. If you read Hebrews 11, you will find a list of people who are being held up as those with great faith. Among that list, you will find a man named Moses who was guilty of murder. You will find a man named Joseph, who spent many years in prison. You will find a lady named Rahab, who the Bible refers to as Rahab the prostitute. And you will also find a man named Noah, who was found drunk, naked, and passed out in his tent. All of these people are known as people of great faith.

So how does God grade? God grades by the heart. David was guilty of at least half of the horrible things listed above and a whole bunch more. Yet he is referred to in the New Testament as a man after God's own heart. God knows your heart. That can be comforting and scary. It's comforting to know that when you make a mistake but truly repent in your heart, God forgives the mistake. It's scary because we can outwardly do good things, but if our hearts are evil, God knows.

Don't buy into the lie of Satan that tells you that your sins in the past have separated you from God forever. And don't buy into the lies of men that say you can do enough good to get into heaven. Have faith in the grace of God. That is the only way to make the grade.

"For it is by grace you have been saved, through faith—and this is not from yourselves, it is the gift of God—not by works, so that no one can boast" (Ephesians 2:8-9).

77. WINNING THE ARGUMENT BUT LOSING THE PERSON

One of my favorite comedians said, "One thing you will never read online: You know what, I think you are right. You have changed my mind." There are some people who have this false belief that they are professional arguers. This belief is amped up when they are typing on their phone or sitting at a keyboard. Do you know anyone like this? Are you one of these people? Would you rather win the argument than win the person? Do you always have to have the last word because you believe whoever speaks last wins? In our house, we have a big plaque on the wall with a verse on it that helps me when I feel the need to straighten someone out or put them in their place.

"And what does the Lord require of you? To act justly and to love mercy and to walk humbly with your God" (Micah 6:8).

These three simple concepts will help you build harmony with others instead of friction. They will help you build relationships instead of discord. First, we must act justly. There is a time for teaching and sharing your opinions. But as followers of Christ, we are to speak the truth in love. Next, we are to love mercy. Mercy is defined as not giving others what they deserve. After we speak the truth in love, take the time to stop speaking and listen intently. Allow others to share what they believe without interruption. The last one may be the toughest one of all: Walk humbly with your God. Humility requires you to check your pride at the door. Humility lets others have the last word. Even Jesus stood silent before His accusers. So, the next time things get a little heated, take the opportunity to show love and grace. You may lose the argument, but you just might win the person.

78. TENNIS, ANYONE?

I have a love/hate relationship with tennis. I love playing tennis. But I hate that I'm not better at playing. I love watching the professionals play tennis. But I hate the scoring system. Tennis has the most bizarre scoring system of any sport. To begin with, there is no such thing in tennis as zero. If you have nothing, that means you have LOVE. I have heard zero referred to as nil, but never LOVE. Then, when you win your first point, the score is 15-LOVE. Why fifteen? I have no idea. When you score the next point, you have 30. Again, it makes absolutely no sense, but I do see the pattern. Until you score your next point, then you have 40. Huh? I don't know the reason for this randomness. If the score becomes 40-40, they call that deuce. I always thought deuce meant two, but what do I know? As I said, tennis has the most bizarre scoring system in all of sports.

But one thing I love about tennis is that you have to win the final point. In sports like football, soccer, and basketball, if you build a big lead, you can just run out the clock. You can literally do nothing until time runs out. Not in tennis. You have to keep playing hard and win the last point.

In our Christian life, we live by a scoring system that the world would look at and say, "It is bizarre." Jesus said, "The first will be last." He also said, "Whoever wants to become great among you must be your servant," and "Whoever wants to save their life will lose it." To the world, this scoring system makes no sense. Also, like tennis, in our Christian lives, we are called to play to the very end. The Apostle Paul wrote this:

"I have fought the good fight, I have finished the race, I have kept the faith. Now there is in store for me the crown of righteousness ..." (Philippians 4:7-8a).

When I show up at the end of time for judgment, I don't want to be well rested and preserved. I want to show up exhausted and beaten from a lifetime of serving the Lord. And when He asks what I have for Him, I will simply respond, "I have nothing." Then I will hear Him say, "No, you have LOVE!"

79. KEEP YOUR EYES ON THE PRIZE

As a sports fan, the spring and summer of 2020 were rough. The Coronavirus robbed me of watching March Madness, the summer Olympics, the college baseball World Series, the softball World Series, spring MLB, and the NBA (who later finished in the "bubble"). The only sport I could find worth watching on ESPN was Cornhole. Up until then, I thought of Cornhole as a game that could be played by anyone, usually at picnics or while tailgating before a football game. Come to find out, there are professional Cornhole players who make a living at it.

Cornhole is a simple game. You simply stand about thirty feet away from a piece of wood with a hole cut in it and toss bean bags. Points are scored if you land one in the hole or on the board. The key to being a good Cornhole player is the keep your eyes on the target and block out everything else.

"And whatever you do, whether in word or deed, do it all in the name of the Lord Jesus, giving thanks to God the Father through him" (Colossians 3:17).

Christianity is actually just that simple. We tend to make it more confusing than it needs to be. We argue over theology. We emphasize the name on the sign in front of our building. We get bent out of shape when the order of worship is changed. We give too much thought to what the group down the street is doing. All of these things, and many others, will distract us from the true goal of pleasing God. If we focus on pleasing God, all of these things will take care of themselves.

Paul understood this concept. He cared very deeply about theology and getting it right. But if you are not pleasing God in the process, you have missed the target. So, whether you are at a picnic on Saturday or in worship services on Sunday, keep your eyes on the prize. Make it your goal to please Him!

135

80. WHINING IN THE WILDERNESS

I am currently teaching through the book of Exodus in our Sunday morning Bible class. The more I study this book, the more I get angry with the Israelites. Let's review: The Israelites were enslaved in Egypt, and they cried out to God for relief. God heard their cry and sent His servant Moses. What followed was 10 plagues that not only gave them their freedom, they left Egypt with flocks of livestock and their pockets full of gold and silver.

But on their way, they got thirsty, and they grumbled saying they would rather have died in Egypt than die of thirst in the wilderness. So, God gave them water. When their tummies growled, they grumbled about having no food. So, God provided manna and quail for them to eat. When they were hemmed in by the Red Sea as Pharaoh's army approached, they grumbled and wished they would have just stayed in Egypt as slaves. So, God not only parted the waters so they could escape, He drowned Pharaoh's army in the sea. If I hear them grumble one more time (and I know I will), I would like to grab my Bible and shake some sense into them. But then I have to stop and remember that they are a lot like us.

> *"Then I thought, 'To this I will appeal: the years when the Most High stretched out his right hand. I will remember the deeds of the Lord; yes, I will remember your miracles of long ago. I will consider all your works and meditate on all your mighty deeds'"*
> *(Psalm 77:10-12).*

God continuously rescued them and blessed them. But the next trial they faced, they forgot all that God had done. When we face challenging times or go through a difficult season of life, we need to stop and remember what all the Lord has done for us. Before we begin to grumble or fall into sin, we need to remember that we have a God who loves us and will not leave us in the wilderness to fend for ourselves. God has always been there. God is with us in our current struggle. And God will always be with us in the future.

81. TAKING A LESSON FROM THE CONEYS

So, just what is a coney? A coney has also been called a hyrax or a rock badger. They are furry little animals that weigh around nine pounds. They are mentioned a couple of times in the Bible.

"The high mountains belong to the wild goats; the crags are a refuge for the hyrax" (Psalm 104:18).

"Hyraxes are creatures of little power, yet they make their home in the crag" (Proverbs 30:26).

Not only do we have a lot in common with these little creatures, we could learn a very valuable lesson from them. They live in families. They never venture too far from home. They spend the majority of their day just basking in the sun. They also sing! They let each other know how they are feeling with all kinds of whistles, twitters, shrieks, and growls.

Here is the weakness of the coney. They have no defense from their predators. Their furry little bodies look delicious to the birds of the air and the scavengers on the ground. The coney is not fast enough to flee, and it does not have claws or teeth to fight off its enemies. So, how do they survive?

They have one great defense. When danger comes, they burrow into the rocks. The rocks are their shield against any would-be attackers. Is there a lesson there for us? We have an enemy who seeks to destroy us. By our own strength, we are defenseless. The coney teaches us to never get too far from our protection. Spend our time basking in the Son (sun) and singing. And to always know that our defender is our Rock. We are as strong as the rock, and our attackers are powerless against it!

"The Lord is my strength and my defense; he has become my salvation" (Psalm 118:14).

82. HAVE A GREAT MONDAY

Do you remember your wedding day? Your friends and family were gathered in their finest clothes. You looked great. Your spouse-to-be looked even greater. You made heartfelt vows to each other and shared a kiss. Could you actually love this person more than on that day? I sure hope so.

Do you remember the day you were baptized? You were surrounded by friends and family. You confessed the name of Jesus. As you entered the water, you were a sinner who deserved an eternity worth of punishment. As you rose from the water, you were a forgiven child of God. Could you love God any more than on that day? I sure hope so.

After years have passed, what is more important to your marriage: the wedding day or how you have lived since then? The wedding ceremony is the foundation of your commitment. But it is meaningless if you forget to live your vows. What is more important: your baptism or how you have lived since that day? Baptism is the necessary step into your relationship with God. But it is meaningless if you abandon that commitment the rest of your life.

This morning, we gather to worship on Easter Sunday to celebrate the resurrection of our Lord and Savior Jesus Christ. We celebrate the most important day in all of history. On that day, death was defeated. On that day, the door was opened for all of us to walk through the grave and spend eternity in heaven. What a great day! But that day is meaningless if we ignore the crucifixion and resurrection of Jesus by living selfishly the rest of our days.

"Praise be to the God and Father of our Lord Jesus Christ! In his great mercy he has given us new birth into a living hope through the resurrection of Jesus Christ from the dead" (1 Peter 1:3).

I hope Easter Sunday is a great day for you. But I hope Monday is even better.

83. PEOPLE PLEASERS

One of the things we try to instill in our teens is the power of peer pressure. We try to teach them that what others think of them is not the most important thing. That is a hard lesson to learn because it starts much earlier than the teen years.

I have two grandsons. The oldest is about to turn 3, and the youngest just had his first birthday. Even at that age, you can see the power of peer pressure. Jordan, the youngest one, not only watches his brother and tries to act like him, he will also do anything he can just to get his brother's attention and approval.

But peer pressure is not just a problem for the kids. My mother lives in an independent living facility. Recently she wanted a very specific new walker. Partially because it would help her, but also so she could show it off to the other residents. The point is, peer pressure is a temptation for all of us, regardless of age.

On Paul's first missionary journey, one of his stops was in Galatia, where many people came to believe in Jesus. When Paul arrived back at his home church in Antioch, he was shocked to hear that the new church established in Galatia had begun to believe a false gospel being preached by false teachers. Paul wrote to them and warned them about going along with what seemed like the most popular thing to do.

"Am I now trying to win the approval of human beings, or of God? Or am I trying to please people? If I were still trying to please people, I would not be a servant of Christ" (Galatians 1:10).

Only one approval really matters in the end. None of us will stand at judgment time hoping all of our peers like us. The only opinion that will decide our eternity will be what God thinks. So, with each decision of our daily lives, we must ask ourselves, "Am I trying to please people or am I trying to please God?"

84. BE STILL AND REMEMBER WHY WE ARE HERE

Do you remember the good old days? I'm referring to just three months ago when everything was "normal." What we called normal was when our days were filled with noise and activity. Get up early, turn on some music or TV, get breakfast for the family, rush out the door to get kids to school and us to work, meetings, deadlines, off to see the kids games or take them to practice, uh-oh, what are we going to do for dinner, try to make it home before dark, see if you can get the house settled enough for at least one quiet moment, off to bed, then do it all again.

That's normal? We have let our normal become organized chaos. And honestly, there was no end in sight. Then along came COVID. Even then we still tried to be "normal." But we were told to quarantine. Stay at home. Only go out when absolutely necessary. At first it was okay. It was like a staycation (a staycation is a vacation where you just stay at home). But after a couple of weeks, it became more like a prison sentence than a vacation. Why? Because we have let busyness become our normal.

What is usually the first thing to go when we are too busy? Our time of spiritual focus on God. I am not one who believes that God caused the pandemic to happen. But I am one who believes that God can use it to our advantage and His glory.

"He says, 'Be still, and know that I am God; I will be exalted among the nations, I will be exalted in the earth'" (Psalm 46:10).

Take time to just be still and refocus your life on God. Find ways to exalt Him in your everyday life. The day will come, soon I hope, when all of this will be behind us. Shame on us if we simply return to our "normal" life. Let this time be a reboot of your life. Commit now that you will not let the noise of this world distract you from your relationship with God.

85. SIMPLE SALVATION

When Jesus was on Earth, He spent His entire life being misunderstood. Around the time of Jesus's birth, King Herod's misunderstanding of Jesus caused him to order the killing of all babies, fearing his earthly throne was threatened. At the age of twelve, Jesus's parents could not understand why He stayed behind in Jerusalem talking with the teachers in the temple. Throughout His ministry years, He was misunderstood by His rivals, friends, and followers. Sadly, even today Jesus is misunderstood. Ask anyone what it means to follow Jesus, and you will get a number of wrong answers.

Wrong answer No. 1: To follow Jesus, you must have an impressive list of accomplishments. On a number of occasions, Jesus took time away from the crowds to spend time with small children. He loved them and blessed them. And what had they accomplished in life? Nothing yet!

Wrong answer No. 2: To follow Jesus, you must have a good reputation. Jesus called a tax collector named Matthew right out of his booth to be one of His disciples. Jesus also spent a day at the house of a tax collector named Zacchaeus. Tax collectors were not respected by the Romans and absolutely hated by the Jews.

Wrong answer No. 3: To follow Jesus, you must be living a good life. When confronted with a woman who had been caught in the act of adultery, Jesus not only saved her, He even refused to condemn her. When coming face to face with a man who was so evil, the community bound him by chains in the cemetery, Jesus saved Him and made him a missionary.

Wrong answer No. 4: To follow Jesus, you must give a lot of money. After watching many rich people give bags of money at the temple, Jesus praised a widow who gave only a couple of pennies.

Wrong answer No. 5: To follow Jesus, you must commit to years of service. Jesus saved a dying criminal on the cross beside Him who had only moments to live and could offer absolutely no future acts of service.

So, what does it take to be a follower of Jesus?

> *"But because of his great love for us, God, who is rich in mercy, made us alive with Christ even when we were dead in transgressions—it is by grace you have been saved"*
> *(Ephesians 2:4-5).*

There is nothing you have done or are doing that can keep you from following Jesus. There is nothing you can do or give that can earn your salvation. Just put your faith in Him, accept the gift of grace, and follow Him. It's really just that simple.

86. MORE LIKE JESUS

Almost thirty-four years ago, I stood in a rented tuxedo in front of 400 family, friends, and neighbors at the Del City Church of Christ. Beside me stood my beautiful bride-to-be, Krista. Adding our ages together, we were still under forty years. We were ready to commit our lives to one another. We were so young and naïve, we really thought we knew what that meant. I remember the preacher reading the following passage:

"'... For this reason a man will leave his father and mother and be united to his wife, and the two will become one flesh'? So they are no longer two, but one flesh. Therefore what God has joined together, let no one separate'" (Matthew 19:5-6).

After a couple of "I do's" and a kiss, we walked up the aisle and headed into our life of matrimonial bliss. We believed every word of the Bible, and we meant every spoken vow that was said that day. But we still had a lot to learn. We spent years trying to put the concept of "two becoming one" into practice. But we are two very different people. Krista loves to travel. I would prefer to stay home. Krista is a morning person. I am a night owl. Krista was cold-natured, and I always wanted to crank up the air conditioner. That has since flipped. And don't get me started on television. She enjoys watching reality shows, and I am happy to watch sports or a mindless sitcom. We were not being very successful at "two becoming one" because we misunderstood the concept. She was trying to change me, and I was trying to change her. It was not working.

In reality, I don't want to change her to be more like me. That would be awful! We don't need to be more like each other. We need to be more like Jesus. The more I become like Jesus and the more she becomes like Jesus, the more we become one. We still have a lot to learn. But we are now headed in the right direction. The pressure of changing each other is off. The challenge to grow deeper in our own spiritual journey is the motivation that drives us. But I still wish she would just sit down with me occasionally and watch an episode of Seinfeld.

87. TOO MUCH BACKGROUND NOISE

A couple of weeks ago, I had the honor of performing the wedding ceremony of Cameron and Layce Grubbs. The night before the ceremony was the rehearsal dinner. We enjoyed a great Tex-Mex meal in a nice restaurant. As we were leaving, I turned to my wife and said, "That was a nightmare." She understood but let me explain my comment to you. My hearing is just fine until I find myself in a room with a lot of background noise. There were about fifty people in a private room. It seemed as if everyone was talking at the same time, and my ears could not focus on anyone individually. While I could hear everything, I could not hear one distinct voice. If we are not careful, that is what our spiritual world can become. We fill our lives with so much noise that the voice of God just gets drowned out in the mix. Last week, our sermon was on Elijah. He was told to stand on a mountain because God was going to pass by.

"Then a great and powerful wind tore the mountains apart and shattered the rocks before the Lord, but the Lord was not in the wind. After the wind there was an earthquake, but the Lord was not in the earthquake. After the earthquake came a fire, but the Lord was not in the fire. And after the fire came a gentle whisper" (1 Kings 19:11-12).

How often do we cry out to God to give us guidance? All the while, we fill our lives with so much background noise, we cannot hear His voice. Truth be told, I have never heard the audible voice of God. But God does speak to me through His Word and through the Holy Spirit. But I will never hear His words if I refuse to quiet my life and tune into His voice.

If you are having trouble hearing the guidance of God in your life, just try this. Turn off the background noise in your life and listen for the gentle whisper.

88. WALK IN LOVE

For the last couple of weeks, we have been keeping our grand dog. And for the last three years, we have been keeping our other grand dog. If you are keeping score, that's our dog, our son's dog, and our daughter's dog. We never wanted to be a three-dog family, but when duty called, we accepted the challenge.

Last Sunday morning, as we were getting ready for church services, we noticed that all three dogs ran into their kennels. Why? Because they are such obedient dogs? No. They went to their kennels because they knew that when we left for worship services, they would get a bacon treat. Last week we also kept our grandsons. For the record, that is too many little creatures for one house. Around 7:30, our little (soon-to-be three-year-old) Judah began picking up his toys and asked if he could take a bath. Why? Because he is such an obedient boy? That's partially true. But also, because he knew that after bath time, he would get to go upstairs and play a game with Pop Pop before he had to go to bed.

The dogs and the grandsons showed me the difference between obedience and compliance. Compliance is doing something because it is the rules or you will receive a treat if your behavior is correct. Obedience is doing what you know is right, regardless of the outcome.

"And this is love: that we walk in obedience to his commands. As you have heard from the beginning, his command is that you walk in love" (2 John 1:6).

Our daily obedience to God should not be motivated solely by the blessings that will come. The mundane tasks, the unpleasant obedience, and the difficult people are report cards on what we've learned about love. As we walk in obedience, it should be because we are walking in love, regardless of how much bacon we receive.

89. LIVING OUTSIDE THE BOX

I'm sure we have all heard the expression, "Think outside the box." But what does it really mean? Let's first understand what it means to think inside the box. Charles H. Duell, Director of the US Patent Office, said, *"Everything that can be invented has been invented."* That was in 1899. Clearly, he was thinking inside the box! So, thinking outside of the box means you are open and willing to consider a new perspective that is different than the way you have always done things or believe they can be done.

I have a question. Would you say that Jesus was an inside-the-box thinker or an outside-the-box thinker? To the Pharisees and the teachers of the law, Jesus was way outside the box. According to the religious leaders of the time, Jesus's outside the box offenses included healing on the Sabbath, not washing His hands before eating, touching the "unclean," eating with sinners, forgiving sin with authority, speaking with women, and many more. We know that Jesus was sinless. So, His outside-the-box of the box thinking and actions were all within God's plan.

I have another question. Would you say that our church is an inside-the-box church or an outside-the-box church? Are we open and willing to consider a new perspective that is different than the way we have always done things or believe that things should be done? Jesus rebuked the inside-the-box thinkers when He said,

"You have let go of the commands of God and are holding on to human traditions" (Mark 7:8).

Human traditions can be a wonderful thing. They can help us build unity and give us stability. But when they begin to hold more power than the commands of God, we have a problem. Those outside of the church probably do not know our traditions, understand our traditions, or even care about our traditions. We are commanded to go into the world and seek the lost. We cannot do that while we are living inside the box.

90. ARE YOU READY TO RUN?

I have often heard it said that the Christian life is not a sprint, it's a marathon. I have run a marathon. It was 26.2 miles where I had to endure wind, hills, and heat. I have also lived the Christian life for almost 50 years. So, is the life of a Christian like running a marathon? At times, it feels more like trying to run the Barclay Marathon. Let me explain.

The Barclay Marathon is an annual event that takes place in the dense woods of Frozen Head State Park in Tennessee. It consists of five 20-mile loops totaling 100 miles, which must be completed in less than sixty hours. There is no exact course laid out; only checkpoints along the way. You are not allowed to use a GPS or your phone. You are only allowed to use a paper map and a compass. The run will take you through forests that are filled with trees, scrub bushes, and lots of thorns. There are also severe elevation changes between checkpoints. One wrong turn can add hours and miles to your journey. Needless to say, no one ever asks, "Did you win?" The only question ever asked is, "Did you finish?" And not many do. For the first thirty-six years the race was held, only fifteen runners crossed the finish line. And by the way, the entrance fee to run is one dollar and sixty cents. That is something that everyone can afford.

"Enter through the narrow gate. For wide is the gate and broad is the road that leads to destruction, and many enter through it. But small is the gate and narrow the road that leads to life, and only a few find it" (Matthew 7:13-14).

How is the Christian life like the Barclay Marathon? Everyone can afford the entrance fee. So, everyone is invited. No one's journey will be exactly the same. Yes, you have a guide (Bible) and checkpoints along the way, but the decision is yours on what exact path to take. There are no shortcuts you can take. If you take a wrong turn, you can recover, but it may add difficulty to your journey. You will encounter hills and valleys along the way, and you will get poked by thorns. But when you cross the finish line, it will be the greatest accomplishment of your life. It will take endurance, but the prize is worth the pain. Are you ready to run?

91. ANOTHER TRAGIC EVENT

You know those signs that hang in a workplace that say the number of days since their last accident? Can you imagine a billboard that says the number of days since the last tragedy in our nation? How big can the number get before we have to change it back to 0? I was born during the Vietnam War. I recently watched a documentary about Three Mile Island. I watched on live TV the tragic end to the standoff in Waco, Texas. I lived in Oklahoma when the Murrah Federal Building was bombed. I watched the Twin Towers in New York City fall to the ground. Since then, there have been countless school, theater, and nightclub shootings. And just last week, there was a shooting in Buffalo that killed ten people. Change the number back to 0 since our last tragedy.

It's hard to live in a world where tragedies happen so often. Like many over the years, I have spent time in prayer for the loved ones of those who have lost their lives. But I have tried to avoid asking the big question, "God, why would you let this happen?" From the Garden of Eden till today, the innocent have suffered and been affected by the evil doings of others. It is easy to lose hope when such tragedies occur.

"Jesus said, 'My kingdom is not of this world. If it were, my servants would fight to prevent my arrest by the Jewish leaders. But now my kingdom is from another place'" (John 18:36).

As Christians, we must live in this world, but we are not of this world. We suffer through these tragedies for a short time, but our citizenship is somewhere else. We should be longing for the day when this world is behind us and eternal bliss is ours forever. In heaven, there will be no need for a billboard telling us when the last tragedy occurred. Evil, death, and destruction will be a thing of the past. Let's all make sure we are prepared for that day.

92. FINDING JOY IN GOD'S WORD

I love listening to '80s music. I graduated high school in 1985, so '80s music is truly the soundtrack of my youth. A few weeks ago on a long drive, I told my phone to play the hits of the '80s. I spent the next couple of hours singing along with every song. It was amazing how the lyrics to each song just seemed to flow out of my mouth. Some of the songs I had not heard in forty years, but the lyrics were still there somewhere in my brain. It made me stop and think, "I wish scripture would just flow out of my mouth the same way these songs did." I pondered the question for a while and found this answer. I have always listened to music just for the joy of it. But reading scripture was usually for study or to get through my daily Bible reading. I read God's Word with a purpose. But joy had not been the purpose.

Let me tell you the story of a man named Scott. Scott Stapp is the lead singer, founder, and lyricist for the band Creed. Scott was raised in a very strict Christian home. When Scott would get in trouble, his punishment was to copy the Psalms in his own handwriting. In an interview, he said that he must have written the 150 Psalms more than a hundred times. Needless to say, as an adult, he has a real love/hate relationship with God and His Word.

"As your words came to me I drank them in, and they filled my heart with joy and happiness because I belong to you, O Lord God of Heaven's Armies" (Jeremiah 15:16).

Scripture should be a joy and not a chore. I guess what I'm saying is, "I Know this Much is True." If you are ever feeling "All out of Love," and you "Want to Know what Love is," "Don't Stop Believing" in the power of God's Word. Approach it with "Open Arms." Drink it in with "Every Breath You Take." God's Word teaches us about the "Power of Love," and you will come to believe that "Sweet Dreams are

Made of This." You will have a "Total Eclipse of the Heart," and then you will be "Walking on Sunshine."

93. A SUICIDE AND A CHICK-O-STICK

Have you ever told someone something about yourself and then instantly regretted it? This happened to me with my family. I can't remember the exact conversation, but I was talking about playing Little League Baseball. After every game, we would make a mad dash to the concession stand. Our coach would allow us to get one item and a drink. I had the same order every time, "I want a suicide and a Chick-O-Stick."

There are several things you need to know before you can understand my regret for sharing this story with my family. A "suicide" drink was when you got a little bit of every kind of soda in the same cup. Yes, it was gross, but it was the cool drink to order. A Chick-O-Stick was a candy bar that was a strange concoction of peanut butter and coconut. Here is the regretful part of the story. I have a slight lisp now. As a child, I had an obvious lisp. The phrase "I want a suicide and a Chick-O-Stick" should never be said by someone with a lisp. My kids and my wife make fun of me to this day because of this story.

I played a lot of Little League games. Therefore, I made a lot of mad dashes to the concession stand. I can't remember how many games we won or lost. I can't remember how many great games I played or how many errors I made. But I vividly remember the reward that followed the games.

"I declare to you, brothers and sisters, that flesh and blood cannot inherit the kingdom of God, nor does the perishable inherit the imperishable. Listen, I tell you a mystery: We will not all sleep, but we will all be changed—in a flash, in the twinkling of an eye, at the last trumpet. For the trumpet will sound, the dead will be raised imperishable, and we will be changed" (1 Corinthians 15:50-52).

In our lives, we will have some victories, and we will make some errors. The only real thing that matters is the reward that follows the game. So, play hard and do your best. And when the day comes, make a mad dash for your reward.

94. MEMORIAL DAY(S)

Last Monday was Memorial Day. To some, that just means a day off from work or a long weekend. But to those who have served in the Armed Forces or those who have lost a loved one who served, the day means so much more. It is a day to remember the men and women who lost their lives serving to protect our freedoms. Every one of us owes a debt to those who gave their lives so we can live ours. Yes, we take one special day out of the year to stop and give them honor. But there is not a day that goes by that we should not be thankful for the sacrifice that was made on our behalf.

Today is Sunday. Every Sunday, we take time during our worship to share in communion. That is a special time we stop and focus on the sacrifice Jesus made for each of us. We consider every Sunday a Memorial Day. We realize we owe a debt to the One who gave His life so we can have life. That is a debt that we can never pay. Jesus willingly became the sacrifice for our sins.

"And he took bread, gave thanks and broke it, and gave it to them, saying, "This is my body given for you; do this in remembrance of me" (Luke 22:19).

"Greater love has no one than this: to lay down one's life for one's friends" (John 15:13).

In response to the sacrifice Jesus made for us, one day a week is not enough. Every moment of every day, we should live in gratitude for the One who gave us life.

95. I LOVE WEST TEXAS!

Have you ever heard the expression "For every closed door, there is an open window"? I know those are supposed to be inspirational words for life, but they sound a lot more like the thoughts of a burglar. In life, you will run into many closed doors. Then you have a decision to make. Will I give up on my hopes and dreams, or will I choose another path and keep moving forward?

Here is a little-known fact about my basketball career (even my wife will hear this for the first time when she reads this). When I played for York College, it was a two-year school. My only hope of continuing college was to get a scholarship for the next two years. My coach called me to his office to fill out some paperwork. A university in Hawaii was interested in me coming and playing for them. I sent in the proper paperwork along with some game films and dreamed of spending two years in paradise. Then the call came, "Thanks, but we are not interested." Needless to say, I was devastated. After a few weeks of wondering if I would ever play again or even finish school, another coach called. How would you like to come play basketball for Wayland Baptist University in Plainview, Texas (never has a town been more aptly named). So, my dreams shifted from a tropical island to the plains of West Texas. In the end, it was one of the greatest blessings of my life.

The Apostle Paul understood what it felt like to have a few doors closed in his face. But through all of his hardships, he never gave up.

"We are hard pressed on every side, but not crushed;
perplexed, but not in despair; persecuted, but not
abandoned; struck down, but not destroyed" (2 Corinthians 4:8-9).

Don't let a closed door define you. Have faith that God has a greater plan for you. Believe it or not, it is better to be in West Texas than in Hawaii if that is where God's blessings await.

96. LIVE FOR AN AUDIENCE OF ONE

It's time to anoint a new king. Saul, Israel's first king, was chosen by the people. However, the second king would be chosen by God. The prophet Samuel had the honor of anointing this new king. God narrowed it down to one family and sent Samuel to Bethlehem to choose one of the sons of a man named Jesse. Samuel was to anoint the son who was chosen by God. It was time for Jesse's sons to stand before the prophet. First up was Eliab, the oldest. Samuel took one look at him and said, "Surely this man is the next king." He is tall, strong, and handsome. Everyone would be proud to serve this man as king. But God said, "No. He is not the one." Next up was Abinadab. Well, he's not as regal as Eliab. But he should do just fine. But God again said, "No." Then Shammah stood before the prophet. God said, "Next!" Four more sons would follow, but God said, "No," to each of them. Samuel looked at Jesse and said, "Are these all the sons you have?" Jesse responded, "There is still the youngest. He is tending the sheep." Jesse never thought his youngest would even be in consideration. But Samuel asked to see this young shepherd boy. And the rest is history. David came in from the field and stood before the prophet. God said, "This is the one!"

"The Lord does not look at the things people look at. People look at the outward appearance, but the Lord looks at the heart"
(2 Samuel 16:7).

We may not all look the part of being a child of God. We may not all have the approval of those around us. We may not all be considered important to other people. But none of that matters to God. God does not see us as others see us. God only looks at one thing: our hearts. And here is the thing I love. We all have a heart. We all have the opportunity to be pleasing and chosen by God. So don't spend your time and energy trying to please others. Just live for an audience of One.

97. KISS

Oh, boy, what is this article going to be about? It is an article for the church bulletin, so I assume it is not about an old rock band that wears too much makeup. It must be about greeting one another with a holy kiss. That's biblical, right? K.I.S.S. is an acronym that stands for Keep It Simple, Stupid. KISS was first used by the US Navy in the 1960s. The KISS principle states that most systems work best if they are kept simple rather than made complicated; therefore, simplicity should be a key goal in design, and unnecessary complexity should be avoided. It is a reminder that we sometimes make things more confusing than they need to be. We are guilty of this in the church also.

Jesus mastered the KISS principle. The Pharisees had not. They studied what we call the Old Testament and came up with 613 laws that God fearing people needed to live by. Jesus boiled it down to two: *Love God and love others.*

When it came to calling His disciples, Jesus did not give them a PowerPoint presentation concerning what they would need to give up, what they should bring, and how long He needed them. Jesus simply said, *"Follow Me."*

The Pharisees tried to trap Jesus with a question on the complexity of divorce. Jesus basically responded by saying, "Just love your spouse.

In the Sermon on the Mount, Jesus addressed all the little things we worry about every day. His advice, *"Seek first the Kingdom of God and all these things will be added to you."*

"Come to me, all you who are weary and burdened, and I will give you rest. Take my yoke upon you and learn from me, for I am gentle and humble in heart, and you will find rest for your souls. For my yoke is easy and my bu0rden is light" (Matthew 11:28-30).

Let's redefine the acronym KISS from Keep It Simple, Stupid to Keep It Simple, Saints. What Jesus asks of us is not easy, but it is simple to understand. Just follow Him, love God, and love people.

98. BAD MATH

One day Jesus took a seat in the Temple courts with His disciples. They were watching as people were making their contributions to the Temple treasury. They watched as people took their bag, or bags, of money and placed them on the table. Occasionally, the trumpets would blow, which got everyone's attention as a wealthy person left a large amount of money. In the midst of this, a woman whose husband had passed away, shuffled to the table. Not wanting to draw any attention to herself, she put her two small coins on the table before she shuffled away. What seemed like a mundane event that would go unnoticed to all caught the eye of Jesus. He immediately turned to His disciples and said, *"Truly I tell you, this poor widow has put more into the treasury than all the others."*

One of my favorite classes in college was Statistics. I loved studying numbers and seeing how they worked together. One lesson I remember from my Statistics class is that numbers never lie. Now here's the problem: there is no earthly way that these two little coins, which were worth less than a penny, could add up to more than the bags of money that others had given to the treasury. And by the way, I'M RIGHT! The numbers don't lie. But Jesus doesn't look at things in earthly ways. Heaven has different scales than we do on Earth. Jesus explained this to His disciples, saying, *"They all gave out of their wealth; but she, out of her poverty, put in everything—all she had to live on."*

The heavenly scales measure two things that our earthly eyes cannot see: They measure our hearts and our faith. The widow's heart was right. She wanted to give what she had to God. She was not guided by what percentage she was required to give. She gave from her heart. And she displayed her faith by putting in everything she had, knowing in faith that God would provide for her.

"Do not store up for yourselves treasures on earth, where moths and vermin destroy, and where thieves break in and steal. But store up for yourselves treasures in heaven, where moths and vermin do not destroy, and where thieves do not break in and steal. For where your treasure is, there your heart will be also" (Matthew 6:19-21).

Are we more concerned about what is required of us when it comes to our giving? Our worship? Our lives? If we would just stop worrying about the earthly scales and start being guided by the treasures we are storing up in heaven, we will not only get Jesus's attention, we will receive His praise. Thank you, Jesus, for making us aware of this easily forgotten woman.

99. ROLE MODEL?

"I am not a role model." This is a famous quote made by Charles Barkley in a Nike commercial back in 1991. At that time, Charles Barkley was one of the biggest stars in the NBA. So, was he right or wrong to say he was not a role model? My answer is yes and no. In the commercial, he went on to say, "Just because I can dunk a basketball doesn't mean that I should raise your kids. Parents should be role models." With that, he was absolutely right. However, kids are watching. So, you do have a responsibility to point them in the right direction with your words and your behavior.

You do not have to be an NBA player to have other people watching you. It doesn't matter if you are a schoolteacher, burger flipper, preacher, waitress, bank teller, retired, friend or neighbor, people are watching you. We all have a responsibility to set a good example that leads people in the right direction. The Apostle Paul had the right idea.

"Follow my example, as I follow the example of Christ"
(1 Corinthians 11:1).

The goal is not to point people to yourself. The goal is to point people toward Jesus. Undoubtedly we all will fail at some point in time. So, in essence, none of us are perfect role models. But there is one who is. Read through the gospels and watch how Jesus treated people. Watch how Jesus dealt with authority. Watch how Jesus reacted to people when they failed or when they were struggling. Watch how Jesus encouraged others to be better than they were. He is our role model.

"… fixing our eyes on Jesus, the pioneer and perfecter of faith"
(Hebrews 12:2).

100. NO EXCUSES

Recently at our church we have been going through the "Fishers of Men" course. The concept of this course comes from Matthew 4, where Jesus invited Peter and his brother Andrew to join Him with this invitation, "Follow me and I will make you fishers of men." Our commission to go out and share the good news about Jesus comes when Jesus is about to ascend into heaven.

"Then Jesus came to them and said, 'All authority in heaven and on earth has been given to me. Therefore go and make disciples of all nations, baptizing them in the name of the Father and of the Son and of the Holy Spirit, and teaching them to obey everything I have commanded you. And surely I am with you always, to the very end of the age'"(Matthew 28:18-20).

Through this study, I have realized that I have been looking at "The Great Commission" all wrong. To be honest, I have been looking at it backwards. I have been trying to figure out what I need to do in order to be equipped to fulfill the great commission. Looking at it that way means I have a built-in excuse not to fulfill the task at hand. I am waiting for God to give me the tools I need to go share the gospel with others. So, here is my new revelation: The minute that I became a Christian, God had already equipped me. My Creator made me with everything I need to be an ambassador for Him. I just need to find my role. It could be going into a foreign land to share the gospel with others. It could be standing in a pulpit every week to share the good news. It could be teaching kids in Bible class. It could be sharing my faith with my neighbors. It could be teaching my own family about my Heavenly Father.

God has equipped you with the tools you need to be a fisher of men. Now you have no excuse. Just go do it!

101. MY MANSION IS BIGGER THAN YOURS

As a former youth minister, I have done many talks on the subject of peer pressure. We are so worried about our children being influenced by others. We try to instill in them that what others think of them is not the most important thing in this world. Yet they still stress over their shoes, their backpacks, their clothes, if they have the latest iPhone, and what type of car picks them up from school. But over the years, I have learned that peer pressure does not end when we graduate high school. When my father was being checked in to an assisted living facility, he asked me for a comb. I haven't carried a comb in my pocket since Junior High School. My dad was worried about what "they" would think of him if his hair was a little windblown. Years later, as we were moving my mother into assisted living, I noticed peer pressure rearing its ugly head again. Whose door is decorated the best? Who has the nicest walker? Whose family comes to visit the most? Who has the nicest pair of dentures?

Does it ever end? Will we be upset if our coffin is not the fanciest one in the cemetery? The truth is, we were each uniquely made by God. So why do we worry so much about what "they" think of us?

"For you created my inmost being; you knit me together in my mother's womb. I praise you because I am fearfully and wonderfully made; your works are wonderful, I know that full well"
(Psalm 139:13-14).

Rather than worry about what "they" think of us, why don't we just strive to please the One who created us? I love the phrase, "Live for an audience of one." If I am pleasing God with my words, my actions, my appearance, my career choice, my worship, and all other aspects of life, does it really matter what "they" think of me? We need to get this one right in our lifetime. I don't want to get to heaven and worry about my mansion being the nicest one on Golden Avenue.

102. DREAM BIG

In 1998, a campaign began called GodSpeaks. An anonymous donor purchased billboard space in South Florida for three months. On the billboards were simple messages of white letters on black space, and each message was signed—God. The campaign became so popular that it was picked up nationwide, showing up on more than 10,000 billboards in over 200 cities. The messages were simple and thought-provoking. Here are a few of them:

We need to talk—God
That "Love thy neighbor" thing … I meant that—God
Let's meet at my house Sunday before the game—God
Loved the wedding, invite me to the marriage—God
What part of "Thou Shalt Not" didn't you understand?—God
Will the road you are on get you to my place?—God
Tell the kids I love them—God

There have been many others, but one I remember reading said, "If you knew without question you would not fail, what would you do with your life?"—God. The reason that one stood out to me was because, without the right mindset, it could be easily misunderstood. The wrong mindset would be if someone were thinking selfishly or with only pleasure in mind. God would not grant them success. But with the right mindset, that simple billboard spoke volumes of truth. Listen to the words of Jesus:

"Very truly I tell you, whoever believes in me will do the works I have been doing, and they will do even greater things than these, because I am going to the Father. And I will do whatever you ask in my name, so that the Father may be glorified in the Son. You may ask me for anything in my name, and I will do it" (John 14:12-14).

If your mindset is on Godly things, then dream big. There is absolutely nothing that cannot be accomplished. Don't let Satan spoil your plans by filling you with doubt. Dream big and act on it. Then don't be surprised by the success that follows.

103. BE A REFLECTION OF LOVE

It's a hard day when we drop our kids off at school for the first time. Our hearts are heavy when we release their hands into the hands of another. Why? Because we only want the best for them. We want them to make friends and be accepted by others. We don't want them to face bullies and get mistreated. We want them to learn and grow and excel. But we have no control over those things once we let them go.

Here is a fact that we don't talk about. It is the other reason our hearts are heavy when we send our kids out into the world. They are representatives of us. If my kid cuts up in front of the other kids, what does that say about me as a parent? If my kid acts out in front of the teachers, what will they think about our family? It is hard when you have to let go of the reins and send your kids into the world. All parents go through this.

God is our heavenly Father, and we are His children. He sends us out into the world with the potential of being good people, making lots of friends, and being a blessing to those around us. God also sends us out into the world with the possibility of being abused or mistreated. At the same time, God also sends us into the world as representatives of Him. We are His ambassadors in this world. That sounds too big, so let's break it down. We are His ambassadors in our community, in our neighborhood, in our classroom, in our office, and in our family. If we fail to reflect the love of God to others, what are they to think about the one we claim to be our Father?

"A new command I give you: Love one another. As I have loved you, so you must love one another. By this everyone will know that you are my disciples, if you love one another" (John 13:34-35).

Let's make our Father proud. By loving others, we will accurately reflect the love our Father has lavished on us.

104. DON'T DRINK THE POISON

We have seven recorded statements that Jesus made while He was hanging on the cross. While all had deep spiritual meaning, one of the things Jesus said not only blesses us today, it challenges us. After multiple illegal trials where powerful people lied to convict Jesus, He was beaten, taunted, spit on, had a crown of thorns embedded into his head, and made to carry His own cross. While on the cross, the Roman soldiers gambled for His clothing, the criminals on either side of Him reviled Him, the religious leaders mocked Him, and the crowd blasphemed Him. Jesus spoke and said, *"Father, forgive them, for they do not know what they are doing"* (Luke 23:34).

There's an old quote you may have heard that says, "Unforgiveness is like drinking poison and hoping the other person dies." Did the people deserve forgiveness for their words or actions? No! Did the people even ask for forgiveness? No! But Jesus understood that holding on to bitterness was a poison He was not willing to drink.

"Do not judge, and you will not be judged. Do not condemn, and you will not be condemned. Forgive, and you will be forgiven"
(Luke 6:37).

Our hearts only have a limited amount of space. When we allow anger, bitterness, and revenge to occupy space in our hearts, it is a poison that will sicken our entire lives. Forgiveness is the antidote that will free up space in our hearts for love, grace, and mercy. So, follow the example of Jesus. Don't drink the poison.

105. ARE YOU A TRUE FOLLOWER OF JESUS?

How do others know that you are a follower of Jesus? When you are sitting around the table with family, when you are talking to your neighbor, or when you meet a stranger, how will they know if you are a follower of Jesus? There are several good answers to that question. You could talk about Jesus. But if you do not have the walk that complements your talk, you could do more harm than good. You could wear a cross around your neck or even have a cross tattooed on your arm. But I have seen a multitude of people and celebrities who will wear a cross while they live in a way that does not honor Jesus in the least. The Bible gives us the answer in one word: LOVE!

"If I speak in the tongues of men or of angels, but do not have love, I am only a resounding gong or a clanging cymbal. If I have the gift of prophecy and can fathom all mysteries and all knowledge, and if I have a faith that can move mountains, but do not have love, I am nothing. If I give all I possess to the poor and give over my body to hardship that I may boast, but do not have love, I gain nothing"
(1 Corinthians 13:1-3).

Paul continues in 1 Corinthians 13 to give the definition of what love looks like in real life. He describes love as being patient and kind to others. He says love will not do anything to discourage or hurt others. He says love is moving yourself out of the way so you can focus on others. He says love is tempering your anger. He says love is forgiving and protecting others.

If you want others to know you are a follower of Jesus, it will cost you. It will cost you time as well as physical and emotional energy. Jesus modeled what love looks like every day of His life. And 2,000 years later, people still follow Him. We all need to roll up our sleeves and start really loving people. That will show them who are and whose we are. Then they will know without a doubt who you follow.

106. NEGATIVE SPLIT

In April of 2006, I ran my first and only marathon. I consider myself a former athlete. I used to love playing football, basketball, and baseball. Basketball became my favorite and in the end, it paid for my college education. I knew what it meant to be in shape. But I was lost when it came to being prepared to run 26.2 miles nonstop. I needed help. So, I called my older brother. He had run three marathons and knew what I would need to do to reach my goal. He gave me tips on everything from breathing, shoes, and taking days off to rest my body. He also introduced me to a term I had never heard before: "negative split." A negative split is when you run the last half of the race faster than you run the first half. In order to have a negative split you must not only be in great shape, you must have focus and self-discipline. Needless to say, on my marathon day I did not have a negative split. The last half of my race was much slower than my first half.

The concept of a negative split has a great application to our spiritual lives. Can you finish stronger in the latter part of your life than in the earlier years? In Matthew 18, Jesus was asked by His disciples, "Who is the greatest in the Kingdom of Heaven?" Jesus presents a child to them and tells them that unless they change and become like a little child, they will never enter the Kingdom of Heaven. Jesus let them know that the pure innocent faith of children is the type of faith adults need to have. The problem is that over time, most adults allow their faith to become stale or jaded. I love doing character studies of Biblical figures. It is rare to find someone in the Bible whose faith stays strong in the final years of their lives. One exception is the Apostle Paul. In his second letter to Timothy, as his life was nearing the end, he made this great declaration:

"I have fought the good fight, I have finished the race, I have kept the faith. [8] Now there is in store for me the crown of righteousness, which the Lord, the righteous Judge, will award to me on that day

—and not only to me, but also to all who have longed for his appearing" (2 Timothy 4:7-8).

Spiritually speaking, negative splits are possible. But just like in running, it will take focus and self-discipline. Here is the challenge for all of us. STAY STRONG! Let's finish with a stronger faith than when we began. There is a great award waiting for you.

107. ARE WE THERE YET?

As vacation season passes and the routine of the school year returns, I remembered some of our vacations when our kids were young. With age and a little more wisdom, I have come to this conclusion: The same people, in the same car, on the same trip can have vastly different experiences. When I was a kid on vacation, I always wondered, "Why is dad in such a bad mood?" When I became a dad, taking the family on vacation, I finally understood. Two of the main roles a dad has on vacation are bus driver and pack mule. As a bus driver, you try to limit the number of bathroom stops and the length of time at each stop. You do this because it directly affects your other role as pack mule. The more mileage you cover each day means the less stops you have to make, which means the fewer times you have to unload and reload the car.

One thing that made me crazy on our trips was when the kids would become impatient. Impatience can show up in a number of ways. Sometimes it is the question, "Are we there yet?" Other times (this is the one that frustrated me the most), they wanted to stop along the way for something that caught their attention. Any billboard, miniature golf course, or go-cart track can derail your entire vacation. I couldn't get them to understand that the place we were going would be so much better than any of these places along the way.

I have a feeling that is the way God feels with us sometimes. He is with us on our journey through life. He is trying to keep us focused on our destination. But all along the way, we get distracted with the things that will only serve to derail our trip. We want what feels good or looks good. All the while God is calling us to stay focused on the main attraction.

"So we fix our eyes not on what is seen, but on what is unseen, since what is seen is temporary, but what is unseen is eternal" (2 Corinthians 4:18).

Don't get lost in the distractions. Stay focused on THE attraction!

108. STUCK IN THE PAST

Do you ever spend time going back through old photos of your childhood? A while back, I found a horrifying picture of myself. Before I give you the description, let me just say, it was the '80s. I remember the occasion, I was leaving for a first date with a girl from high school. As I was walking out the door, my mom said, "You look so nice. Let me take a picture." So, here it goes. Let's start with the hair. After a summer of being a lifeguard, my hair was a few shades more blond than usual. Today, my hairstyle back then would be described as a mullet. It was parted down the middle in the front and permed in the back with way too much moose. Again, let me remind you, it was the '80s. As for the clothing, I was wearing blue jeans and a nice T-shirt. Over my T-shirt I was wearing a thin cotton sports coat with the sleeves pushed up to my elbows Miami Vice style. (If you don't know what that means, Google it.) At the time, I thought I was looking good. However, with the benefit of hindsight, I can see that it was a nightmare. Fortunately, I have evolved.

"When I was a child, I talked like a child, I thought like a child, I reasoned like a child. When I became a man, I put the ways of childhood behind me" (1 Corinthians 13:11).

Hopefully my faith has matured and grown also. I would hate to think that my faith in God today was the exact same as the faith I had as a teenager. Yes, my faith is in the same God. But through the years, my faith has grown deeper, my commitment has grown stronger, my study of God's Word has grown more intense, my service in the name of God has grown more productive, and my reflecting the love of God to others has grown more passionate.

Don't let your faith in God grow stale. Keep growing. Keep digging deeper. Keep expressing your faith in new and exciting ways. I guess what I am saying is, don't let your faith continue to sport a mullet.

109. THERE'S MORE WHERE THAT CAME FROM

Have you ever found yourself in a situation where you felt absolutely overwhelmed? Where you felt completely depleted mentally, physically, financially, or spiritually? You did as much as you could. Your tank was empty. You are all prayed out, and no answer can be found. Maybe you are there today. If not, that situation may be in your near future. When you come to the end of our rope, open your Bible and read Luke 9.

The disciples had just returned from an exhilarating but exhausting journey. They had gone into the villages, preaching to all who would listen and healing those who were in need. Upon their return, they needed some R&R&R time. They needed to report, rest, and recuperate. Instead of peace and quiet, they were engulfed by a large crowd. It is easy to understand why they told Jesus to dismiss the people. The crowd was huge, needy, and hungry. Jesus responded with a challenge. "You give them something to eat." What Jesus asked them to do was overwhelming. All they could scrounge up was five small loaves of bread and two little fish. There was nothing they could do. Nothing, except put what little they had into the hands of Jesus. Jesus blessed the small amount of food and told the disciples to begin passing it out. I wonder what was going through their minds as they kept passing out food, and the supply never ended.

"They all ate and were satisfied, and the disciples picked up twelve basketfuls of broken pieces that were left over" (Luke 9:17).

With Jesus, there is not only always enough; there are leftovers. They ended up with more leftovers than they had to begin with. When life overwhelms you, remember to put your problems in the hands of Jesus. Not only will He satisfy, you will have leftovers.

110. JOY

Do you remember attending Vacation Bible School when you were younger? I can't remember much from my college history classes, but I can remember those songs from VBS. Very few of these songs ever made the transition from VBS to Sunday morning worship. Some for good reason. (I could never figure out why that rooster was so grouchy.) One song that should have made our Sunday morning worship playlist has a simple thought that the church could really use today.

"I've got the joy, joy, joy, joy down in my heart. Where? Down in my heart. Where? Down in my heart to stay."

I'm not sure why that song never made its way into our Sunday morning worship. Maybe because it is hard to sing that song with a frown on your face. Take a minute to look around during our worship service and count the smiles you see. It seems like we have lost our joy. Not only have we lost our joy in worship, we have lost our joy in living.

As a church staff member, we are always looking for a way to "advertise" our church to the community. Do you know what would be the best advertisement? JOY! If people were to see our enthusiasm for life and in particular our relationship with God, we would need to build a bigger auditorium. Last night, the first ten minutes of the national news included the pandemic, racial tensions, hurricanes forming in the Gulf, and wildfires. The world needs some joy.

If you want to find some joy in the Bible, read the book of Philippians. The overall theme of this book is JOY. In this short book of only four chapters, Paul mentions joy five times and rejoice six times. Keep in mind that Paul is writing this book while he is a prisoner in chains. What Paul teaches us about joy is that joy is different from happiness. Happiness is dependent on circumstances. Joy rises above our circumstances.

"Rejoice in the Lord always. I will say it again: Rejoice!"
(Philippians 4:4).

111. EXCUSES, EXCUSES

People will come up with all kinds of excuses to skip church services. Here are some of the usuals:

- I overslept.
- The Cowboys (or the Saints) are playing the early game.
- Last time I went, someone was in my seat.
- It's raining.
- I can't get a good parking spot.
- I'm feeling a little sick.
- Someone there may be sick.
- It's full of hypocrites. (So is the grocery store, but you still go there.)

(Let us hold unswervingly to the hope we profess, for he who promised is faithful. And let us consider how we may spur one another on toward love and good deeds, not giving up meeting together, as some are in the habit of doing, but encouraging one another—and all the more as you see the Day approaching" *(Hebrews 10:23-25).*

Last week, Krista and I were on vacation in New York City. On Sunday morning, we decided which church service we wanted to attend. I must admit that I had prejudged the people of New York City. I thought we would be sitting in a small church with very few people. I could not have been more wrong. We got up early, rode the subway, and then walked a few blocks to find the church. What I saw shocked me. The doors weren't open yet but that didn't deter people. There was a line of people more than a block long, waiting in the sun. During the service, they made an announcement that surprised me even more. The church had negotiated with a nearby parking garage. They informed the congregation that on Sunday mornings, it would only cost $8 to park their car during services.

As we left, I was thinking about the barriers that the early church had to overcome to attend a worship service. Not only was it inconvenient for them, it could literally cost them their lives. We live in a privileged time and in a privileged place. So, what's your excuse?

112. GIVE FROM YOUR HEART

"Well, if I win, I promise I will …" How many times did you hear that over the last several weeks as the Powerball Lottery was approaching 2 billion dollars? If history teaches us anything about big jackpot winners, it shows us that winning does not build character; it exposes it. If you have ever spent time imagining what you would do if you had millions of dollars, stop and ask yourself, "What are you doing with the blessings you have today?" We have all been blessed with time, talents, and treasure. How are you spending yours? The more important question is, how are you sharing yours?

There's a story in the Bible about a widow who gave a small amount of money to the temple treasury. She was surrounded by people who were giving large sacks of gold while she quietly donated her few pennies. Her few pennies went unnoticed by everyone except Jesus. Jesus told His disciples that she put more into the treasury than all the others. If you are looking at this event while wearing your "worldly glasses," this makes no sense. But if you look at this event while wearing your "spiritual glasses," it makes all the sense in the world. God does not look at the amount that is given; He looks at the heart of the giver.

"And my God will meet all your needs according to the riches of his glory in Christ Jesus" (Philippians 4:19).

The excuse we give ourselves for not sharing more of our time, talents, and treasure is that we don't believe we have enough to spare. Never forget that we serve a God who loves us and meets all of our needs according to the riches of His glory. That means that we have a bucket that will never be empty as long as we are sharing what we have for God's glory. You don't have to win the Powerball Lottery to bless others. God notices the smallest things you give when you give from your heart.

113. FROM PERSEVERANCE TO PROMISE

When I was young I begged my dad to put up a basketball goal at our house. He refused. I continued to beg. I promised I would use it every day. Finally, he caved in and put a goal in our backyard. And true to my word, I went out and shot hoops every day. I remember one particular winter day when school was called off because of an ice storm. Mom and I were arguing because I wanted to go outside and play, and mom wanted to keep me healthy. We compromised. In order to keep my promise to my dad, I was allowed to run into the backyard and shoot one layup. I made the shot, but my ball got stuck in the frozen net. I had to wait for it to thaw days later before I could get my basketball back. In the end, Dad loved the goal in the backyard. I always thought he just loved to watch me play. But with hindsight, my playing never let the grass grow, so it was less for him to mow. If you are wondering what ever became of my love of basketball and the commitment to play every day? Basketball paid for my college education. I never played for a "big time" program that you could have watched on television. But I was able to graduate from a Christian university, which we could have never afforded.

"You need to persevere so that when you have done the will of God, you will receive what he has promised" (Hebrews 10:36).

There is power in perseverance. Any worthwhile commitment you make will have challenges that will make you want to quit. That is the enemy trying to defeat you. Jesus faced discouragement, persecution, frustration, threats, and people who didn't understand His purpose. But He persevered to the end because His mission was greater than anything that could stand in the way. So don't let an ice storm or anything else stop you from keeping your commitments. There is a promise in the end that is greater than any hardships you face.

114. GIVE THANKS

How many Christmas carols can you name? It seems like there are an endless number of songs written about Christmas. There are the old carols and an infinite number of newer songs written for the holiday season. There are even more songs that would be appropriate for Valentine's Day. Songs that celebrate someone's love for another. There are even songs written for Halloween. Who doesn't love the Monster Mash? But Thanksgiving is different. No artist has ever released a CD of Thanksgiving songs.

However, we are given the lyrics to some beautiful songs of Thanksgiving. We have to go all the way back to the Old Testament, to the book of Psalms, to find them. Here is just a sample:

"I will give thanks to the Lord because of his righteousness; I will sing the praises of the name of the Lord Most High" (Psalm 7:17).

"I will give thanks to you, Lord, with all my heart; I will tell of all your wonderful deeds" (Psalm 9:1).

"Let us come before him with thanksgiving and extol him with music and song" (Psalm 95:2).

"Enter his gates with thanksgiving and his courts with praise; give thanks to him and praise his name" (Psalm 100:4).

"Give thanks to the Lord, for he is good; his love endures forever" (Psalm 107:1).

"I will give you thanks, for you answered me; you have become my salvation" (Psalm 118:21).

"Give thanks to the God of heaven. His love endures forever"
(Psalm 136:26).

Giving thanks should be at the heart of every believer. Our God has blessed us in numerous ways. During each day of this week, as you realize another blessing, pause and give thanks to God, the giver of all good and perfect gifts. Have a wonderful Thanksgiving holiday.

115. THE WAITING

One of my favorite country singers is Brad Paisley. One of his songs that I love is called "Waiting on a Woman." The song is about two men sitting on a bench in a shopping mall waiting on their wives. The older man is passing on his wisdom to the younger man. He talks to him about having to wait on his wife to get ready for their first date. Then he had to wait on her while she planned their wedding. Since then, he has had to wait on her every time they were getting ready to go out. The song ends by saying that men are usually the first to die. So, when he dies, he will find a bench in heaven, have a seat, and wait on his woman.

That is a sweet song with a lot of truth. We spend a great deal of our life waiting. We wait at red lights. We wait in line at the grocery store. We wait for the doctor's results. We wait for our kids to grow up. Then we wait for our kids to visit. There's an old expression that describes our busy lives perfectly: "Hurry up and wait." We often do the same thing with God. We pray, and then we wait on God to give us an answer. We spend our time waiting on God to give us a sign to help us make a decision .

"I wait for the Lord, my whole being waits, and in his word I put my hope" (Psalm 130:5).

Consider this for a moment: Maybe while we are waiting on God, He is actually waiting on us! God has promised to never leave us or forsake us. So, while we are standing still waiting on God to act, He is waiting on us to take a step in faith. God's desire for His children is not for us to stagnate while we are waiting for a sign. Jesus said that He came to give us an abundant life. So, stop waiting and start living.

116. BROTHER MUD

I have worked with many elders throughout my years of being a minister. Almost all of them have been very good men. Several I would describe as exceptional. But quite often, I will talk about one elder named "Brother Mud." Actually, there is no Brother Mud. He is just a compilation of all the worst characteristics I have seen in elders. Brother Mud is the elder who, after hearing a great idea, would say, "I'm against it." Or if you are from the South, "I'm agin' it." When pressed for a reason why he was against the great idea, we would hear one of his two favorite answers. The first answer: "We've never done that before." The second answer: "We tried that before, and it didn't work." With either of those answers, it was almost guaranteed that the great idea would never see the light of day.

One morning, Peter and his crew of experienced fishermen were washing out their nets after an extremely unsuccessful night of fishing. Jesus showed up with a crowd of people and used Peter's boat as a pulpit to preach. Peter sat and listened to the entire sermon. When Jesus wrapped it up, He turned to Peter and said, "Put out into deep water, and let down the nets for a catch." As an experienced fisherman, Peter knew that you didn't go net fishing during the day, and you sure didn't cast your nets in the deep water. In Peter's response to Jesus's request, you can hear the battle going on between Brother Mud and faith.

"Peter answered, 'Master, we've worked hard all night and haven't caught anything. But because you say so, I will let down the nets'"
(Luke 5:5).

The morning ends with an amazing catch of fish and Peter deciding to follow Jesus for the rest of his life. We all have a little Brother Mud in us. But if we let Brother Mud make our decisions, we will miss out on an eternal adventure we will never regret. So, politely tell Brother Mud that you understand his concerns, but you have decided instead, to live by faith.

117. MAMA RAISED YOU RIGHT

I have often been asked, "Phillip, why are you such a big Oklahoma Sooners fan? Did you go to school there?" No, is the answer to the second question. So let me try to give you an answer to the first question. I was raised in Oklahoma. Some of my earliest memories are from Saturday afternoons in the fall when mom and I would watch the Sooners play football on television. One of my favorite memories is the day that Oklahoma beat Ohio State on a last-second field goal. I got so excited that I jumped up and knocked over my mom's favorite potted plant in the living room. There was shattered porcelain and dirt all over our living room carpet. Mom just looked at the mess and said, "You are lucky he made that field goal."

Mom also bought me OU football jerseys and shirts that were always the first things worn after laundry day. In elementary school, about once a month, we would have movie days. The entire school would come to the gym for an afternoon of movies. Often, they would show us highlight films from the previous Sooners football season. I went to college in Nebraska and Texas. But by that time, my loyalty to OU was so deep that I remained a fan even while living in enemy territory. Now I am living back in Texas surrounded by Longhorns and Bear fans, but I still stand proudly for my Sooners. In the environment I was raised in, I thought everyone was a fan of the Oklahoma Sooners. By the time I was old enough to know differently, my commitments were so deep that no one was going to change me.

"Start children off on the way they should go, and even when they are old they will not turn from it" (Proverbs 22:6).

Being a fan of the Sooners was not the greatest gift Mom gave me. Growing up, I cannot remember a Sunday morning that mom did not take my brother, sister, and me to church. Much like the post office, through rain, snow, sleet, and hail, we were always there. There were some Wednesday nights when I would have to leave my Little League Baseball game in the middle of an inning to go to church in my uniform. That's just how I was raised. Thank you, Mom, for starting me off on the way I should go. Now that I am older, even though you are gone, I will not turn from it.

118. STEPPING OUT

When our kids were young, we took a vacation to Sandusky, Ohio. Sandusky is the home of Cedar Point Amusement Park, known as the roller coaster capital of the world. The highlight of the trip was when we came face-to-face with the Top Thrill Dragster. This roller coaster took you from zero to 120 miles per hour in 3.5 seconds. At that point, you were shot up 420 feet at a 90-degree angle. (By comparison, the Statue of Liberty is only 305 feet tall, including its pedestal.) After reaching the top, you immediately begin the descent. You are twisted 720 degrees before the track flattens out, and you come to a stop. The entire ride takes seventeen seconds.

My daughter Tori, who was ten at the time, said, "Dad, let's go do it!" My son Brandyn, who was twelve at the time, said, "No way!" So, my daughter and I stood in line for two hours to experience the most exciting seventeen seconds of our lives. Two years later, we went back to Cedar Point, and my son and I rode the Top Thrill Dragster while my daughter stood on the sidelines. If you are keeping score, that's Philip—2; Brandyn—1; Tori—1; and Krista—0.

The decision that each of my kids faced is actually one that we face in the church today. Am I willing to step out in faith for an adventure, or do I want to stay in the safety and comfort of where I stand today? It feels safe and comfortable to say as a church that this is how we have always done it, so why would we do anything different? Sadly, that is the formula for slowly killing the church. We need to follow the example of Peter. On a stormy night, the disciples were in a boat fighting to keep it afloat. Jesus came walking on the water toward them. They thought He was a ghost.

"But Jesus immediately said to them: 'Take courage! It is I. Don't be afraid.' 'Lord, if it's you,' Peter replied, 'tell me to come to you on the water.' 'Come,' he said. Then Peter got down out of the boat, walked on the water and came toward Jesus"
(Matthew 14:27-29).

If we are earnestly seeking Jesus, we must be willing to get out of the boat and take a few steps. We may stumble along the way. But Jesus will immediately reach out His hand to lift us up. Which one of the disciples displayed actual faith? Was it the 11 who stayed in the boat? Or was it the one who stepped out?

119. THE FUTURE

Does anyone remember picking up your landline in your kitchen and dialing 411? That was the information line. At best, it could give you someone's phone number. Now think of that person having a conversation with someone from 2022. The conversation might go something like this:

First of all, no one has landlines anymore. Everyone carries their own phone in their own pocket. And here is just an example of what these little pocket phones can do. I can immediately know the current weather of any place in the world. I can not only know when and where every movie is playing, I can know who is in the movie, what other movies they have been in, and what thousands of other people think about the movie. I can find out more information than I would ever want to know about people I haven't seen in 30 years. I can immediately listen to any song ever recorded. I can see a satellite picture of the place I am standing (and also downtown Baghdad, Iraq, if I really wanted to). I can know the score of any game of any sport that has ever been played. I can also get directions to any address anywhere in the nation and see how the traffic is flowing along my route.

There is so much more our little phones can do. But I think that is enough to blow the mind of someone just forty years ago. Here's a scary thought. If someone forty years in the future came to talk to us today, what would they tell us that would blow our minds? I can't even imagine!

"Now to him who is able to do immeasurably more than all we ask or imagine, according to his power that is at work within us, to him be glory in the church and in Christ Jesus throughout all generations, for ever and ever! Amen" (Ephesians 3:20-21).

God is not surprised by our advancements in technology. In fact, the best we can do today is still elementary to God. But here is the amazing part. God, who can do more than we can even imagine, is at work within us! So, what does the future hold for us? I can't even imagine.

120. STAY WITH THE SHEPHERD

There are two things that I haven't heard said in a long time. First, "I wish I had a camera right now." I used to hear that a lot when I was younger. We would have never believed then that someday every person would always have a camera with them. The other thing that you don't hear anymore is, "Can you give me the directions?" Back in the day, when you needed to find a specific place, you had to have detailed directions on how to get there. Now all you need is an address. Who would have believed that every person would carry their own personal GPS in their pocket? We didn't even know what a GPS was. But now, I don't know how I would travel without it.

While we may not have always had a GPS, we have always had an EPS. A GPS is a Global Positioning System that will tell you where you are and how to get to where you are trying to go. An EPS is an Eternal Positioning System. You may better know it as the Bible. By reading and knowing the Bible, you will always know where you are and how to get to where you are trying to go.

"Whether you turn to the right or to the left, your ears will hear a voice behind you, saying, 'This is the way; walk in it'" (Isaiah 30:21).

Jesus worded it a couple of different ways. In John 14:6, Jesus said, *"I am the way, the truth, and the life. No one comes to the Father except through me."* And in John 10, Jesus refers to himself as "The Good Shepherd." If you feel lost in life, here is a good rule of thumb: Stay close to the shepherd. If we are walking through life with the shepherd, where we are at any particular moment is not really all that important. But if we stick with the "Good Shepherd," we know He is leading us to the Father.

121. THE REST IS STILL UNWRITTEN

From the moment Moses was born, he was living on borrowed time. Moses was a Hebrew boy and was supposed to be killed, according to a decree by Pharaoh. But Pharaoh's daughter had compassion and adopted him. About forty years later, Moses saw an Egyptian beating a Hebrew slave. In a fit of rage, Moses killed the Egyptian. When the murder became public knowledge, Moses ran. He spent the next forty years tending the livestock of someone else and looking over his shoulder. But at the age of eighty, Moses's life was forever changed. He noticed a bush on fire that would not burn up. From the bush, God spoke to Moses and said, "I'm sending you back to Egypt to bring out my people."

It is easy for us to believe that our mistakes disqualify us from any future service or usefulness in the Kingdom of God. Our guilt and shame can lead us to believe God is finished with us. Surely He has no use for a sinner like me. That is not our God! Our God will meet you where you are today and lead you down the road to a better story. Our God hates where you have been. But He refuses to leave you there. The Apostle Paul knew this. Listen to the words he wrote to Timothy.

"But for that very reason I was shown mercy so that in me, the worst of sinners, Christ Jesus might display his immense patience as an example for those who would believe in him and receive eternal life" (1 Timothy 1:16).

We all have ugly chapters in our lives. But we have yet to reach the final chapter in our book. We have a choice. We can spend the rest of our lives doing busy work and looking over our shoulders. Or we can accept the grace and mercy that God offers and get busy making a difference in this world. God has made His choice. He offers you forgiveness and a purpose for your life. The only choice left is yours.

122. HIDE IT UNDER A BUSHEL, NO!

I recently heard a comedian say that 2020 was his favorite year. His explanation was that everyone was wearing a mask, most people stayed home, everyone kept their distance from each other, and nobody wanted to hug. If you are an introvert or people just really get on your nerves, you are living in a golden age. To avoid the risk of running into someone at the grocery store, you can just order it and have them bring it to your car. Honestly, you don't have to go shopping for anything. You can order just about anything from Amazon, and they will bring it to your door. You don't even have to talk to the delivery person. They will just drop your package on your porch and leave.

The same is true with our churches. By necessity, most churches broadcast their worship services online now. You can now "worship" while you are wearing your pajamas in the privacy of your own home. It is now very easy to become a recluse and avoid people altogether. But that is not what the children of God are called to do.

> *"You are the salt of the earth. But if the salt loses its saltiness, how can it be made salty again? It is no longer good for anything, except to be thrown out and trampled underfoot. "You are the light of the world. A town built on a hill cannot be hidden. Neither do people light a lamp and put it under a bowl. Instead they put it on its stand, and it gives light to everyone in the house. In the same way, let your light shine before others, that they may see your good deeds and glorify your Father in heaven"(Matthew 5:13-16).*

It is hard to be salt and light while locked in your house. Locking yourself in your home may be the best example ever of putting your light under a bowl. As children of God, we are not "of this world," but we are called to be in this world. We are to reflect the love that God has shown us into the darkened world. That doesn't happen when you stay behind a locked door. So be wise and take care of yourself. But let's get out there and be salty!

123. THE GREAT REUNION

Krista and I spent last weekend in Granite City, Illinois. That is the first place where I served as a preacher. They asked me to come back and speak at their Heritage Day to celebrate eighty-five years as a church. We lived there for almost ten years. That is the place my kids say they were raised. The nearest family member we had lived over 500 miles away. However, we found a new family: our church family. Krista and I found new brothers and sisters. Our kids had dozens of new friends and grandparents. It was seven years ago when we left Granite City. This was the first time I made it back. We saw a lot of familiar faces. But there were many faces missing. Some dear family members had passed on.

I chose to speak on "The Bride of Christ." The church is called the Bride of Christ, and Jesus promised to return someday to claim His bride. That promise brings both joy and fear. It brings joy to those who have been added to the church, knowing that for all eternity we will be together in paradise in the presence of God. It brings fear to those outside of the church, knowing they will spend eternity in torment, separated from God.

I hope that realization will bring you joy and give you the motivation to live as a child of God. There will be a great reunion someday. Not only will we get to see our fellow church brothers and sisters, but we will also get to be reunited with those who have gone before us. We will be reunited with our ancestors who passed the faith down to the next generation. We will also get to meet those great people of faith that we read about in the Bible. It will be a great reunion. I don't want to miss it. Do you?

"After that, we who are still alive and are left will be caught up together with them in the clouds to meet the Lord in the air. And so we will be with the Lord forever. Therefore encourage one another with these words" (1 Thessalonians: 4:17).

124. MASKING THE REAL PROBLEM

Last week, we had a leak that resulted in about an inch or so of standing water throughout our house. Once discovered, I leapt into fix-it mode. I grabbed the wet vac and tried to get out as much of the water as possible. My next step was to get all of the area rugs out of the house and onto the driveway to dry them out. Next, I got everything I could off the floor. My hope was to dry out everything, put everything back, and go on living life as if the leak never occurred. Fortunately, my wife knows me well enough that she called in the professionals. They knew what I refused to see; the problem was not just a surface problem. Baseboards had to be torn out, carpets had to be ripped up, and professional drying machines had to be brought in to prevent mold from growing in our walls. I was trying to cover up the problem. They actually came in to fix the problem.

We are guilty of doing the same thing with our spiritual lives. We mistakenly believe that if we look the part on the outside, we can hide the problems that are going on in our hearts. We may fool some people with that. But we don't fool God, and the problem will only grow worse. God has no desire for you to look good to others while there is mold growing in your heart.

"I will give you a new heart and put a new spirit in you; I will remove from you your heart of stone and give you a heart of flesh"
(Ezekiel 36:26).

We will all experience floods in our lifetime. Our typical answer is to dry out the floors and go on living. But that does not fix the problem. If you have mold growing in your heart, God is the solution. It starts with getting your heart right. We must recognize the problem, confess our inadequacies, and submit ourselves to God. We can only cover up the problem. God can fix the problem.

125. WHAT'S YOUR EXCUSE?

"Jesus is coming to town today. I'm not exactly sure why, but I know I need to see Him. Oh, look, there is already a crowd along the street, and I'm so short I will never even get a look at Him. I guess I'll just head back to my tax collector's booth."

"Our friend desperately needs to see Jesus. Since he is unable to walk, let's put him on a mat and take him. Oh, look, the place is packed. We will never get him to Jesus. I guess we'll just carry him back home. Maybe he will see Jesus some other time."

"I am unclean. I have been this way for twelve years. I've tried everything, but I just can't get this bleeding to stop. I know that Jesus is in town. And I know He can help. But just look at the crowd. I'll never get to Jesus. Besides, he seems to be busy helping that other man. I guess I'll just keep on bleeding and hope for another opportunity."

If you know your Bible, then you know that each of these stories has a different ending from what I just described. Zacchaeus didn't let the crowd or his stature stop him from seeing Jesus. He climbed a tree, and his life was changed. The four friends didn't let a few adversities stop them from bringing their friend to Jesus. They scaled a wall, cut a hole in the roof, and lowered their friend to Jesus. And their friend stood and walked. The lady would not let her health condition, the crowd, or a few laws stop her from pushing her way through and just touching Jesus. Once she did, she found a blessing and healing.

"But as for me, I am poor and needy; come quickly to me, O God. You are my help and my deliverer; Lord, do not delay" (Psalm 70:5).

We can all find excuses not to reach out to Jesus today. Satan is notorious for putting roadblocks between you and your Savior. Reaching out to Jesus may never be convenient. But I promise, it will be worth the struggle!

126. ONE VOICE

I love my dog Scout. She is seventy-five pounds of lovable fur and the sweetest-natured dog I have ever known. Many people have asked about her pedigree. Our answer was always, "We have no idea." So, we did a doggy DNA test on her. The results came back, and we found out she is a mixture of about ten different breeds. The truth of the matter is, Scout is a mutt. Scout is the perfect dog except for one thing: She is lazy. Her typical day consists of slowly moving from one place to another to lie down. We always say her spirit animal is Eeyore. The only things that perk her up are the sounds of food hitting the bottom of her bowl and two things that we say. If we say the word "walk" or "check the mail," she leaps to her feet, wags her tail violently, and runs for the door. She could be in a dead sleep, but if we say those words, she is up and ready to go.

"My sheep listen to my voice; I know them, and they follow me"
(John 10:27).

This world is full of a lot of noise. During your typical day, you will hear dozens, if not hundreds, of voices. Voices on the news tell you what is happening in our world. Voices of our children asking for things. Voices of our bosses telling us what to do. Voices on commercials telling us what to buy. Voices of our teachers trying to instruct us. Voices of strangers that we overhear. We are constantly hearing voices. But what voice do you react to? In John 10, Jesus says that He is the Good Shepherd. He goes on to say that His sheep hear His voice and they follow Him. We could learn a lot from my dog Scout. She hears everything, but she only reacts when she hears my voice. God speaks to us through His Word and through His Spirit. Listen for His voice. And when God says it's time to walk, get up, start wagging your tail, and run to follow Him.

127. FOLLOW YOUR PASSION

When I was in the sixth-grade, I thought I found my real passion and purpose for life. It was basketball. I continued to play football and baseball, but they were just something to do until basketball season started. As high school graduation neared, my next step was not decided by where I wanted to go; it was decided by where basketball would take me. Basketball took me to York College in York, Nebraska, and later to Wayland Baptist University in Plainview, Texas. As I was completing my junior year of college, I had my future all planned out. I was going to complete my degree as an education major and begin teaching and coaching. But God had different plans. As my faith in God matured, my priorities began to shift. During my senior year of college, not only had I changed my major, I was working as a part-time youth minister. I have now been a full-time minister for over thirty-four years, and I wouldn't change a thing.

*"Each of you should use whatever gift you have received to serve
others, as faithful stewards of God's grace in its various forms"*
(1 Peter 4:10).

One day, a man was fired from his job at a newspaper in Kansas City because his editor said he "lacked imagination." That man's name was Walt Disney. Could we all stop for a minute and thank that editor for his decision? I believe we all know what this man who "lacked imagination" did with the rest of his life. Walt Disney followed his passion, and now we have Mickey Mouse, Donald Duck, and Space Mountain.

God created us individually with different passions and talents. My passion for basketball took me to a place where I could find my deeper passion. I questioned God after spending a few cold winters in Nebraska and a couple of years in the plains of West Texas. But God had a plan. So, pray hard and follow your passion. Along the way, remember to love and serve others. Following my passion did not lead me to the NBA or to the sidelines with a clipboard in my hand. It is leading me to a better place. Heaven!

128. GIVE THANKS WITH A GRATEFUL HEART

At some point in time this week, I hope you will have the opportunity to sit around a table full of food. I also hope that before you dig in to your Thanksgiving meal, you will stop and give thanks. A tradition in our family is to stop and give thanks for a particular blessing in each person's life. I must admit that due to COVID, 2020 was a hard year to find a wonderful blessing. Then 2021 came along. That year, we had two deaths in our immediate family and a cancerous tumor was found in my kidney. As we gathered around the Thanksgiving table, I was still recovering from surgery. There are times when wonderful blessings are hard to find.

Each of the gospels tells the story of a time when Jesus and the disciples were surrounded by a massive crowd. When it came time to eat, food was scarce. All they could find was one boy's lunch that consisted of five small pieces of bread and two fish. Instead of dwelling on the things they did not have, Jesus instructed everyone to sit down, and then …

"Taking the five loaves and the two fish and looking up to heaven, he gave thanks and broke the loaves. Then he gave them to his disciples to distribute to the people. He also divided the two fish among them all. They all ate and were satisfied" (Mark 6:41-42).

Rather than complaining about the meager amount of food, Jesus looked up to heaven and gave thanks. By the end of the meal, not only was everyone full, they ended up with twelve baskets of leftovers. So, if you are having a hard time this year finding a blessing, just follow the example of Jesus. Find a small blessing and lift it up to God. Then stand back and watch what God can do with a small blessing and a grateful heart. Hope you have a wonderful Thanksgiving.

129. I KNOW MY PLACE

I want to share with you one of the most hurtful things ever said to me. It was my junior year of college. I was a scholarship player on the university basketball team. We were in a team meeting when our coach asked us to write down what role we believed we had on the basketball team. He gave us several options, including star of the team, defensive stopper, scoring threat, clutch shooter, role player, rebounder, just happy to be on the team, and a few others. I considered my strengths and weaknesses. I knew I was in no way the star player. I was not the most athletic, so I marked off rebounder and defensive stopper. I wrote down role player. I knew that when I was given the opportunity to play, I would give maximum effort. And he recruited me because I held multiple shooting records in junior college. Coach walked by to look at my paper. When he saw role player written down, he just laughed. He took his pen and crossed it out and said, "Phillip, you should just be happy to be on the team."

That hurt my pride because I thought I had more talent than that. It hurt my heart because my coach thought I had nothing to offer the team other than just being there. I thought more highly of myself than he did. But on a team, the coach's opinion is really the only opinion that matters. One thing I realized that day is that the world can be a cruel place. But God's kingdom doesn't work like the world. Jesus said the real heroes are the servants. He said our impact isn't measured by our accolades, but by the sacrifices we make.

"The last will be first, and the first will be last" (Matthew 20:16).

I never made the cover of *Sports Illustrated* or signed a pro contract. Now I try to walk humbly and remember my place, just happy to be on God's team. You know what? That's a pretty good place to be!

130. DON'T FORGET THE BREAD

I love the traditional Thanksgiving meal. The turkey and dressing are a must. But when you add the side dishes, they make the meal complete. Some of my personal favorites are sweet potatoes with melted marshmallows on top, green bean casserole, cheesy rice, deviled eggs, mashed potatoes and gravy … I could go on and on. And no Thanksgiving meal would be complete without dessert. When given the choice of pecan pie or apple pie, I usually choose both. There are some traditions I don't care for. I have never developed a taste for cranberry sauce. And I know this will sound un-American, but I don't care for pumpkin pie. I agree with the great American storyteller Garrison Keillor when he said of pumpkin pie, "It is the ultimate example of mediocrity. The best pumpkin pie you have ever eaten wasn't that much better than the worst pumpkin pie you have ever eaten."

As good as all that food sounds, the meal would not be complete if you forgot the bread. Whether it is dinner rolls or fresh-baked bread, it is what pulls the meal together. Bread stands alone in diversity for all types of meals in most every culture.

When you read through the Bible, it is amazing how often bread shows up. Unleavened bread was a must in the Passover meal that marked the freeing of God's children from slavery in Egypt. God rained down bread from heaven during the forty years the children of Egypt journeyed through the desert. David was delivering bread to his brothers on the battlefield when he encountered a giant named Goliath. Jesus multiplied five loaves of bread along with some fish to serve the 5,000. Jesus broke bread with His disciples at the Last Supper. The early church was known for meeting together to break bread. But most importantly, Jesus took bread and broke it saying, *Take and eat, this is my body.* Jesus also referred to Himself as the "Bread of Life."

"For the bread of God is the bread that comes down from heaven and gives life to the world" (John 6:33).

Here is a good rule for Thanksgiving is also a good rule for life, "Don't forget the bread!"

131. FOUL TROUBLE

In my youth, I was a three-sport kid. I loved playing football, basketball, and baseball. As I was entering high school, my basketball coach told me I needed to pick one and stick with it. With hindsight, he was right. I might have been good at all of them, but I wouldn't have excelled at any of them. I chose basketball, and it ended up paying for my college. I still love basketball. I don't play much anymore, but I enjoy watching. Basketball is considered a non-contact sport. But anyone who has ever played competitive basketball will tell you there is a lot of contact that goes on once the ball is tossed. However, if there is too much contact, the whistle blows, and you are called for a foul. In high school and college, you get five fouls; in the NBA, you get six. When you reach your limit, you are banished to the bench to watch the rest of the game. You are helpless to do anything to help your team. So, at the beginning of the game, players are very aggressive. But after a couple of fouls, a player will back off for fear of getting into foul trouble.

"If you, Lord, kept a record of sins, Lord, who could stand? But with you there is forgiveness, so that we can, with reverence, serve you" (Psalm 130:3-4).

Sadly, many people live their Christian lives like they are in foul trouble. We stop living a bold Christian life because of a few mistakes in our past. And some feel banished to the bench, believing that their past mistakes have left them unable to help the team. We serve a God who not only forgives, He forgets. With grace, you are never in foul trouble. When you confess your mistakes, they are erased. So, get off the bench and play hard. Our team needs you!

132. NO FEAR IN LOVE

I remember the early summer of 1989. I had just graduated from college and was ready to start my career. But even bigger than that, I was in love with the woman of my dreams. I bought a ring and was ready to pop the question. I asked Krista to go to the zoo with me. (Please don't ask why I thought proposing in front of the gorilla cage would be romantic.) Thankfully, my sister asked us to take her daughter with us that day, so the proposal was postponed. Plan B was to take Krista to the Myriad Gardens in downtown Oklahoma City the next day. As we stood on the bridge, I fumbled to get the ring out of my pocket. Then I asked Krista Starr to become Krista Treat. She said "Yes," and thirty-four years later, we are both glad I didn't drop the ring off the bridge. Thank goodness she didn't want to hyphenate our last names; it would sound like a Dairy Queen product.

Sadly, that proposal would be shameful in today's world. For a guy to propose today, he has to fly in friends and family, rent out a venue, write some poems, get the lighting just right, hire a photographer, hire a videographer, and book an after-party. My question is this: What if she says "No"? That would be my greatest fear if I were the young man proposing. But every guy I have asked confidently told me the same thing, "She is going to say 'Yes.'" It reminds me of a verse written by John, the disciple whom Jesus loved.

"There is no fear in love. Perfect love puts fear out of our hearts. People have fear when they are afraid of being punished. The man who is afraid does not have perfect love" (1 John 4:18 NLV).

The "proposer" may have a fear of her saying "No" or his plans going awry. But the love he has is bigger than any of those fears. Could you imagine if we had a love like that for our God? Our expressions of love to God would be extravagant. We would not concern ourselves with the cost, inconvenience, or the potential of failing. Our expressions of love to God would be public. Who cares who is watching and what they may think of me? We would be confident in our expressions of love to God. The question of "What if we fail?" would not even be on the radar. We would be assured that our expressions of love to God would be well-received.

I want to have that perfect love for my God. Wouldn't that be a real star-treat? (Sorry, I couldn't help myself.)

133. GOODBYE 2021

This week, we all get to do something I am very excited about. We get to say goodbye to 2021. It's time to put a lid on 2021 and shove it in the back of the closet. It has been a year that, for the most part, I would like to forget. In 2021, I had to say goodbye to my father in January. February brought in one of the worst snowstorms I can remember. In the midst of that snowstorm, Krista's sister passed away. Throughout the year, we kept thinking we were saying goodbye to COVID, but it kept coming back. Later in the year came the great colonoscopy debacle. After three colonoscopies in three weeks, plus an ambulance ride, it was discovered that I had a cancerous tumor on my kidney. So, back to the hospital for a four-day stay and surgery to remove part of my kidney. Twenty-twenty-one has not been an easy year for me, and I have the scars to prove it!

Here is the scary part about all of that: When 2020 was over, I thought it had to be the worst year ever. Twenty-twenty introduced us to COVID and new phrases like "social distancing" and "quarantine in place." The year 2020 literally shut down our schools, churches, the Olympics, and many businesses. We adapted, but we struggled. So, dare I say, what will happen in 2022?

The best way we can face 2022 is to take a page from the life of Abraham. He had a life that was full of ups and downs. Abraham was chosen by God to be the father of a nation. But along the way, he had to visit Sodom and Gomorrah, he got caught in a lie on several occasions, he often doubted the promise of God, and he was asked by God to sacrifice his son. But do not forget how it all started.

"The Lord had said to Abram, "Go from your country, your people and your father's household to the land I will show you"
(Genesis 12:1).

The story of Abraham starts with God telling him to put the past behind him, step out in faith, and trust God. So, as we conclude 2021 and venture out into 2022, let's take a cue from Abraham. Listen to God and step out in faith. Our God is faithful. He will never leave or forsake us. So come on, 2022. Let's see what cha got!

SECTION THREE:

OUR
love
FOR OTHERS

134. SEVEN IS NOT THE LUCKY NUMBER

Peter thought he had arrived as a follower of Jesus. This former fisherman had learned about forgiveness by watching Jesus. So, one day, he decided to show Jesus all he had learned by posing a question to Jesus. Peter asked, *"Lord, how many times shall I forgive my brother or sister who sins against me? Up to seven times?"* Peter then waited for the praise of Jesus. Forgiving someone seven times went above and beyond what even a good person might do, right? Jesus's response surprised Peter. Jesus said, *"I tell you, not seven times, but seventy-seven times."* I imagine Peter's first thought was, "How can someone keep track of seventy-seven times?" Which was exactly Jesus's point. If you live your life always looking at the scoreboard keeping track of who has wronged you then your heart is not the heart of a true follower of Jesus.

Immediately following this discussion of forgiveness Jesus told the disciples a story about a man, (we'll call him Scrooge), who was drowning in millions of dollars' worth of debt. After some begging, the king forgave his debt, no strings attached. The newly debt-free Scrooge walked out of the palace and found a man, (we'll call him Bob), who owed him a couple of dollars. Scrooge demanded payment. When Bob could not pay, Scrooge had him thrown in jail. The king heard what happened, so Scrooge's forgiveness was revoked, and Bob got a new cellmate.

"Bear with each other and forgive one another if any of you has a grievance against someone. Forgive as the Lord forgave you"
(Colossians 3:12).

Living your life always keeping score of the sins of others is a miserable way to live. If you are a scoreboard watcher, it is time to get on your knees and thank God that heaven doesn't have a scoreboard. God has forgiven you. Our response has to be forgiving others. Otherwise, we lose the game.

135. IT'S A BEAUTIFUL DAY IN THE NEIGHBORHOOD

Do you have a least-favorite neighbor? I've had a few in my days. When I was a kid, my next-door neighbor got a mean dog just to keep me from climbing the fence to get whatever ball I accidentally threw into their yard. In college, your neighbors are the other guys who live on your hall in the dorm. My least favorite was the metal head who wired his alarm clock through his stereo. So, whenever Metallica woke him up at 6 a.m., we were all up (even on Saturday mornings).

As an adult, bad neighbors have continued to show up. One hillbilly neighbor threw a dead squirrel into our back yard because he thought our miniature schnauzer would enjoy eating it. We had a neighbor whose hoarding grew out of their house, onto their porch, and into their driveway. In Tulsa, we had a homeowner's association that introduced us to a whole different genre of annoying neighbors. I received a written citation because others could see my trash bin from the street.

Why would God put difficult people into our lives? Wouldn't life be easier if we didn't have to deal with difficult people? I believe God has a purpose for this. In Matthew 14, Jesus gave His disciples a little glimpse into heaven.

> *"My Father's house has many rooms; if that were not so, would I have told you that I am going there to prepare a place for you? And if I go and prepare a place for you, I will come back and take you to be with me that you also may be where I am" (Matthew 14:2-3).*

One thing is certain about heaven—there will be other people around us. Maybe, just maybe, God is using difficult neighbors on Earth to prepare us for our eternal dwelling. One of my favorite preachers tells the story about being in the lobby after services when a very disgruntled older lady took the opportunity to tell him how much she disliked him and his preaching. He hugged her and said, "I'm going to make sure I live next door to you in heaven so we will have a lot of time to work this out." It may be a good idea to learn how to love the people around us now. They may be your neighbor for longer than you think!

136. LOVE ONE ANOTHER

I don't know if you are a New Year's resolution type of a person. But it is that time of year. It's not the time of year to make resolutions. That was a couple of weeks ago. It is that time of year when we begin to break those resolutions. The most common resolution is to get in shape and lose some weight. But one excuse for one day leads to another excuse for the next day. Before you know it, that resolution is a forgotten memory.

This year I didn't even think about making any New Year's resolutions. Considering how unpredictable last year was, why bother? If we resolved to go to the gym more last year, we had a perfect excuse: They closed down the gyms. If we resolved to attend church services more regularly, we had a perfect excuse: They closed the doors to our church buildings. So why make resolutions if someone else can come in and derail them?

I have a resolution for all of us to strive for this year: Let's resolve to love others. To simply love others may not come easy. Some people can really try your patience. To love others may not come naturally. It is a choice. But one thing is certain—no pandemic can take away your opportunity to love others. No government shutdown can keep you from loving others. Social distancing and having to quarantine will only make us be more creative with how we love others. To love others sounds like a good bumper sticker, but it is more than that for those who strive to please God. It is a command. Resolve today that you will love others. It will not only make this world a better place; it will make our God smile.

"For the entire law is fulfilled in keeping this one command: 'Love your neighbor as yourself'" (Galatians 5:14).

137. YOU ARE THE LIGHT OF THE WORLD

Have you ever had one of those days when it seems like the world is just trying to frustrate you? Your first errand of the day is to go to the bank. The lines are long, and you try to be patient. The other people in line are grumbling, and they take their anger out on the tellers. Next stop is the grocery store. Everyone seems to be walking in slow motion like it is the first time they have ever been shopping. Then there is the mother with four kids in tow, who has parked her cart in front of the items you need. Then you are faced with the choice of which checkout line to choose. And of course, you get in line with the people who insist on telling their life story to the checkout person, who was supposed to go on break thirty minutes ago. Last stop is a restaurant. Finally, you can sit down, relax, and enjoy a meal. But the service is slow because a couple of the waitstaff called in sick that day. The meal is slow to arrive, and your drink glass remains empty for most of the meal.

With each of these scenarios, you have a choice. You can voice your frustrations and let everyone around you know how inconsiderate they are and how much they are messing up your day. Or, you could bite your lip, say nothing, and just boil on the inside.

Let me give you a third option.

"Do not let any unwholesome talk come out of your mouths, but only what is helpful for building others up according to their needs, that it may benefit those who listen" (Ephesians 4:29).

Take a moment and put yourself in the shoes of the bank teller, the mother of four, the checkout person, and the overwhelmed waitress. What if, instead of making a bad day worse for others, you choose to make their day better by smiling and speaking words of love? Rather than tear them down, build them up. At the end of the day, you'll feel better about yourself, and you will have been a spark of light in the life of another who was having a dark day. We are called to be light in this world, not to add to the darkness.

138. I HAVE A HARD OUT

I heard a phrase used the other day that I had not heard before. It happened to be two celebrities talking to each other when one of them said, "I have a hard out at three o'clock." I have since learned what the phrase "hard out" means. Hard out means that I have to leave, no matter what is happening. People who use the phrase "hard out" typically have a very full calendar. I understand deadlines and commitments. It is the need to get things done and not leave others waiting. However …

Picture a husband talking to his wife as she is pouring out her heart about a particular struggle she is facing, and he says to her, "I have a hard out in ten minutes, so you need to wrap this up." There is a real good chance that he would be sleeping in the doghouse that evening.

Picture a father listening to his child talk about their day, and the father says, "I have a hard out in five minutes, so get to the point." What does that tell the child about their importance?

Picture a friend talking to another friend and saying, "I have a hard out, so maybe we can catch up with each other later." What kind of friend is that?

"Be completely humble and gentle; be patient, bearing with one another in love" (Ephesians 4:2).

Read through the book of Mark sometime and notice the busyness of Jesus. Watch how Jesus never minded a delay or an interruption to His busy schedule. People and relationships were more important to Jesus than staying on schedule. In Ephesians 4:2, Paul reminds us how we should treat others. We need to be humble, gentle, and patient while we bear with one another in love. Don't let your busy schedule destroy your relationships.

And by the way, how patient has God been with you? Have you

ever been praying and heard God say, "I have a hard out in two minutes, so can you hurry up and get to the Amen"? If God is patient with you, then we owe it to Him to be patient and loving with others.

139. BE ABOUT THE BUSINESS OF LOVING OTHERS

Carly Pearce is a singer/songwriter who has a song out called "What He Didn't Do." In this song, she is reminiscing about a love gone wrong. During the song, she lists the things that he didn't do, like treat her right, put her first, be a man of his word, and stay home because he wanted to. So, the relationship is over, not because of the things he did, but the things he didn't do.

The Bible has plenty to say about the things that we should not do to others: We should not lie to others; we should not steal from others; we should not murder others; and we should not mistreat others. While all of those (and more) are true, the Bible overwhelmingly has even more to say about how we should treat others.

"A new command I give you: Love one another. As I have loved you, so you must love one another. By this everyone will know that you are my disciples, if you love one another" (John 13:34-35).

"Let no debt remain outstanding, except the continuing debt to love one another, for whoever loves others has fulfilled the law" (Romans 13:8).

"And this is his command: to believe in the name of his Son, Jesus Christ, and to love one another as he commanded us" (1 John 3:23).

If this world would spend more time loving one another, we would spend less time hurting or neglecting one another. If you want your world to change, be about the business of loving others.

140. MIXED MESSAGES

I have a book in my office titled, *How to be a Christian without Being Religious*. Just the title forces us to ask the question, "Is there a difference between being a Christian and being religious?" In the church, the answer is yes, there is a big difference. However, the world sees them as one in the same. Being religious includes things like attending worship services, dressing correctly, and practicing the spiritual disciplines, such as reading scripture, praying, giving, and fasting. For the record, there is nothing wrong with any of these activities. Jesus did all of these things. But so did the Pharisees. And Jesus called them out on their hypocrisy. How can you do all of these great things and still not be right with God? The answer is two things: the heart and others.

All these religious activities can be done ritualistically. They may or may not connect with your heart, and they have no connection with others. To understand what it means to be a Christian, we just have to look at the life of Jesus. Yes, He went to the Temple and the Synagogue. Yes, He read scripture and prayed. But most of the text we have on the life of Jesus shows Him loving and forgiving others, sitting down and spending time with children, feeding hungry people, and healing the lame.

"By this everyone will know that you are my disciples, if you love one another" (John 13:35).

If your car breaks down in rush hour traffic, do you want someone to send you a detailed diagnostic of what went wrong? Or would you prefer a pair of jumper cables, a lift, or a call for a tow truck? If you know a single mother who lost her job, do you think she would rather have a lecture on what went wrong in her life or a gift card to a grocery store? The world will know what we believe by seeing what we do.

Religion is important. But without Christ-like living, it sends a bad message to others.

141. WORDS

Words have tremendous power. With four simple words from God, He created day and night. Just reading Genesis 1, we see the power of God's words as He spoke our world into existence. But words also persuaded Eve to disobey God and cause the fall of mankind. With words, Jesus cast out demons and called Lazarus out of the tomb. Words were also used to put Jesus on the cross. Words were spoken at Pentecost that changed the hearts of thousands of people. Words will also be spoken on judgment day that will tell us of our eternal existence.

Have words shaped your life? Did you hear words of encouragement from your parents that gave you the courage to get out there and face life? Did you hear words from a teacher or coach that gave you the confidence to succeed? Did you hear words from a friend or mentor that guided your career path? Or maybe you have allowed the words of others to keep you down or hold you back. Maybe words have kept you from having the confidence to move forward and try new things.

What about your words? Yes, God's words have the power to create life. But your words have the power to shape lives. You can use your words to encourage someone who is depressed. Your words can give confidence to someone who is doubting. Your words can also cut deep and hurt others. The two words, "I do," can launch a lifelong commitment. But other words can tear that commitment to shreds.

"Do not let any unwholesome talk come out of your mouths, but only what is helpful for building others up according to their needs, that it may benefit those who listen" (Ephesians 4:29).

Let's be very picky about the words we say. You alone control the words that come out of your mouth.

142. CHOOSE LOVE

One evening I sat down and watched the movie *Divergent* with my daughter. I was just enjoying the movie when she exclaimed, "This is my life!" I had to ask for clarity on what she meant by that. *Divergent* is a movie set in a futuristic time when society is divided into 5 factions. At the age of sixteen, each person must choose which faction they belong to. This decision is permanent. They will be a part of that faction for the rest of their lives. If they choose a faction they were not raised in, they will be separated from their parents.

My daughter, who was finishing high school and starting college at the time, said she could relate to the main character, Tris, who was struggling with her decision. The pressures of choosing a college and deciding on a major made her feel like these were permanent decisions that would set her course for the rest of her life. In some ways, she was right. But in other ways, she was completely wrong.

I believe we all feel that pressure when we are forced to make a decision. Some decisions definitely have a right answer and a wrong answer (like the choice to sin or not to sin). But here is a secret: God is not overly concerned with where we go and what we do. If we start down one path and realize that it is not a fit, just get off at the first exit ramp and choose another path. What God is concerned about is who we are and how we treat others.

"Therefore, as God's chosen people, holy and dearly loved, clothe yourselves with compassion, kindness, humility, gentleness and patience. Bear with each other and forgive one another if any of you has a grievance against someone. Forgive as the Lord forgave you. And over all these virtues put on love, which binds them all together in perfect unity" (Colossians 3:12-14).

Who you are is more important than where you are. If you find yourself teaching in a classroom, love your students. If you find yourself working in a hospital, love your patients. If you find yourself serving in a law office, love your clients. If you find yourself waiting tables, love your customers. If you find yourself in a home, love your family. No matter where you are and what you are doing, choose love.

143. PEOPLE

"People, they're the worst." That is a quote from Jerry Seinfeld on an episode of his show. It was, of course, said in jest. But it is very easy to adapt this quote to your everyday life. People can drive you crazy. There are those people who drive too slow in the left lane on the interstate. There are those people who haven't even thought about their order until they are the first person in line at the drive-thru. There are those people who will take two baskets of groceries through the self-checkout line while you are behind them with one loaf of bread. There are those people who will talk on their phones in the movie theater. And to take a few more from Seinfeld: There are those people who are close talkers, low talkers, regifters, anti-dentites (prejudice against dentists), and people who double dip their chips. Sometimes it feels like people were put on Earth just to give you anxiety.

It would be no surprise to me if Jesus felt the same way in His short time on Earth. What type of people would drive Jesus crazy? People who pick up stones before looking in the mirror at their own lives. People who ignored the value of children. People who worry about things they can't control. People who judge others. People who place themselves ahead of others. People who are blessed and don't give thanks. People who would use religion for their own profit. People who look good on the outside but are rotten on the inside. People who would betray Him. People who make promises and break them before the rooster crows. People who chose not to follow because they are too busy with other things.

If you didn't find yourself in that last list, read it again. Jesus had every excuse in the world to write off people because of their behavior, including you and me. But He didn't. And we shouldn't either.

"But God demonstrates his own love for us in this: While we were still sinners, Christ died for us" (Romans 5:8).

Jesus gave us the example of loving and being with the people who could have potentially driven Him crazy. So, when your patience gets worn thin, just follow the example of Jesus and love them anyway. "People, they're the best! Or maybe at least they are tolerable.

144. EVERY ONE NEEDS ONE

There are many ways for a person to come into a relationship with Jesus. The typical way that people come to know Jesus is through their family. Other ways include a friend, an invitation from a stranger knocking on your door, a post on social media, shared reading material, a podcast, television, radio … The list could go on and on. But they all have one thing in common. One person reached out to another. We have all come to know God because at least one person in your life invited you to church services, friended you when you were lonely, handed you a Bible, shared their story with you, or just stood out as an example of how a follower of Jesus lives.

The latest statistics say that there are at least 2.38 billion Christians living in our world today. That is around a third of the estimated 8 billion people who currently populate our planet. Here is what makes this hard to believe: This started with just eleven people who were charged with reaching out and sharing the gospel message about 2,000 years ago. We read in the book of Acts that the number grew from eleven to 150 before the day of Pentecost. On that day, the number grew to over 3,000. A short time later, the number grew to 5,000. And since that time, there have been billions and billions of Christians around the world.

"We are therefore Christ's ambassadors, as though God were making his appeal through us" (2 Corinthians 5:20).

There are two reasons that Christianity has spread across the world and has grown to this number. First, it is not only good news, it is THE GOOD NEWS. But the second reason is that when someone received the good news, they did not keep it to themselves. They shared it with others. Will you be Christ's ambassador and do the same?

145. THE TIME IS NOW!

I have been a minister for thirty-five years. I spent fourteen of those years in youth ministry, and now twenty-one years preaching. In that time, I have been blessed to be in and out of the lives of many people. Looking back, God gave me the opportunity to minister to hundreds of young people at a crucial time of their spiritual development. I pray that God worked through me to introduce them to Jesus and encourage them in their relationship with God. As a preacher, I have had the opportunity to walk beside many people through births, deaths, weddings, and struggles. But that is only one side of the coin. I think of the people who were there with Krista and me when our children were born. I am thankful for those who were there to encourage me when I was depressed or going through job transitions. God has a way of putting just the right people in just the right place at just the right time.

In the book of Esther, we read about a young Jewish girl named Hadassah, who is also known as Esther. Esther was taken from her village to be one of many young ladies who would possibly become the King of Persia's next queen. Esther was chosen to be queen even though the King was unaware of her Jewish heritage. Subsequently, an edict was put in place condemning all of the Jewish people to death. Esther had to make a decision. She could risk her life and go before the king and plea for her people or say nothing. Listen to the challenging words sent to Esther from her cousin/foster-father, Mordecai.

"And who knows but that you have come to your royal position for such a time as this?" (Esther 4:14).

God places certain people in certain places at certain times to speak lifesaving words. Who has God placed in your life today who needs to hear the lifesaving words that Jesus came to give them new life? Who do you know right now who is lost and hurting and needs to know God loves them? You may be the only one they will listen to. And who knows but that you have a relationship with them for such a time as this? Will you speak up or say nothing?

146. LIFE ON BEAVERS BEND ROAD

Contrary to popular belief, a lot of ministers are introverts. I definitely fall into that category. Yes, I love preaching and seeing everyone on Sunday. But there is a reason that Monday is my day off. I need a day of solitude to find some balance in my life. Five years ago, Krista and I bought a house on Beavers Bend Road. On our dead-end street, there are twelve houses. I'm embarrassed to admit that after living there two years I only knew a few people's names. Then COVID hit, and we were all stuck in our houses. I'm thankful that one neighbor had the initiative to get us all together. On Easter Sunday of 2020, when all our churches were closed, we all agreed to have a sunset Easter service in the cul-de-sac at the end of our street. Every household attended. And yes, we all had our masks on and kept our social distance. But we got together to sing, pray, and listen to God's Word. Then, last year, one family took it a step further. They decided that every Tuesday evening, they would open their home and invite every family to come share a meal together. And we continue to do that each week. Thank goodness for eager extraverts. I now know all my neighbors on Beavers Bend Road.

"Dear friends, since God so loved us, we also ought to love one another. No one has ever seen God; but if we love one another, God lives in us and his love is made complete in us"
(1 John 4:11-12).

We all understand the importance of loving God. But Jesus says that we are not fulfilling our purpose here if we do not love others. In order to love our neighbors, we must first get to know our neighbors. I'm thankful that I got a firm nudge to get to know those who live around me.

147. BEST MEAL EVER

What is the most memorable breakfast you have ever eaten? Ponder this question for a minute and see where your mind takes you. As I thought about it, my mind went two places. First was breakfast on Wilderness Trek in the mountains of Colorado. My youth group and I woke at sunrise to an amazing smell. It was meat being cooked on an open flame. Come to find out the meat was SPAM from a can. But we were starving, and it tasted great to us. The second place my mind went was to my grandmother's house. One morning, she made waffles from scratch that she cooked on an old waffle iron. Then she let me put peanut butter and syrup on my waffle. YUM!

The more I thought about it, the more I realized that my most memorable breakfasts had very little to do with the food. Waffles are a dime a dozen. And SPAM? If it was that good, why have I not eaten it since that day? The reason these meals stood out to me was because of the atmosphere and the people.

One morning, Jesus made breakfast for a couple of His disciples. Not long after Jesus rose from the dead, Peter and a few buddies went back to what they knew best, fishing. Earlier, when Jesus was arrested, all of the disciples scattered. Peter even went so far as to deny even knowing Jesus. He figured that his life as a follower of Jesus was over, so why not fish? After a bad night of fishing, they heard a voice from the shore. When Peter realized it was Jesus, he leapt from the boat and swam to shore. There was Jesus with bread and fish on the fire. No one asked where Jesus got the fish and bread. I'm sure they all remembered that Jesus could produce some fish and bread from next to nothing. What's most amazing about this meal is what Jesus didn't say. He didn't chastise them for scattering. He didn't give them the biggest "I told you so" of all time. Jesus just provided a meal and some time for them. And that was enough.

*"Jesus said to them, 'Come and have breakfast.' None of the
disciples dared ask him, 'Who are you?' They knew it was the Lord"
(John 21:12).*

Never miss an opportunity to share a meal with someone. When you
do get to share a meal together, quit worrying about the food and just
cherish the moment.

148. JUST TRY

Matthew was a tax collector when Jesus invited him to follow. Luke 5:28 says that Matthew, also known as Levi, left everything to follow Jesus. Being a tax collector, Matthew would know a lot about money. So, it is no big surprise that Matthew would relay a parable that Jesus taught in which money played the lead role. The story goes like this … The master was leaving home for a while, so he entrusted his money to three servants. To one he gave five bags of gold, the next servant received two bags of gold, and the final one received one bag of gold. When the master returned, the first two servants had doubled the gold that was entrusted to them. The servant who was entrusted with one bag of gold buried it out of fear of losing it. So, he was only able to return the one bag of gold to the master. Needless to say, the master was not pleased. He told the servant that he could have at least put the money in the bank and received a little interest.

Why was the master so upset? He was upset because the third servant didn't even try. By doing nothing, he missed every opportunity to please the master. Our heavenly Father has blessed each of us individually with time, talents, and opportunities to expand His Kingdom. Some people make the most of every opportunity to share the love of God with others. While others, out of fear, do nothing with the opportunities that are given to them. How does that fear manifest itself? Some are ashamed of their faith and refuse to share it with others. Some use the excuse of being too shy. While others just assume that they will be rejected, so they don't even try. The third servant was chastised by the master, not because he didn't double the amount, but because he refused to try.

When you are presented with an opportunity to share your faith, just TRY. The results will be in God's hands. Our responsibility is to TRY. Those who try will hear the master say these beautiful words …

"His master replied, 'Well done, good and faithful servant! You have been faithful with a few things; I will put you in charge of many things. Come and share your master's happiness!'"
(Matthew 25:23).

149. THE GREATEST OF THESE

Stop and think of the person or persons who have made the greatest difference in your life. Who has made a positive impact on you becoming the person you are today? For me, several people come to mind. I've had a couple of coaches who worked hard not only to make me a better player, but a better person. I've also had a few teachers who, for some unknown reason, took a special interest in me because they could see something in me that I could not see myself. There have been a few friends along the way who stood by my side and lifted me up when I was down. But two special people come to mind. First, my mother made sure that I knew who Jesus was and that Jesus is the most important relationship I would ever have. But the one person who has made the greatest difference in my life is my wife of thirty-three years. She knows the good and the bad, and she has never given up on me. She has made me a better person than I ever thought I could be.

As a quick side note, are you that person to anyone? Are you inspiring someone to be a better person? Are you sharing with others what is most important in life?

"And now these three remain: faith, hope and love. But the greatest of these is love" (1 Corinthians 13:13).

Every single one of us has a heavenly Father who is eternally faithful. He has given us hope for today and hope for an eternal home with Him. He loves each one of us in a special way. He knows every good thing about us, and He knows all of our dark secrets. And the amazing thing is, He loves us anyway.

Very few things in this world are eternal. We know that faith, hope, and love will stand the test of time. But the greatest of these is love. So, get out there and start loving others. Your love may just change someone's eternity.

150. ACCEPT ONE ANOTHER

I believe that most of us are familiar with Leonardo Da Vinci's painting of *The Last Supper*. It portrays the twelve disciples chosen by Jesus sitting around a table the night before Jesus was crucified. At this meal, Jesus instituted what we call the Lord's Supper. The moment that Da Vinci captured in his painting was when Jesus told the twelve disciples that one of them would betray Him. But even that moment was not the most controversial thing about this supper.

The most controversial thing about the Last Supper was the twelve disciples themselves. Each of these twelve men was personally chosen by Jesus to be in His inner circle. If we were choosing the Son of God's twelve closest friends for the short time that He was on Earth, I imagine we would have chosen differently. We would have chosen a few scholars, a few charismatic speakers, and maybe a few politicians who had some influence among the people. But Jesus chose an assortment of common, uneducated men from small towns. He chose a tax collector. which was one of the most hated professions a man could have. He chose a political zealot who would strike fear in most people and would be the archenemy of a tax collector. And He chose a few fishermen who were not known to be the most reputable people. Also, Jesus associated Himself with the Pharisees, with the diseased, with the tax collectors, with the prostitutes, with a five-times-divorced woman, and with another woman caught in the sinful act of adultery.

All of this makes me ask the question, would we accept Jesus as a member of our church? He seemed to be accepting of people from all walks of life. In all our modern churches, the people tend to look the same. We congregate with groups of people who are similar to ourselves. And we struggle to accept and welcome those who live different lifestyles and who don't seem to be the "upright citizens" that we claim to be. Jesus was sinless and never condoned the sin of others. But at the same time, He was accepting and loving of all people. We can learn a lot from the example of Jesus.

"Accept one another, then, just as Christ accepted you, in order to bring praise to God" (Romans 15:7).

151. THANK YOU, MOM

I would love to tell you that even as a child, I was always focused on spiritual matters. But that just isn't true. I would love to tell you that I was a joy to raise and never gave my parents any problems. But that just isn't true. I would love to tell you that from my childhood on, I was always focused on being a minister in the church. But that just isn't true either. Well … sorta

My fourth-grade teacher at Townsend Elementary in Del City, Oklahoma, told my mom a story that she loved to tell anyone who would listen. Our teacher asked us one day what we would like to be when we grew up. When it came my turn to answer, I said, "I would like to be a preacher or a garbage man." Even at that age, I enjoyed trying to get a laugh.

When I was sixteen, my parents divorced, and I really lost my way. I often lied to my mom because I knew it would break her heart if she really knew the truth about what I was doing. My brother and sister were both grown and out of the house during my high school years. It was just mom and me. I would stay out past curfew. Sometimes I would come home on time only to sneak out to be with my friends. That behavior continued till my second year of college. I finally committed my life to be in a real relationship with God.

Even though I thought I was really sneaky, Mom knew all along what was really going on. When my kids were teenagers, and I had a new perspective, I had a few questions for my mom. One of them being, "How did you make it through those years knowing that I was out there messing up?" She answered, "I just stayed home and prayed for you."

Thank you, Mom, for raising me in the church. Thank you, Mom, for being patient with me. Thank you, Mom, for praying for me. I am blessed. I hope now I can be a blessing to others.

"Start children off on the way they should go, and even when they are old they will not turn from it" (Proverbs 22:6).

152. PRAISE HER

There are many things in life that are not appreciated at the moment. It takes time for true value to surface. That can be said about our mothers. Not many young children truly appreciate their mothers until later in life. I remember calling my mother multiple times as my children were growing up just to tell her, "Thank you." It took being a parent to realize all that my mother had done for me and all I put her through. So, as we celebrate Mother's Day, I want to highlight a passage of scripture that is often read on this day. Proverbs 31 describes a wife of noble character. She is a woman of:

DIGNITY—She is worthy of praise and a woman of great value. She adds value to her home, church family, community, and to the world.

PATIENCE—The scripture tells us that she "considers a field and buys it." She is willing to wait patiently and make the best decisions.

DILIGENCE—She is a hard worker. Her work is not only fruitful, it makes her stronger.

GENEROUSITY—With all that she had worked for and acquired, she freely gives to the poor. She truly is a blessing as she intentionally seeks opportunities to help others.

COURAGE—She can laugh at the days to come because she is encouraged in the truth that God has ordered her steps. Because she trusts God with tomorrow, she can have peace for today.

WISDOM—With God as her guiding source, she has clarity on the decisions she makes, how she lives her life, and the words she chooses.

DEVOTION—She's praised because she is first devoted to God. All of her virtuous qualities are founded on her devotion to the Lord.

"Charm is deceptive, and beauty is fleeting; but a woman who fears the Lord is to be praised" (Proverbs 31:30).

Choose this day and every day to love and honor your mother. She is a gift from God.

153. KOINONIA

When I was first introduced to the word Koinonia, I was a freshman at York College. It was the name of one of the campus social clubs. When I asked what the word meant, I was told it means fellowship. Actually, it is a Greek word that means to share together, take part together or to give to one another. I was thinking about that word this week and realized that it is what I have been missing. I love the fact that we have been able to communicate together during this time of social isolation. We are able to talk by telephone, see each other through FaceTime and Zoom, and worship 'together' through the use of social media. But it is just not the same.

After creation, the first words we have from God are, *"It is not good for man to be alone."* He created within us a need for fellowship. When we are baptized into Christ, we are added to the Body of Christ. Instantly, we not only have a local family, but also a worldwide family and an eternal family. Listen to the description of the very first church members in Jerusalem following Pentecost.

"They devoted themselves to the apostles' teaching and to fellowship, to the breaking of bread and to prayer. All the believers were together and had everything in common. Every day they continued to meet together in the temple courts. They broke bread in their homes and ate together with glad and sincere hearts, praising God and enjoying the favor of all the people. And the Lord added to their number daily those who were being saved" (Acts 2:42, 44, 46-47).

This has been a strange few months to say the least. Yes, we have survived. But no, we are not thriving. Why? Because we were created to be together. That is what we are missing. The church has survived severe persecution in the past, and it will survive the isolation that we are having to endure today. I hope to see you all in person soon. I miss you. I need to be in fellowship with you.

154. THE BLESSING OF FRIENDSHIP

As I look around my office, I see a large number of pictures. Most are of my two grandchildren. Those two boys bring so much joy into my life. There are several pictures of my wife, my children, and their spouses. I have one picture of me crossing the finish line of a marathon I ran in my younger and skinnier days. Then there is one picture of four friends and me that was taken about thirty years ago. This picture has been in my office since the day it was taken. Let me tell you why this picture is so special. The other four guys in the picture are Scott, Randy, Todd, and Tim. It was taken at a golf course in Kansas. That day it was twelve degrees and windy, but that didn't keep us from golfing. We were all there because Tim's young son had been diagnosed with cancer. So, we weren't there that day to golf. We were there to support our friend. Golfing was a side note.

"A friend loves at all times, and a brother is born for a time of adversity" (Proverbs 17:17).

The five of us were all youth ministers at the time. That is how we became friends. What made us brothers was just going through life together. All five of us have had job changes along the way. Randy lost a child during childbirth. Tim's son had cancer and later passed away. And just recently, we lost Todd due to a brain tumor. Even though distance separates us, we are still brothers.

Jesus modeled life for us in so many ways. Yes, Jesus loved all people. But Jesus found twelve guys and pulled them in closer than all others. Jesus loved His friends. He taught them, He forgave them, He corrected them, He washed their feet, and eventually He laid down His life for them. Yes, Jesus was their savior. But Jesus was also their friend.

"One who has unreliable friends soon comes to ruin, but there is a friend who sticks closer than a brother" (Proverbs 18:24).

If you have a few friends, count yourself among the blessed. To make friends, we have to follow the example of Jesus and invest in people. Friendships will cost you time and energy. But the investment will be worth it.

155. LOVE IS DIFFICULT

God is love. John said it twice in 1 John 4. You can see God's love poured out in creation from the smallest intricate details to His eternal plan. God's love was best shown through His son, Jesus. As you read the gospels, you see what love looks like when it walks on our ground and breathes our air. When you read Paul's definition of love in 1 Corinthians 13, you can see the true characteristics of God the Father and His Son, Jesus Christ.

"Love is patient, love is kind. It does not envy, it does not boast, it is not proud. It does not dishonor others, it is not self-seeking, it is not easily angered, it keeps no record of wrongs. Love does not delight in evil but rejoices with the truth. It always protects, always trusts, always hopes, always perseveres. Love never fails"
(1 Corinthians 13:4-8).

When the entire mission of man is boiled down to two statements: We are to love God and love others. God has shown His love for us. Our first response is to love God. Now comes the difficult part. Equally as important to loving God is loving those who are in our lives every day. We are called to reflect the love that God has shown us to our family, to our brothers and sisters in Christ, to our friends, to strangers, and to our enemies.

Now look over Paul's definition of love again. How are you doing? Are you showing love to your family by being patient with them and not flying off the handle at the drop of a hat? Are you showing love to your church family by putting their needs ahead of your own needs and by not keeping score of how many times they have wronged you? Are you showing love to your friends by honoring them and not being jealous of the things they have? Are you showing love to strangers by your kindness toward them? Are you showing love to your enemies by hoping and praying that good things happen to them?

Love is difficult. But whoever said that being a Christian was going to be easy?

156. CONSTRUCTION OR DESTRUCTION?

A couple of weeks ago in my study of Job, I asked the question, "Are you a builder or a destroyer?" I mentioned the house that is being constructed at the end of my street. Over a year ago, they began cutting down trees. Then the ground was leveled. Eventually a foundation was poured and construction began. Now there is the shell of a beautiful house that is still being worked on every day. I assume that in a few months, there will be a family living inside this home. The thought occurred to me that it would only take a matter of minutes with a wrecking ball to reduce this structure to a pile of rubble. This house, which has been carefully planned and meticulously constructed, is really fragile when the right (or wrong) thing comes along with the intentions of destruction.

People are a lot like that house. As we grow up, parents, teachers, ministers, friends, mentors, and others work to build a child into a good person. Yet one moment of abuse or one harsh word can destroy all the time and effort put into construction. It all comes back to the question, "Are you a builder or a destroyer?"

"Therefore encourage one another and build each other up, just as in fact you are doing" (1 Thessalonians 5:11).

I want to follow the example of Jesus. He was absolutely a builder. When Jesus walked by Matthew, He didn't see a tax collector who was ripping people off. He saw a friend who would stick with Him like a brother and who would eventually write a book about His life. When He saw another tax collector up in a tree, and He didn't ignore or shame him. Jesus befriended Zacchaeus, and as a result, his life was changed and he began to bless others. When a woman, who had been caught in a scandalous love affair, was thrown at the feet of Jesus, He didn't see an adulterous. He saw a person who was about to begin living a better story. Jesus sets an example for us of how to live our daily lives as builders and not destroyers. He did it by telling others who they are becoming, not who they used to be.

157. BEFORE IT'S TOO LATE

Over the past four years, I have had the privilege of speaking at the funerals of my father, my sister-in-law, my mother, and my mother-in-law. Speaking at the funeral of a loved one is both heartbreaking and a joy at the same time. I have found it to be great grief therapy. While working through the pain of losing someone close to me, I get to spend the time dwelling on the memories that brought joy to my life. Then I get the opportunity to stand before others and share those precious memories that made them special.

One of my favorite authors and speakers is Garrison Keillor. He once said, "Isn't it a shame that you live your whole life and then miss your funeral by only a couple of days?" What would it do for you if you were able to hear the people you love gather together and share all the great things about your life and how you have touched them and encouraged them? Why do we wait until it is too late?

> *"Therefore encourage one another and build each other up, just as in fact you are doing. Now we ask you, brothers and sisters, to acknowledge those who work hard among you, who care for you in the Lord and who admonish you. Hold them in the highest regard in love because of their work. Live in peace with each other"*
> *(1 Thessalonians 5:11-13).*

We shouldn't wait until it is too late to let others know how special they are. Take the time to reach out to loved ones, friends, and even acquaintances and tell them how they have positively affected your life. Not only will it be good for you, it will bring joy and may just extend the life of another.

158. LOVING OTHERS IN SPITE OF …

Last Monday morning, I woke up and drove to North Richland Hills. I had several reasons for making this trip. I was meeting my wife there in order to bring her back home. I was going to see my daughter and her husband. But the big motivation was to see my two grand boys. The added bonus that day was to celebrate Judah's third birthday. As I walked in the door, Krista said, "Jordan is waking up from his nap. Will you go get him?" Jordan is my one-year-old grandson. The moment I opened the door, I could smell the smell. You know what I'm talking about! Not thirty seconds into being there, I was changing a dirty diaper. The diaper was full, and the baby was upset. But I was smiling and loving every minute of it.

"Therefore, as God's chosen people, holy and dearly loved, clothe yourselves with compassion, kindness, humility, gentleness and patience" (Colossians 3:12).

That is a hard command to keep. Why? Because people can be difficult at times. People will push your boundaries. People are not appreciative. People will test your patience. People tend to be rude. And as Christians, we are supposed to be compassionate, kind, humble, gentle, and patient with these people who could seemingly care less. How can we do it? One word changes everything: LOVE! I love my grandson, so I could put up with his fussiness while I did one of the nastiest jobs on Earth. He did not appreciate what I was doing at the time, but in the end he was clean and happy, and I enjoyed getting to love on him for the entire day. God loves us and has changed plenty of our dirty diapers. So, the least we could do is love on others in spite of their messes.

159. SPEAK LIFE

A few months ago, Krista and I went to a Toby Mac concert along with our children and their spouses. Toby Mac is a Christian artist who Krista and I first saw in concert long before our kids were even born. As fun as his songs are, they are also spiritually deep. One song of his that has stuck with me is a song called "Speak Life." The idea of speaking life to someone intrigues me. What does it mean to speak life to someone? Here are two examples. It should be pretty clear which one is speaking life to someone.

First example: Adam and Eve are in the Garden of Eden. Eve and the serpent are having a discussion about eating fruit from the tree in the middle of the garden. The serpent said to Eve, "God knows that when you eat from it your eyes will be opened, and you will be like God, knowing good and evil."

Second example: Jesus had a woman thrown at His feet who had been caught in the act of adultery. The people were ready to stone her. After dismissing the crowd, Jesus said this to her, "Then neither do I condemn you. Go now and leave your life of sin."

In the first example, the serpent literally spoke death into humankind. In the second example, Jesus literally spoke life into a woman who was broken and hurting.

"Words kill, words give life; they're either poison or fruit—you choose" (Proverbs 18:21 MSG).

Consider the words that come out of your mouth. To those who hear, are you speaking life to them? The choice is yours.

160. TEAMMATES

I have always loved team sports. Growing up, I was on a team throughout the year. In fall, I was on the football team. In winter, I was on the basketball team. During the summer, I was on the baseball team. I have forgotten a lot of classmates' names, but I can remember the names of all of my teammates. My favorite team was the basketball team in my sophomore year of college. That was thirty-five years ago, but I could tell you each of their names, and I could tell you stories for days about that season.

What makes a team so special? I believe there are several elements. The first thing that makes a team special is that we have common goals. We wanted to win our conference (something York College had never done) and go to the national tournament. The next thing that made that team so special is that we worked hard together to bring out the best in each other. Sweating, running, and competing against each other not only helped unite us, but it also helped sharpen our skills. And finally, we had a common enemy. At times, it felt like our coach was the enemy because he pushed us so hard. But the ultimate enemy was the other teams we played. All of those things combined made us a brotherhood that I cherish to this day.

"A friend loves at all times, and a brother is born for a time of adversity" (Proverbs 17:17).

When we become a Christian, we are placed in a family of brothers and sisters. We should all be working together to reach our common goals, which are to expand God's Kingdom (team) by seeking the lost. As we work together, we should be united and spurring one another on to grow in our faith. And together we can fight and eventually defeat our common enemy.

Remember that you are a part of a team. And here is the best news, our team wins in the end!

161. THE LENS OF LOVE

I have heard the story of a father and his two young children who were riding on the subway in New York City. The two children were acting up by running up and down the subway car and shouting at each other. They were bumping into other people and being an annoyance to everyone around them. Meanwhile, there sat the father of these two children. He stared forward, not paying a bit of attention to the chaos around him. Finally, one passenger had enough and said, "Maybe if you paid attention to your children, they wouldn't act like that!" The father responded and said, "We are on our way home from the hospital. Their mother, my wife, just died. None of us knows how to act." It is easy to make judgments about people without knowing the entire story. We see people through the lens of our own understanding. That lens is clouded by our own judgments, understanding, and prejudices. What we should strive to do is see people as Jesus sees them—through the lens of love and compassion.

When others saw a man who was crazy and to be avoided at all costs, Jesus saw a man who could be useful in His kingdom once the demons who possessed him were removed.

When others saw an adulterous woman who was worthy of being stoned to death, Jesus saw a broken woman who was worthy of being saved.

When others saw a thief on a cross who was receiving the death sentence he deserved, Jesus saw a repentant man who would join Him in Paradise.

If we can learn to see people through the eyes of Jesus, not only will we treat them with compassion, but God's Kingdom will grow.

"Let no debt remain outstanding, except the continuing debt to love one another" (Romans 13:8).

162. WE ARE A WORK IN PROGRESS

"Be patient, God isn't finished with me yet." I've heard that phrase my whole life. As each day passes, I understand it at a deeper level. After graduating high school, with a basketball scholarship in my hand, I was headed off to greener pastures (if you can call York, Nebraska, greener pastures). I knew who I was and what I wanted to become. Fast forward three years. My competitive basketball days were behind me, I was changing my major after my junior year, and I was dating a girl I knew our futures did not align. I was truly a work in progress. Just two years later, I was married to the girl God had planned for me all along, and I was starting a career in church work that is continuing to this day. Now I have been married for over 30 years, Krista and I are empty nesters, both of our children are doing great, and I have a grandson who is almost a month old.

How did I get here? There is only one answer to that question: BY THE GRACE OF GOD. God has been faithful every step of the way. When I took a good step, God smiled. When I took a misstep, God was patient and said, "We can work through this." And the exciting thing is, God isn't finished with me yet! God is still working on me every day to make me the person that He created me to be.

"Therefore we do not lose heart. Though outwardly we are wasting away, yet inwardly we are being renewed day by day"
(2 Corinthians 4:16).

I say all of this not just to be nostalgic. But to acknowledge God's patience with me. And God was not alone. So many people in my life could have written me off, but they didn't. They extended grace when I failed and patience when I stumbled. So, when you encounter someone who is failing or stumbling, extend a little grace and show a little patience. Just remember, God isn't finished with them yet either.

273

163. SEEING POTENTIAL

A while back on a Sunday afternoon, I was watching golf on television and fading into my traditional Sunday afternoon nap when I heard a commercial that made me sit up in my chair. It was just a typical golf commercial with amateurs trying to improve their game. The tagline at the end of the commercial said, "Inside every golfer is a better one." As an athlete (or former athlete), that rang a bell with me. Why did I go to basketball camp every summer of my teenage years? Why did I practice shooting on my backyard goal until there was no grass left? Why did I play summer league basketball when I could have been swimming with my friends? Because I knew there was room for improvement. Why did coaches invest their time and energy in me? Because they knew I could be a better player.

Jesus had that same attitude when He looked at people. When Jesus saw a short little tax collector sitting on the branch of a tree, He saw a person with a benevolent heart. When Peter was sinking in the water because of his lack of faith, Jesus saw a man who could preach in such a way that thousands would respond. When Jesus saw a demon-possessed man living in the tombs, He saw a missionary who was capable of teaching others. When the disciples saw little children who were disrupting the meeting, Jesus saw members of the kingdom of God. When Jesus saw a 5-time divorcee, He saw a woman who was worthy of carrying the gospel to an entire city.

"Now to him who is able to do immeasurably more than all we ask or imagine, according to his power that is at work within us" (Ephesians 3:20).

The potential within us is greater than we can even imagine when we allow God to work through us. When you look in the mirror, do you see a better you in there? God does! When we look at others, can we see them through the eyes of Jesus, who sees them for what they could be rather than what they used to be?

164. HOW TO TRAIN YOURSELF

Last week I took seven campers and two staff members to Camp Horizon. On Saturday night, the two staff members had meetings, so I decided to take the rest to see a movie. They chose to see the movie *How to Train Your Dragon*. This is a movie I never would have seen on my own. But the truth is, I enjoyed the movie. Here is a quick plot summary. In the mythical Viking village of Berk, dragons often attacked, stealing livestock and endangering villagers. A sixteen-year-old mess-up, aptly named Hiccup, is told to stay inside during an attack. Wanting to prove himself, he sneaks out and actually shoots down a rare dragon. He searches for the dragon, determined to kill it. However, when he finds it wounded he decides not to kill it and instead befriends it. Spoiler alert!! In the end, this decision saves the future of the entire village. When Hiccup was asked why he didn't kill the dragon, he responded, "I wouldn't kill him, because he looked as frightened as I was. I looked at him, and I saw myself."

When I heard that line, I pulled out my phone and wrote it down. Over the next five days at camp, I taught a class on "Compassion." The goal for my class was to teach the campers that God has shown compassion to them by sending Jesus to die for our sins, even though we are worthy of death. And because God has shown such great compassion for us, we should show compassion for others.

"Be kind and compassionate to one another, forgiving each other, just as in Christ God forgave you" (Ephesians 4:32).

We are all in the same boat. All of us are sinners. We all stand in need of compassion from God. So, when we look at others, we should not only see someone who was made in the image of God, but we should see ourselves. Someone who is in need of compassion.

165. IS IMAGE ANYTHING?

There is an old expression that says, "Image is everything." The amazing thing about that expression is that it was popularized long before social media ever existed. Not only did social media solidify that old expression, it practically made it law. Facebook, Instagram, and others are now places where people only show you the image of themselves that they want you to believe. Every picture posted seems to be staged and filtered. There are many reasons that I don't show much of my life on social media. One reason is that I have not found the right filter that can make me look good.

Over the years, Krista and I have tried to take selfies when we have been at various events. The results are always a disaster. We stretch out our arms, smile big, and snap the picture. When we look at our picture, the horror begins. We have many questions. Do I really have that many chins? What is going on with my hair? Is that a bald spot? Why do I look so tired? Am I really that old? So, we do the old person thing and ask another old person to take our picture. The results are usually not much better.

Yes, image is important. But image is not everything. Take Jesus, for example. One day, Jesus was approached by a man with leprosy. Jesus felt compassion for the man, reached out and touched him, and the man was instantly healed. If Jesus had a publicist, they would have snapped a few pictures and posted them immediately (however you would have done that in biblical times). But Jesus had a different approach.

"Jesus sent him away at once with a strong warning: 'See that you don't tell this to anyone'" (Mark 1:43-44).

In Jesus's life, He did not focus on what the masses thought about Him. Instead, Jesus simply loved who was in front of Him at the moment. And in the end, His life blessed the masses. If we follow the example of Jesus, we will not be focused on our own image. Instead, we will be focused on seeing the image of God in others and loving them.

166. A PART OF THE FAMILY

It always makes me laugh when someone calls me with car problems and asks me to come over and help. I will, but I promise you, the last thing you want is me with my head under your hood trying to diagnose the problem. The same is true if you are building something. If you ask, I will do my best to help. But I will pass on what my seventh-grade shop teacher said to me. In a fit of frustration, he looked at me and said, "Treat, I can't even trust you to use a hammer!" However inept I am in some fields, I do have skills in other areas of life.

When it comes to spiritual matters or relationship problems, let me encourage you to give me a call. I can either help you or point you in the right direction to find help. I love to listen to the great American storyteller, Garrison Keillor. In one of his stories, he was talking about Clint Bunson, who was a very capable handyman in the town of Lake Wobegon, Minnesota. Everyone would call on Clint when anything went wrong at their house. They called on him so much that he said that he began to envy the incapable.

One of the greatest things about being a member of the church is that God has equipped everyone with talents that can be helpful to others. Just take a look at the early church.

"All the believers were together and had everything in common. They sold property and possessions to give to anyone who had need" (Acts 2:44-45).

The most important thing about being a member of the church is that we are saved by our commitment to God through His Son, Jesus. Not only are we a family, we are a community. We spend time together, and we help out those who are in need. God has gifted you in some way to be a blessing to His family. Do not hide or neglect your gift. Do everything you can to help your family members in their time of need.

If you find yourself in need, please reach out to the family. We are here for each other. However, if you need help building your house, you are welcome to give me a call. I will show up with a word of encouragement and cold water for all the workers. Just don't let me pick up a hammer.

167. OH, TO HAVE A HEART LIKE JESUS

Romans 3:23 says, *"For all have sinned and fall short of the glory of God."* I'm sure we can all agree on that. I believe that we could also all agree that we would rather not have the details of our sin broadcast on the evening news or make headlines. That is what makes the woman's story in John 8 so tragic.

Jesus was teaching a crowd in the temple courts when the teachers of the law and the Pharisees brought in a woman and made her stand before all the people. They proceeded to publicly announce her sin, "We have caught her in the act of adultery." Her private sin was now aired out for public consumption. They pressed Jesus for an answer, "In the Law, Moses commanded us to stone such women. Now what do you say?"

Oh, to have the heart of Jesus! His priority was not following the letter of the law or pleasing the religious leaders. Also, Jesus did not make His own reputation a priority by trying to please the majority of the people. His first priority was the broken and shame-filled heart of this woman. Jesus responded by kneeling and writing in the dirt with His finger. People often speculate on what Jesus wrote. It doesn't matter to me what He wrote. I believe that Jesus wrote on the ground just to take the attention off of this lady. At this moment, no one was looking at her. With the people distracted by Jesus writing in the dirt, He said, "Let any one of you who is without sin be the first to throw a stone at her." Stones dropped, and people shuffled away until it was just her and Jesus.

"Jesus straightened up and asked her, 'Woman, where are they? Has no one condemned you?' 'No one, sir,' she said. 'Then neither do I condemn you,' Jesus declared. 'Go now and leave your life of sin'" (John 8:10-11).

For the first time that day, she was treated with dignity. She left that day having met the Son of God, found forgiveness, and focused on living better. Let us all live daily like Jesus. Let us love others, treat people with dignity, and shine the light of His love and grace on all of those who cross our paths.

168. BE THE LIGHT

Long ago, I saw a great sign that was posted inside a church building. The sign read, "You are now entering your mission field." What made this sign so great was its location. It was not posted by the classrooms to remind teachers of the importance of their time teaching the Bible. It was not posted by the door of the auditorium to help get your heart and mind right before worship. It was posted by the exits. As the congregation left their time of worship and headed for their cars, they were reminded, "You are NOW entering your mission field."

It is easy to believe that the church building is sacred and our time of worship is the most important part of a Christian's week. That is the way many of us were raised. On Sunday, we not only put on our finest clothes, but we also put on our finest faces. We wash and press our clothing so we look sharp. We wash our faces, comb our hair, and brush our teeth, so we will shine on Sunday morning. But that is not where Christians are called to shine.

"You are the light of the world. A town built on a hill cannot be hidden. Neither do people light a lamp and put it under a bowl. Instead they put it on its stand, and it gives light to everyone in the house. In the same way, let your light shine before others, that they may see your good deeds and glorify your Father in heaven"
(Matthew 5:14-16).

We were not saved just so we could come to worship on Sundays and look good. We were saved to go and be a light in dark places. Jesus tells His disciples to "Go into all the world." We have come to believe that if we are not going to some village off the grid in Brazil, then we are off the hook on that command. Go into all the world starts on your car ride home from church. All the world is your dinner table. All the world is your family get-togethers. All the world is the office where you work. All the world is the classroom and the cafeteria at school. All the world includes everyone you encounter on social media. Take the Light of God's love to dark places. This world is full of dark places that need a glimpse of hope. Be the light you are called to be.

169. SUMMIT DAY

I have a love/hate relationship with an event that is called Wilderness Trek, which I have done six times. At Wilderness Trek, you leave everything behind except a couple of sets of clothes, a few cooking supplies, a tent, a sleeping bag, and whatever food you can carry. We would spend five days hiking through the Colorado mountains. On the last day, we tried to summit one of the 14,000-foot peaks. My first year on Trek, we started hiking at 5 a.m. on summit day. About 5:15, one of my youth group girls named Carrie started crying. Through her tears, she said that she was never going to make it and wanted to go back to her tent and lie down. I spent the next six hours walking with Carrie and constantly encouraging her to keep going. A little after 11 a.m., we summited the mountain. She was elated, and I was exhausted.

The next summer, I took for granted how good of shape I was in and slacked off on my training. As we started out early in the morning on summit day, I thought to myself, "I am never going to make it to the top." During the next six hours, different youth group kids would walk with me and give me encouragement to keep going. Several offered to carry my backpack. As we made it to the summit and began hugging and taking pictures, I realized I would have never made it there without the encouragement of others.

"Therefore encourage one another and build each other up, just as in fact you are doing" (1 Thessalonians 5:11).

We will all have times in our lives when we are in desperate need of encouragement. We will have that feeling that we will never make it through this difficulty or this season of life, and we just want to quit. At other times, we will see someone who has reached their limit, and they are in need of a word of encouragement. This is the beauty of being in a church family. We walk beside one another giving others what they need and receiving what we need. Be an encourager. And receive the encouragement you need from others. The summit is just ahead.

170. CHANGE FROM THE INSIDE OUT

Have you ever had to spend a lot of time with an angry person? I don't mean someone who just gets angry in the moment. I mean someone whose default setting is anger. If they won the lottery, they would be mad about the taxes they would have to pay. On a beautiful sunny day, they complain about the heat. If the doctor gave them a clean bill of health, they would be upset at the cost of the co-pay. And even worshiping God, they are upset at the length of the sermon or the song selections. Do you desire to spend time with that person, or do you try to avoid them?

On the other hand, have you ever been around a person whose default setting is joy? If it's raining outside, they are happy because the lawn needed water. If they are stuck in traffic, they just crank up the radio and sing along. If the airlines lose their luggage, they are excited to buy some new clothes. I like to be in the presence of that type of person. I'd like to be that type of person.

I have come to believe that anger and joy are not reactions; they are habits. Habits are simply comfort zones. If I am an angry person, I can look at any situation and find a reason to get mad. If I am a joyous person, I can look at any situation and find the silver lining. Paul tells us in Philippians 4:4 to rejoice in the Lord ALWAYS.

How can an angry person change? You can try with all your might to change your outer reactions to situations, but the only way to truly change is to change from the inside out. When we are baptized, we are given the gift of the Holy Spirit. You can squelch that Spirit, and it will only reside as a seed within you. Or you can embrace the Spirit and let it produce the fruit that will make you more Godly.

"But the fruit of the Spirit is love, joy, peace, patience, kindness, goodness, faithfulness, gentleness, self-control"
(Galatians 5:22-23).

That is the type of person I want to be. It is also the type of person I want to be around.

171. THE POWER OF OUR WORDS

This week, I read a great quote from an author who goes by the name "Unknown." Here is the quote:

"The tongue has no bones, but it is strong enough to break a heart. So be careful with your words."

We live in a time and place where some choices are taken out of our hands. We do not decide how much we pay in taxes. We do not decide on which side of the street we drive. We do not decide who deserves to live and die. Those decisions have been made, and they are given to us as laws. If we break them, we pay a stiff penalty.

Here is one thing that each of us gets to decide for ourselves: what we say. We even have laws in place that guarantee us the right to free speech. I call that a scary blessing. It is a blessing that we can say what we think and feel. But at the same time, it is scary because of the destructiveness that words can have on people.

"A bit in the mouth of a horse controls the whole horse. A small rudder on a huge ship in the hands of a skilled captain sets a course in the face of the strongest winds. A word out of your mouth may seem of no account, but it can accomplish nearly anything—or destroy it!" (James 3:3-5 MSG).

When you take the opportunity to speak, choose your words wisely. The words you say reflect who you are. They have the power to build others up or tear them down. Here is another quote from that great author "Unknown":

"Words are seeds that do more than blow around. They land in our hearts and not on the ground. Be careful what you plant and careful what you say. You might have to eat what you planted one day."

172. EFFECTIVE EVANGELISM

How did you come to know about Jesus? Maybe a stranger approached you and asked you about your eternal life. Possibly, but not likely. Maybe a preacher or teacher stood up and proclaimed the good news that touched your heart. That's more likely, but how did you come to hear that teaching in the first place? The most effective type of evangelism happens when a friend or loved one first lives a Godly life, shares their story, and then guides another to the scriptures.

I came to know about God because my mother took me to church services from the time I was born. I knew the stories of Noah and the ark and Daniel and the lion's den before I was able to read. My growth in my relationship with God was nurtured by my brother and sister, Bible class teachers, camp counselors, friends, and then eventually youth ministers, preachers, and evangelists. My Christianity was not one giant leap. It was a series of baby steps that started at home.

"Hear, O Israel: The Lord our God, the Lord is one.
Love the Lord your God with all your heart and with all your soul
and with all your strength. These commandments that I give you
today are to be on your hearts. Impress them on your children. Talk
about them when you sit at home and when you walk along the
road, when you lie down and when you get up"
(Deuteronomy 6:4-7).

If we want to save our children, it should not be left up to others. Hopefully, Bible class teachers, youth ministers, and preachers can all be a part of nurturing their relationship with God. But the most effective work is done at home.

173. FACEBOOK VS. FRIEND

Words will evolve over time. We all know what the word "bully" implies—someone who is cruel to those weaker. Its original meaning was lover or sweetheart. Just in my lifetime, several words have different meanings. The word "bad" evolved from being unacceptable behavior to something really cool. The word "bomb" was and still is something destructive. However, if you just add "da" in front of it, the meaning changes completely. If something is described as "da bomb," that means it is the best thing ever. And today, if a young person describes something as "sick," that means it is exciting and amazing.

Growing up, if I called someone my friend, that meant that I was close to them, we were in a relationship, and we were there for each other in good times and in bad times. Then Facebook came along and just destroyed the notion of being a friend. With just a quick glance at my Facebook profile, I see that I currently have 882 "friends." I never knew I had that many friends. Upon closer examination, 882 is a gross overstatement. There are classmates I haven't seen or heard from since high school graduation. There are people I have only met once in my life. And there are a number of names that are unrecognizable to me. Do I really have that many friends? Solomon gives us a great definition of what it means to be a friend.

"Two are better than one, because they have a good return for their labor: If either of them falls down, one can help the other up. But pity anyone who falls and has no one to help them up"
(Ecclesiastes 4:9-10).

Here is a different take on "friends." Have you ever thought about who your neighbors are going to be in heaven? We are told that Jesus is preparing a room for us in heaven. But who will be next door? I believe it will be people from other countries who we have never met.

And some people who lived long before me, or some who have yet to be born. Thinking of it that way, I have a lot more than just 882 friends!

174. BE KIND, REWIND

Do you remember this phrase? This phrase was made popular by Blockbuster Video. For the Millennials and the Generation Z people out there, let me give you some history. Long before streaming services and DVDs, if we wanted to watch a movie, we had to get into our cars and drive to video rental stores like Blockbuster. Once there, we would walk up and down aisles full of VHS tapes. After picking a few, we would take them home and have a couple of days to watch them. When we finished a movie, we had to rewind it before returning it. If we failed to rewind them, we would receive a $2 late fee. So, the phrase is a warning/rule: Be Kind, Rewind.

"Therefore, as God's chosen people, holy and dearly loved, clothe yourselves with compassion, kindness, humility, gentleness and patience" *(Colossians 3:12).*

Kindness is quickly becoming a lost art. Kind words, kind actions, and kind attitudes are rarely seen anymore. They have been replaced by rude words, selfish actions, and negative attitudes. General kindness is now seen as a weakness and is taken advantage of. But as Christians, we are called to clothe ourselves with kindness. None of us would leave the house without clothes. So, we should not leave the house without kindness. Can I repurpose the phrase "Be Kind, Rewind"? Why should we be kind in a world where it is not appreciated? Because God has been so kind to us. The next time you have an opportunity to show kindness, STOP and REWIND to a time when God has shown kindness to you. Do you deserve the kindness of God? No, we have all sinned and stepped outside of the will of God. But God continues to show kindness to us. So, when given the opportunity, "Be Kind, Rewind."

175. COULD I HAVE A MOMENT OF YOUR TIME?

Striving to be more like Jesus is a lifelong process. When you start making some headway in one area, another weakness is exposed that needs some attention. One such weakness became very apparent to me recently. I struggle with interruptions. I like to focus on the task at hand, complete it, then move on to the next task. But life does not always cooperate with my agenda. Someone will interrupt my schedule with a need. My tendency is to put them off so I can complete my task. But Jesus has been working on my stubbornness and my attitude.

If anyone had the right to tell others to wait their turn, it was Jesus. But as you read through the gospels, you will discover that Jesus did not seem to have a problem with interruptions. Jesus had a crowd of people who were in need of teaching and healing, but the little children also needed some playtime and a blessing. On another occasion, a synagogue leader's daughter was dying, and Jesus was on His way to their house when a woman touched His garment with the hope of being healed from her ailment. Jesus stopped what He was doing to give her His full attention. And later, Jesus, the disciples, and a large crowd were on their way into the city of Nain when a funeral procession was headed out of town. Jesus stopped and raised the widow's son from the dead before continuing on into town. There are many other examples, but I think we get the point. Jesus did not mind interruptions when others were in need.

"Do nothing out of selfish ambition or vain conceit. Rather, in humility value others above yourselves, not looking to your own interests but each of you to the interests of the others"
(Philippians 2:3-4).

Being more like Jesus is as much about attitude as it is about behavior. We must see the value of others and set our own interests aside for the moment. I am far from mastering this attitude and behavior, but I commit to working on it. How about you?

176. COMMAND VS. FEELING

I grew up playing sports. As a teenager, I played football, basketball, and baseball. That meant I had a lot of coaches along the way. One phrase that I just instinctively never said to a coach was, "No, I don't feel like it." I thought it quite often, but I never said it. Could you imagine being in basketball practice and the coach says, "Everyone on the baseline, we are going to run some sprints." And one player says, "Not right now, coach, I don't feel like it." I know what the end result of that conversation would be: more sprints! What I learned from sports is that coaches have a purpose for their commands. If they wanted us to run sprints, it was because they wanted us physically fit enough to finish the game strong.

One command that Jesus gave us is to forgive one another. He taught us that when we pray, we should say, "Forgive us as we forgive others." He taught us that if we do not forgive others, God will not forgive us. He taught us parables that emphasized the need to forgive others. He gave us multiple examples of forgiving others of their sins, including forgiving those who nailed Him to the cross. We are called to be forgiving people.

Sometimes forgiving others is difficult. However, are you willing to look God in the eye and tell Him, "I don't feel like forgiving them"? We have to move the command ahead of the feeling. Why? Because our God has a purpose. Going through the difficulty of forgiving others when we don't feel like it will build the character we need to finish the game strong. The bottom line is that we are not deserving of God's forgiveness. But in the midst of our messy lives, God sent His Son so we can have forgiveness.

"But God demonstrates his own love for us in this: While we were still sinners, Christ died for us" (Romans 5:8).

Move the command ahead of the feeling. Let's finish strong.

177. THE PROCESS OF CONVERSION

One of my favorite conversion moments in the Bible is when Simon Peter made the decision to follow Jesus. It's the best fishing story I know. Peter and the other fishermen were washing their nets after a frustrating night of fishing with no success. Jesus borrowed Peter's boat to use as a pulpit to speak to the crowd. After the sermon, Jesus was in the mood to do a little fishing. After a catch that almost sank two boats, Jesus issued Peter an invitation.

"'Come, follow me,' Jesus said, 'and I will send you out to fish for people'" (Matthew 4:19).

But that is just part of the story. Jesus and Peter had met at least two times before Jesus asked for a commitment from Peter. The first time they met was thanks to Peter's brother Andrew. In John 1, Andrew met Jesus for the first time. He immediately found his brother Peter and introduced him to Jesus. This is when Jesus told Simon that you will now be known as Peter.

Their second recorded meeting is found in Matthew 8. Peter had Jesus come to the house for lunch. Peter's mother-in-law was sick and in bed. Jesus healed her, and they hung out and had a meal together.

Their third meeting happened on the shore of the lake. After the enormous catch of fish and the invitation of Jesus, Luke 5:11 tells us Peter 'left everything' and followed Jesus.

Notice the invitation was not the first thing Jesus ever said to Peter. The invitation came after a relationship was built. In our church, a conversion can happen simply as a response to the invitation. But the Jesus method (in the case of Peter) is a more likely scenario. It comes after a relationship has been built. Spend time with people. Find a common interest to share. Share a few meals together. Build a relationship. Then invite them to join you in following Jesus. In doing so, you may just find a fishing buddy for life.

178. SURROUNDED BY PEOPLE

Have you ever wondered what heaven will be like? I have come to believe that our human brains cannot comprehend heaven. But the Bible gives us glimpses that we can understand.

Things that we hate on Earth, like death, crying, mourning, and pain, will not be in heaven.

"He will wipe every tear from their eyes. There will be no more death or mourning or crying or pain, for the old order of things has passed away" (Revelation 21:4).

There will be plenty of room—and rooms.

"My Father's house has many rooms; if that were not so, would I have told you that I am going there to prepare a place for you?" (John 14:2).

We will be with God.

"And I heard a loud voice from the throne saying, "Look! God's dwelling place is now among the people, and he will dwell with them. They will be his people, and God himself will be with them and be their God" (Revelation 21:3).

Many places in the Bible refer to heaven as a city, meaning there will be a lot of "people" around. Here is a little-known fact about me: I am a self-admitted introvert. The "shelter in place" time of 2020 was no problem for me. I've always thought that if I were ever to go to prison, solitary confinement would be fine with me. The problem with that is that my profession is very public and requires me to be among people. Believe it or not, I know many preachers who suffer from this same affliction. One thing the Bible does not mention about heaven is that there will be doors with locks. So, when we make it to heaven, we'd better be ready to be surrounded by other people.

If I am going to accept the great commission and go into all the world and preach the gospel to all creation, and I'm going to love my neighbor as myself, I'm going to have to overcome the desire to be isolated. Being among the people is good training, so I will be ready when I receive my eternal residence in heaven. Let's all get out there and love others now. We introverts can just consider this training for eternity.

179. WE HAVE FOUND OUR PEOPLE

My wife Krista and her identical twin sister Kara spent last weekend in Twinsburg, Ohio, at the Twins Day Festival. More than 2,000 twins and multiples attended the event. As they walked around the park, meeting people and taking pictures, Kara posted this comment, "We have found our people." It is a great feeling when you can truly be in fellowship with others. When you can be amongst people who understand what you are going through on a deeper level. It is comforting to know that there are others like you. It is a blessing to be with your people.

But there is an old saying, "You can't live in Twinsburg forever." Actually, I just made that up. But the point is that visiting Twinsburg is a nice vacation, but your life and your purpose are outside of Twinsburg. As a church family, we get to come together to worship and spend time in fellowship. Think of it as a football game. The team huddles up before every play. But no team has ever scored a touchdown while they were in the huddle. You have to "break" and go run the play. It is a blessing when we get to be with others who have the same commitments and the same goals. But that is not our calling in life.

"Therefore go and make disciples of all nations, baptizing them in the name of the Father and of the Son and of the Holy Spirit, and teaching them to obey everything I have commanded you. And surely I am with you always, to the very end of the age"
(Matthew 28:19-20).

Our calling in life is not to stay together in the church building. That is simply a wonderful blessing. Our calling is to go out into the world and shine. That will bring glory to God, and just maybe "those people" can become "our people!"

180. ARE YOU READY TO CHANGE THE WORLD?

Have you ever met anyone famous? Being an athlete, I had the privilege of sharing the court with some great players. While in high school, I played against Stacey King. He went on to play with the Chicago Bulls. As a teammate of Michael Jordan, they scored a combined seventy points in a playoff game. (Michael Jordan scored sixty-nine and Stacey King scored one.) While in college, I played against Larry Johnson. He played in the NBA for eleven seasons and made the All-Star team twice. But even more impressive is that he was in the original Space Jam movie. But those are not the greatest people I have ever met.

I had a young man in my youth group named Brandon who grew up to be a husband, father, and professor at Abilene Christian University. I was friends with a man named Mike who, before dying of COVID, ministered at a church in Colorado for more than forty years. I have a friend named Stacy who was a stay-at-home mom who homeschooled her five children. So, who are the real heroes? Listen to the words of Jesus …

"Very truly I tell you, whoever believes in me will do the works I have been doing, and they will do even greater things than these, because I am going to the Father" (John 14:12).

What makes a hero? It's not playing in the NBA. It's doing the work of the Lord by investing in people. Each of us has the ability and the opportunity to be a real hero. It begins by committing your life to God then sharing the love that He has given you with others. Those are the real heroes who change the world.

181. WALK IN THE WAY OF LOVE

What if it were just you and God in the world? God could keep an eye on you pretty easily. God would not only know you personally, He would know everything about you. He would not only know what you do, He would know why you do it. The second you made a mistake, He would know it. And God would love you anyway. Even if it were just you and your mistakes in the world, God would still send His Son as a sacrifice to offer you the gift of grace. God would give you a second chance, and a third chance, and a fourth chance …

But it is not just you and God in the world. God has surrounded you with people He knows everything about and loves them just as dearly as He loves you. When it seems like some people are put on this planet just to annoy you, remember that they are loved dearly by God.

"Follow God's example, therefore, as dearly loved children and walk in the way of love, just as Christ loved us and gave himself up for us as a fragrant offering and sacrifice to God" (Ephesians 5:1-2).

Our job in this world is not to play God by judging and condemning others when they fail to live up to the expectations we have. Our job is to follow the example of God by loving others. God loves them just as God loves you. God knows more about them than you do, and He loves them anyway. God sent His Son as a sacrifice for their mistakes, the same way He sent Jesus for your mistakes. God has shown you an abundance of patience. When we show patience to others, we are truly walking in the way of love.

182. A REAL HERO

If you are in search of a real biblical hero, you need to look no further than a man named Paul. Paul is the author of around half of what we call The New Testament. Paul was a great missionary and church builder. He made three missionary journeys, establishing and encouraging churches. He was an inspiring preacher and teacher. He also suffered tremendously for the sake of Christ, being beaten, imprisoned, and shipwrecked. What a hero!

But Paul is not the hero I want to write about today. Before Paul accomplished all the things written above, he was known as Saul of Tarsus. He was a well-educated man who stood in direct opposition to Christianity. It was his mission to arrest and imprison anyone who believed that Jesus was the Son of God. Believers in Christ feared Saul. While on his way to Damascus, Saul was struck blind and spoken to by Jesus. He was told to go into the city and await further instructions. God sent a man named Ananias to touch, teach, and baptize Saul. Ananias obeyed.

"Then Ananias went to the house and entered it. Placing his hands on Saul, he said, 'Brother Saul, the Lord—Jesus, who appeared to you on the road as you were coming here—has sent me so that you may see again and be filled with the Holy Spirit'" (Acts 9:17).

Ananias is a different type of hero. Ananias never wrote a book. Ananias never traveled around the world establishing churches and preaching. Ananias was simply a faithful man who feared for his life but shared the gospel with another because Jesus called on him. Maybe we can't all be a hero like Paul. But all of us can be a hero like Ananias. Be faithful and obey God. That is being a real hero!

183. GATHER AROUND THE TABLE

After my first month of being the minister here at the Eastern Hills Church of Christ I had one question in my mind, "How are these people not the fattest church on Earth?" I asked that because in my first four weeks here, we had three potluck dinners. Through the years of being a minister, I have learned a few things about potluck dinners. First, most men have no idea how much effort goes into the meal. They just show up, get in line, and fill their belly. Second, most of the women who make the potluck happen experience too much stress. They worry about the plates, silverware, napkins, tablecloths, set-up, clean-up, and constantly wonder if there is going to be enough food. Third, the children seem to always take the best pieces of chicken. I don't know if that is true, but that is the complaint I hear most. And lastly, almost everyone misses the point of the potluck dinner.

Acts 2 tells us about the birth of this new thing called "The Church." The first sentence in the Bible after the church was formed says this:

"They devoted themselves to the apostles' teaching and to fellowship, to the breaking of bread and to prayer" (Acts 2:42).

It is important as a church to devote ourselves to learning and prayer. But the other things are equally important for a healthy church: eating and fellowship. Remember when Jesus and the disciples were joined by five thousand plus people on a hillside. The disciples suggested that Jesus dismiss the people so they could each head their own way and get something to eat. Jesus said, "No. Break them up into small groups, and I will give them something to eat." Was it all about the food? No! It was all about the fellowship.

I'm so glad that we still have potluck dinners together. But next time, remember that the food is just an excuse for us to spend some time in fellowship. And by the way, I'm sorry about that fat comment earlier!

184. ONE WAY TO CHANGE THE WORLD

It was a day that I will never forget. It was a Friday afternoon. I was loading the bus to take the youth group on our winter retreat. My wife and our two toddlers were on their way to Oklahoma City to spend the weekend with Nana. Just as the bus was about to pull out, someone from the church ran out to tell me that I had a message on the church answering machine from Krista. This was long before the day when everyone had a cell phone. As I listened to her frantic voice, she explained that while on the turnpike between Tulsa and Oklahoma City, our car caught on fire. She and the kids were safe, but the car was a total loss. One of my youth deacons took my place on the retreat while I raced to find my family. The important part was that we were all fine. The tough part was that we were a one-income family at the time, and there was no way we could afford to replace our car. The next Sunday at church, my church treasurer handed me a check for $5,000. He said an anonymous member wanted us to get a car for our family. That church member will never know the burden that was lifted off of our young family.

*"But when you give to the needy, do not let your left hand know
what your right hand is doing, so that your giving may be in secret.
Then your Father, who sees what is done in secret, will reward you"
(Matthew 6:3-4).*

That day I learned about a thing called "R.A.K.'s." That stands for Random Acts of Kindness. We have been on the receiving end of several Random Acts of kindness. And we have also tried our best to be on the giving end as well. The thing about Random Acts of Kindness is that when they are done to receive glory, they lose their randomness and their purpose. But when a true Random Act of

Kindness is done, only God receives the glory. Oftentimes after performing a miracle, Jesus would say, "Tell no one." Jesus was introducing us to another way to change the world. Bless others in a way that points them to God. The less focus we receive and the more focus God receives will make this world a better place.

185. IT TAKES LIGHT AND TIME

Here's a phrase you haven't heard recently: "Oh, I wish I had a camera." Today everybody has a camera with them all the time. Back in my younger days, you had to buy a device that was just a camera and carry it around in a special bag. And compared to today's technology, pictures were a nightmare. You had to snap a picture and hope you got a good one. Then, only when your entire roll of film was complete, you would take it in to be developed. It may take an hour, it could take a week, but eventually you would get your pictures and get your first look to see if the lighting was right or if you had cut anyone's head off by your bad angle. Then it happened! The invention of the Polaroid camera! With this big device, you could snap a picture, and it would shoot right out. But there was still a waiting period. The picture needed light and about a minute to develop. People would often try shaking the picture to speed up the process, but it didn't help. It just needed light and time.

The Polaroid picture is a good illustration of how we try to develop people. We want the final picture instantly. But the development of people takes a little time. Abraham was an impatient liar while he developed into a great man of faith. Joseph had to go through a series of ups and downs before he became a forgiving leader. Moses was a murdering fugitive before he led God's children out of Egypt. The disciples had their fair share of faith struggles and personal struggles before they boldly stood and proclaimed that Jesus was the Son of God.

> *"… being confident of this, that he who began a good work in you will carry it on to completion until the day of Christ Jesus"*
> *(Philippians 1:6).*

We want people to change immediately. And when change does not happen instantly, we treat them like a Polaroid picture. We try shaking them until we get the results we want. Remember that we serve a patient God. He continually works while they are being molded into the image of Himself. So, learn to be patient with others. And while you're at it, give a little patience to yourself. Allow time for God to develop you into His beloved child. And remember what it takes to develop: light and time. Continue to walk in the light and be patient.

186. GROW UP!

I have to confess something that I caught myself doing a while back. It is shameful and embarrassing. I was watching a daytime talk show about couples who could not get along. As they argued about things that are no big deal but seemingly important to them, Dr. Phil stopped them in their tracks with one question. "Would you rather be right or happy?"

I grew up in a family of five. I am the youngest of three siblings, so it always felt like my opinion mattered the least. But that didn't keep me from whining and crying to get my way. I wonder sometimes if God made a mistake by putting us in families. It seems to be the place where we first learn how to say and do things that hurt the ones we love. Krista was telling me the other day that when she was younger and got mad at her identical twin sister, she would call her ugly.

Families are not a mistake. God knew exactly what He was doing. Family is a place where we learn to love and work out our differences. Family should prepare us for the rest of our lives, where we will encounter many people we disagree with every day. Jesus calls us to love those we disagree with and even love our enemies. But what if they are wrong and I know I can win the argument? Well, would you rather be right or happy?

"When I was a child, I talked like a child, I thought like a child, I reasoned like a child. When I became a man, I put the ways of childhood behind me" (1 Corinthians 13:11).

187. HOW DO YOU LOVE GOD?

Answer this question: How do you love God? The answer can seem rather obvious. I love God by reading His Word every day. I love God by showing up to worship every week. I love God by teaching a class or sweeping the floors at the church building. I love God by obeying Him and doing the good things I read about in the Bible. I love God by not doing the bad things I read about in the Bible. All of those are great, but if that is all you do, you are really missing the point.

In Matthew 22, a highly "religious" man, who was an expert in what we call the Old Testament, posed a question to Jesus. He asked, *"… which is the greatest commandment in the law?"* His motives for the question may have been legit. Or maybe he wanted to stump Jesus. Or maybe he just wanted to get a pat on the back. Regardless of his motives, the answer Jesus gave him truly answers the question, "How do you love God?"

> *"Jesus replied: 'Love the Lord your God with all your heart and with all your soul and with all your mind.' This is the first and greatest commandment. And the second is like it: 'Love your neighbor as yourself.' All the Law and the Prophets hang on these two commandments" (Matthew 22:37-40).*

I love the phrase, *"And the second is like it."* We correctly assume that loving God is a total commitment to keep the commandments. What we often miss is that loving people is just as important. One without the other is useless, spiritually speaking. As a parent of two adult children, nothing warms my heart more than my children still loving each other. God must have that same feeling when He sees His children loving each other.

These two commands go hand in hand. You can't truly love God if you can't love others. And you can't truly love others if you can't love

God. Everyone is made in the image of God, so every person reflects a part of God's creative expression in this world in one way or another. So, if you are having trouble loving a God you cannot see, try loving those you can see.

188. KINGDOM UPSIDE-DOWN

This week, Krista and I have been on vacation with our son, his wife, our daughter, her husband, and our two grandsons. As nice as we all are, we have a competition problem. Krista and I arrived at the cabin first, followed by my daughter's family, then my son and his wife. We win! At the cabin, they had the old arcade game called Frogger. I sat there till I set the high score. I win! The first night we were all together, we played a number of board games. I lost, lost, won, and then lost. I was pretty bummed about that. With our grandsons, who are two and four years old, everything is a competition. Tomorrow we are all going bowling, and I definitely plan on winning. Coming in first place really feels good. Through the years, I have learned to be a gracious loser, but I don't like it. The same could probably be said about most of us. Like Ricky Bobby says in Talladega Nights, "If you ain't first, you're last." That's the reality of the world in which we live. But that is not the order of things in God's Kingdom.

"So the last will be first, and the first will be last" (Matthew 20:16).

"The greatest among you will be your servant. For those who exalt themselves will be humbled, and those who humble themselves will be exalted" (Matthew 23:11-12).

One of Coach Vince Lombardi's famous quotes is, "Winning isn't everything; it's the only thing." That may be true on the football field, but it is not true in God's Kingdom. God's Kingdom is upside-down from the rest of the world. To be a follower of God, we must learn to put others ahead of ourselves. In order to please God, we must learn to exalt others and humble ourselves. Jesus is our ultimate example. He humbled Himself and became obedient to death, even death on a cross. He did this so that we may have the greatest victory.

I'm trying to learn humility and putting others' needs ahead of my own. But I still want to beat the family at bowling.

189. WORDS CHANGE LIVES

It is hard to imagine that a few simple words can change a life. We all say and hear thousands of words every day. Could just a couple of words really have a great impact? The year was 1979. I was in the sixth-grade at Townsend Elementary School in Del City, Oklahoma. Every day, our principal, Seah A. Sanders, would speak over the intercom with our daily announcements. To a sixth-grader, the principal was equivalent to the president of the United States. He was the ultimate authority. One afternoon during the announcements, Mr. Sanders was talking about the school's basketball game from the previous day. I remember his exact words. He said, "Phillip Treat scored twelve points. He is Townsend's own Larry Bird."

Larry Bird had just led his Indiana State Sycamores to the NCAA finals. He was my favorite basketball player. People in the school started calling me Larry Bird. For me, basketball was just another sport that I played. But with that encouragement, I began to practice basketball every day. In high school, I was a good enough player to get a college scholarship. Did Mr. Sanders's words have an effect on my life? Well, not only can I quote them word for word forty years later, they gave me the opportunity to get a Christian education in college.

Yes, a few simple words can change a life. Positive words spoken to another can build that person up. While just a few negative words can tear someone down. The first words that Simon heard from the mouth of Jesus were, "You will now be called Peter (which means rock). This wishy-washy man would later stand and deliver the first gospel sermon that proclaimed Jesus as the risen Son of God. Those few words from Jesus changed the life of Peter. On the other hand, just a few words from Jezebel made the powerful prophet Elijah contemplate suicide. Words can change lives.

"Gracious words are a honeycomb, sweet to the soul and healing to the bones" (Proverbs 16:24).

Thousands of words will leave your mouth today. Will they be words that build others up or tear them down? Choose your words wisely.

190. HOW TO LOVE PEOPLE

Have you ever met someone who is really hard to love? I know we are supposed to love all people, but sometimes that can be a real challenge. Usually, the reason we struggle to love someone else is because they are different. It may be their looks, their attitude, their heritage, their education, their morals, etc. The challenge in loving someone who is different stems from a lack of understanding them.

The last couple of Sunday nights, we have studied "The Mockingbird Parables." We have taken samples from one of my favorite books, *To Kill a Mockingbird*, and found biblical truths that can help us daily. While working on my lessons, I was reminded of one of my favorite quotes from the book. Scout Finch, a young girl, was struggling to understand someone who was a mystery to her. Her father, Atticus Finch, told her this, "You never really understand a person until you consider things from his point of view … until you climb into his skin and walk around in it."

If we spend the time and effort to get to know someone, it makes them much easier to love. If we can see life from their perspective, we begin to understand them a little more. When I get real honest with myself, I have to admit I can be one of those people who are hard to love. I sometimes joke when I shouldn't. I sometimes forget to filter what I say, and it comes across as insensitive. I'm sometimes in my own world and don't notice the people around me who are hurting. I could go on and on, but I will stop there.

From a spiritual perspective, we all must be hard to love. We have all sinned and fallen short of the glory of God. But here is the good news:

"In the beginning was the Word, and the Word was with God, and the Word was God" (John 1:1).

"The Word became flesh and made his dwelling among us. We have seen his glory, the glory of the one and only Son, who came from the Father, full of grace and truth" (John 1:14).

How is God able to love us? Not only is He our creator, but He climbed into our skin and walked around in it.

191. CONFESSION IS PART OF THE HEALING PROCESS

Several years ago, while I was attending a youth minister's seminar, we were in an afternoon class that had about thirty people. The teacher was just getting started when one man entered the classroom late. The teacher jokingly said to him, "Come on in and take a seat. We were just going around the room confessing our greatest sin. You're next!" Without skipping a beat, the man who entered late said, "My greatest sin is gossip. Who's next?" The teacher was only joking, but that man's answer would have shut down the confessions really quick.

We are all familiar with the verse, "The prayer of a righteous person is powerful and effective." That is just part of the verse. Here is the entire verse:

"Therefore confess your sins to each other and pray for each other so that you may be healed. The prayer of a righteous person is powerful and effective" (James 5:16).

Twice in that verse, you will read the phrase "each other." That means we are all in this together. Somehow, being part of a church family has come to mean that we put on our best Sunday face and leave all of our imperfections swept under the carpet at home. There are several problems with that. One problem is that when we get together, it seems like every other household is so perfect that we will never fit in. Another problem is a concept I learned long ago: You can't heal or change what you refuse to acknowledge.

There are two ways to read the following sentence: There is a time and place to confess your sins to each other. One meaning is that there are some times when it would be inappropriate for a full confession to others. But don't let that override the meaning of James 5:16. We need faithful brothers and sisters we can share our struggles with, who will not only keep our confessions to themselves but will also love us and pray for us. That is one of the greatest blessings of being a part of God's family.

192. LET IT GO

During the summer of 2005, I lived in the St. Louis area. That summer and fall, I was able to attend several St. Louis Cardinals baseball games in Busch Stadium. One of the things that made those games more interesting was going to the upper deck on the first-base side because I could look down into the new stadium being built next door. As the summer turned to fall, the new stadium was taking shape. They named the new stadium "Busch Stadium." (I guess they really liked that name.) In the fall of 2006, they used a wrecking ball to destroy the old stadium as they finished up the new stadium for the next season.

The old stadium had a scoreboard in center field that displayed the current scores of all the games around the league. When the final out of the final game was recorded in "old" Busch Stadium, the scores on that scoreboard did not change. Instead, the scoreboard was moved into the "new" Busch Stadium. That scoreboard is in the walkway down by the concession area. All the scores from closing day 2005 are frozen in time on that scoreboard. It is still there today.

So often we treat others like that old scoreboard. Not only do we keep score, we lock in on the past and hold on to it. Then every time we see them, we remember their wrongs, and it rekindles bitterness and hurt. In the Sermon on the Mount, Jesus tells us that we are to forgive others. Yes, that can be a difficult task. But Jesus goes on to give us the motivation we need to forgive others. In Matthew 6:15, Jesus says that if we refuse to forgive others, God will not forgive us of our sins. And God knows we all need forgiveness. Let God be our example of how to forgive.

"As far as the east is from the west, so far has he removed our transgressions from us" (Psalm 103:12).

If you are guilty of carrying around that old scoreboard, just remember—your name is on someone's scoreboard that they are carrying around. How can we love and have unity when we keep looking at the scoreboard? Let's learn to forgive as God forgives.

193. JESUS REALLY KNOWS WHAT HE IS TALKING ABOUT

Will Rogers is quoted as saying, "I never met a man I didn't like." Well then, Will Rogers needs to run into some of the annoying people that I do, and we'll just see if he can still say that. It seems that some people are put on this Earth just to bother me. Maybe it can be as simple as someone cutting me off in traffic or ramming my Achilles tendon with a shopping cart. We tend to forget those things rather quickly. But how do you handle it when you are hurt deeply by someone, and you just can't seem to let it go? Several years ago, a group of people hurt me in a way that greatly affected the course of my life. The anger I felt occupied my thoughts day and night. I tried to get over it, but deep down in my heart, I was secretly hoping for their demise. As a Christian, I knew this was wrong, but the feelings remained.

"But to you who are listening I say: Love your enemies, do good to those who hate you, bless those who curse you, pray for those who mistreat you" (Luke 6:27-28).

I knew these words of Jesus in my head, but my heart was having a hard time applying them to my current situation. Over time, I realized that I was the only one suffering. My bitterness was giving me heartburn, high blood pressure, and continual negative thoughts. So, I thought I would give the words of Jesus a try. I began to pray for them. I prayed for them to have peace, joy, and success. As time passed, I continued that prayer until I actually meant it. The results? The negativity in my life subsided, my physical health improved, my mental health improved, and most importantly, my spiritual health improved. It finally dawned on me that Jesus really knew what He was talking about.

As Jesus hung on the cross, He prayed for forgiveness for those who put Him there. Yes, I believe Jesus truly meant for them to find forgiveness. But Jesus also knew that He did not want to face death with bitterness in His heart. So, I say again, Jesus really knows what He is talking about. Maybe we should listen.

194. BECOMING A HOLY TEMPLE

"Consequently, you are no longer foreigners and strangers, but fellow citizens with God's people and also members of his household, built on the foundation of the apostles and prophets, with Christ Jesus himself as the chief cornerstone" *(Ephesians 2:19-20).*

There is a lot of power packed into this passage of scripture. Paul is writing this letter to the church in Ephesus, which had become a blended church of Jews and Gentiles. To the outside world, there was a huge difference between the two. But inside the church, those distinctions were dissolved. In our church today, I've never heard of a problem between Jews and Gentiles. We have other problems that try to divide us. There are racial differences, financial differences, age differences, educational differences, and background differences that try to keep us from being a unified family. Paul is saying when we become a part of God's family we are no longer foreigners and strangers; we are members.

The one thing that has the power to unify people who are so different is Jesus. Jesus reached out to people of all races. Jesus honored the widow who only had two pennies to her name, and He invited the rich tax collectors to follow Him. Jesus taught the older generation and invited the children to come to Him. Jesus spoke in a way that challenged the teachers of the law and encouraged the common man. And Jesus loved the Pharisee Nicodemus and the five-time-divorced Samaritan woman.

Our church needs to follow the example of Jesus. We not only need to be diverse, we need to love our diversity. In the next verse in Ephesians 3, Paul used a beautiful analogy of a church family with diversity.

"In him the whole building is joined together and rises to become a holy temple in the Lord" (Ephesians 3:21).

Satan will always try to divide us. With Jesus as our cornerstone, we will come together to build a holy temple in the Lord. That can only happen when we each embrace and love those who are different from ourselves.

195. TOGETHER AGAIN

Last Sunday morning, my family and I were at the Clark Avenue Church of Christ in Granite City, Illinois. That was the first church to hire me as their pulpit preacher. We spent almost 10 years with that church family. They were patient with me as a new preacher, and they truly helped us raise our kids. It was great to worship with them again. During our worship, I had a moment of clarity. While I was happy to worship and fellowship with them, my mind was back in Marshall, Texas, wondering how things were going with my Eastern Hills family. I have no desire to return to Granite City on a permanent basis, but it was a good feeling being with them.

Here was my epiphany. We started worship at a different time. We were singing different songs. The order of worship was different. We were hearing (and delivering) different sermons. The manner of dress was a little different. The average age was different. But one thing was not different at all. As communion was being served, it hit me: They are doing the exact same thing at Eastern Hills. We are all taking the bread and the fruit of the vine that represent our Savior's sacrifice. As I thought about it a little more, the world got a lot smaller. The church in San Antonio, where my son is a youth minister, is doing the exact same thing. The other church families I have been a member of through the years are doing the exact same thing. Churches all around the world are doing the exact same thing. Miles may separate us, but Jesus unifies us.

"Whoever eats my flesh and drinks my blood has eternal life, and I will raise them up at the last day" (John 6:54).

So, while we were away last Sunday, we were still with you. You may be separated from family and friends today, but Jesus brings us together. This thought took me to the next level of unity through Jesus.

In the future, miles will no longer separate God's children. We will be together, gathered around one table, in His presence, sharing a meal together. What a day that will be.

196. WE ARE ALL PART CHAMELEON

A while back, I found a large box in the garage that was taped shut. This box had made it through several moves from state to state and hadn't been open in years. The box was labeled "Tapes." It was a box full of hundreds of cassette tapes that I kept from Junior High through early adulthood. I found everything from George Strait to Ozzy Osborn, from Run DMC to Accapella, from Michael Jackson to Van Halen, from Devo to Def Leppard, from Air Supply to the Beastie Boys, and everywhere in between. Was my musical taste really that random? I realized that the music I listened to corresponded with the friends I had at the time.

My friends in Junior High listened to pop music and dabbled a little bit into rock and roll. Then MTV hit, and we watched Devo and Michael Jackson videos. While I was in the youth group at church, we went to several Accapella concerts. When I had my first High School crush, I finally figured out what Air Supply was singing about. On the basketball team, I was introduced to rap music. In college, I buddied up with a few guys who were into country music. Here was my realization as I dug deeper and deeper in my box of tapes: Who you are friends with influences who you are.

"One who has unreliable friends soon comes to ruin, but there is a friend who sticks closer than a brother" (Proverbs 18:24).

We are all part chameleon. We tend to look like what surrounds us. Jesus set an example for us. Yes, He reached out and loved all people, but He was very choosy when it came to those who were closest to Him. We need to be the light of the world, reaching out into dark places. But we must choose our close friends very carefully.

197. WARNING LABELS

Have you ever noticed the stupidity of some warning labels placed on the products we purchase? Here are a few examples: A warning sticker on a baby stroller reads, "Remove child before folding." A warning label on a box of Nytol Sleeping Aid reads, "May cause drowsiness." On a Vidal Sassoon blow dryer, the warning label reads, "Do not use while sleeping." Most irons have a warning label that reads, "Never iron clothes while wearing them." A warning label on the box of a child's Superman costume reads, "This costume does not enable flight or super strength." After reading a few of these, you have to ask yourself, "How many hours were spent in a boardroom making the decision on the wording of these labels?" Or "How many frivolous lawsuits were filed to make these companies feel they had to place these labels on their products?"

We tend to put warning labels on people, also. We label people as crazy, or they have issues, or they don't look like us, or believe like us. When we do that, we keep people at a distance. But Jesus never let labels keep Him from engaging with people others avoided. Jesus talked with the "crazy man" in the cemetery, who everyone else avoided. Jesus touched the lepers and a bleeding woman, who others shunned. Jesus spoke with the Pharisees, who were out to get Him. Instead of avoiding them, Jesus chose to engage them.

"On hearing this, Jesus said to them, 'It is not the healthy who need a doctor, but the sick. I have not come to call the righteous, but sinners'" (Mark 2:17).

Instead of seeing warning labels on people, we need to see welcome labels. We avoid them because of the fear of them influencing us. In doing so, we miss the opportunity to influence them. Jesus never met a person who wasn't worth saving. God, please give us the courage to see people as Jesus did.

198. IT'S THAT SEASON AGAIN

The season is starting. I'm not talking about football season; it's already in full swing. And as much as I love having my heart broken every year, that is not my topic. And I'm not talking about the holiday season. It's not even Thanksgiving, and all the Christmas decorations are already going up. The season I am talking about is election season. We are about to enter a presidential election year. The debates, commercials, ads, texts, and phone calls will be invading our daily lives very soon. This is the time that we are all reminded just how divided we are as a nation. Even those from the same political party turn against each other during the primaries. It seems that each candidate's goal is getting your vote by making you despise their opponent. Very few candidates try to win your vote on their own merits. Instead of building up their own character, they sow discord by discrediting their opponent. The ugliest element of our human nature is on full display.

As Christians, we need to remember the words of Jesus as He introduced His first recorded sermon.

"Blessed are the peacemakers, for they will be called children of God" (Matthew 5:9).

I may not agree with you politically, but that does not give me the justification to make you my enemy. We will not agree on all things, but we must not lose sight of the fact that we are all made in the image of God. Instead of bringing about division, how can we bring about unity? Before you speak or post something online, keep these scriptures in mind.

"Whatever happens, conduct yourselves in a manner worthy of the gospel of Christ" (Philippians 1:27).

"Let us therefore make every effort to do what leads to peace and to mutual edification" (Romans 14:19).

"And over all these virtues put on love, which binds them all together in perfect unity" (Colossians 3:14).

199. THE LIVING BIBLE

My first memory of "going to church" is attending Bible study. Does anyone else remember flannel graphs? Bible stories were told to us with little paper characters on a flannel board, showing us the story. Later, we were rewarded for memorizing scripture. I eventually moved into the youth group, where we would have devotionals and Bible studies. Every semester that I was in college, I took at least one Bible class (usually more). When I became a youth minister, we were involved in Bible Quiz, where teens studied a book of the Bible and tested their knowledge by competing against other youth groups. As an adult, I have been a part of several small groups that met weekly and studied the Bible. All the while attending our church services where had Sunday morning and Wednesday night Bible classes. That's a lot of Bible study.

Let me propose a radical thought: Maybe we need a fewer Bible classes and a few more BIBLE DOING activities. Now, there is absolutely nothing wrong with Bible study. However, Jesus did not say, "Study me." He said, "Follow me." When we read about Jesus, do you see Him studying the Bible or living the Bible? A little bit of both, but I believe He spent a lot of time *living* the Bible. When you read in Matthew 25 about judgment day, the discussion is not about how many scriptures have been memorized or if you had perfect attendance at worship services. The discussion was about whether or not you fed someone who was hungry, gave water to someone who was thirsty, visited the sick and imprisoned, clothed the needy, or welcomed strangers.

Knowing the Bible is important. But not at the expense of doing the Bible. What can you do today to live the Bible?

"The world and its desires pass away, but whoever does the will of God lives forever" (1 John 2:17).

200. JUST PART OF THE FAMILY

We have officially entered the holiday season. Thanksgiving is quickly approaching, and Christmas is just around the corner. And you know what that means—family is coming! For the most part, that is a good thing. But if your family is like my family, there are always a few uncomfortable moments. We all have an uncle who insists on loudly sharing his view of politics. We all have that aunt with an annoying laugh. Our grandpa is over there talking with turkey stuck in his teeth and green bean casserole on his shirt. And I'm pretty sure we all have that one cousin who is just plain weird. But we still love them. Why? Because they are family!

One day, Jesus was talking with a crowd of people. He was told that his mother and brothers were standing outside and wanted to speak with Him. Listen to Jesus's response.

> *"He replied to him, 'Who is my mother, and who are my brothers?' Pointing to his disciples, he said, 'Here are my mother and my brothers. For whoever does the will of my Father in heaven is my brother and sister and mother'" (Matthew 12:48-50).*

I have always struggled with this passage of scripture. Was Jesus saying that His mother and His brothers were no longer important to Him? Not at all. What Jesus was saying is that when you become a follower of God, your family grows. Your family now includes that one lady who sings just a little off-key; she is your sister. And that old man who blows his nose really loud and can't stop himself from looking at it; he is your brother. Your family also includes those teenagers who are cutting up and that baby who won't stop crying. They may drive you crazy. But you still love them. Why? Because they are family!

201. DOES OUR LOVE HAVE AN AGENDA?

At this point in my life, I have been a full-time minister for more than thirty years. I spent fourteen years in youth ministry and the rest as a preaching minister. That is what makes this embarrassing to say: I think I have been doing it wrong the whole time. That's not to say that everything has been wrong or sinful. Let me explain.

While I was a youth minister, I tried to have an incredibly active group. Yes, we would have Bible studies and devotionals. But my calendar was also full of lock-ins, movie nights, game nights, laser tag, paintball, professional sporting events, amusement parks, and on and on. My motivation for all of these activities was pure. Establish a relationship with teens, then teach them about Jesus. Moving into the preacher role, the activities were different, but the formula was the same. We not only have a benevolence program where we help those who are in need, but we also give out food baskets for Thanksgiving, fruit baskets at Christmas, candy and games around Halloween, and on and on. All of this is done with the hope of telling others about Jesus. Is there anything wrong with what we are doing? No. But we need to make sure that our agenda aligns with Jesus's agenda.

When Jesus fed the multitude, He did so because they were hungry. When Jesus healed the sick and lame, He did so because He wanted them to have a better life. When Jesus changed water to wine at a wedding, He did not stop the celebration to offer an invitation to follow Him. Jesus shows us an example of loving and blessing people with no strings attached.

"Dear friends, since God so loved us, we also ought to love one another. No one has ever seen God; but if we love one another, God lives in us and his love is made complete in us"
(1 John 4:11-12).

We need to love and bless others simply because we have been loved and blessed. If they want to know about a relationship with God, by all means let us lead them to the cross. But the question I have been asking myself is this: If I love others with an agenda, is it really love?

202. LOOKING AROUND THE TABLE

It's Thanksgiving week, so let me ask you a question … Who is going to be sitting around your table to eat? The answer is most likely family. So, let me ask the question another way: Who would you like to have sitting around your table to eat? Hopefully, your answer is the same. But if you could add anybody to the family list, who would it be? Maybe your favorite actor or actress. Maybe your favorite singer or author. Or maybe someone from your past who has inspired you. I assume you would not desire to sit down for a meal with someone who has wronged you or someone who has let you down.

"And he said to them, 'I have eagerly desired to eat this Passover with you before I suffer'" (Luke 22:15).

As Jesus sits down for what we call the Last Supper, He is in the midst of His twelve disciples. They didn't crash the party. They were all cordially invited by Jesus. Yet Jesus knew that before the morning would dawn on the following day, one of them would betray Him, one would deny Him, and all of them would scatter the moment of His arrest. Surely Jesus could have found others who were more loyal to Him. He could have invited the ladies who would follow Him to the cross and be the first ones at His tomb on Sunday morning. Or He could have spent His last night with His mother and brothers. But instead, He chose to eat with the twelve who were going to fail Him. Why? Two words, love and grace.

We are all invited to a last, last supper with Jesus. This supper will last for an eternity. And just like the disciples, we have all failed Him. Why do we still get the invitation to attend? Love and grace. So, just like Jesus, as you sit around the table this week, make sure you offer love and grace to your family and friends.

203. GOD WITH US

I was asked the other day about who my groomsmen were at my wedding. I had to stop and think for a minute. Well, there was my best man, Jim. Last I heard, he was working with a big firm in Wichita. Then there was Paul. The last time we talked, he was preaching at a church in Denver. And then there is Bob. He is a golf pro, managing a country club somewhere in Oregon. It seems like there was one more. Oh, yeah, my brother, Kent. I do know all about him. How easy it is to let very important relationships just slip away. Of the three groomsmen I haven't talked to in more than a decade, none of us had a falling out. We just lost touch with each other. Facebook helps, kinda. We are friends on Facebook, but that's not a real relationship.

In 2018, a movie called *TAG* came out. The movie is based on a true story of a group of friends who committed to never lose touch with each other. When they were kids, they loved to play tag. They decided as adults they would keep playing. Even though they lived all over the United States, for one month of every year, the game was on. Whoever was 'it' would fly across the country just to sneak up on their friend to tag him and say, "You're it." The movie was written after the real friends were featured on the front page of the *Wall Street Journal*. My favorite quote from the movie is, "We don't stop playing because we grow old. We grow old because we stop playing."

That is not reality for most of us. Through our lifetime, relationships come and go. Even the relationships we once characterized as best friends will fade over time. That is what makes one of the names for Jesus so special.

"All this took place to fulfill what the Lord had said through the prophet: 'The virgin will conceive and give birth to a son, and they will call him Immanuel,' which means 'God with us'"
(Matthew 1:22-23).

Our God will never lose touch with His children. The name Immanuel means that God is with us today, tomorrow, and forevermore.

204. SACRED TIME

To a child, thirty-three years seems like an eternity. As I near my 60s, thirty-three years doesn't seem like a long time at all. But it is estimated that Jesus lived about thirty-three years on Earth. That's thirty-three precious years in all eternity that Jesus walked on our ground and breathed our air. So, this short period of time must be sacred and filled with only the most important things, right? Stop and think about some of the ways Jesus spent His time.

We read about Jesus sharing a meal at Peter's house, Matthew's house, Simon the Leper's house, Simon the Pharisee's house, and at the home of Mary and Martha. Jesus attended a wedding in Cana. Jesus spent a lot of time in a boat with His disciples. Jesus spent time with little children. Jesus cooked breakfast for a few of His disciples. Jesus spent some time alone with a Pharisee named Nicodemus and later with the Samaritan woman at the well. He also spent time with the lame, sick, blind, demon-possessed, crippled, and the family of Lazarus as they mourned his death. Jesus also took an afternoon to spend with a tax collector named Zacchaeus.

"Jesus replied: '"Love the Lord your God with all your heart and with all your soul and with all your mind." This is the first and greatest commandment. And the second is like it: "Love your neighbor as yourself"' (Matthew 22:37-39).

It is clear that during the precious time Jesus had on Earth, He spent investing in people. When we think of Immanuel (God with us), we usually look at the manger, but it goes much further than that. Jesus lived the words He said, He loved God, and He loved others. Like Jesus, the short time we have in our life is precious. Take the time to invest in people. It will not be time wasted.

SECTION FOUR:

OUR *love* FOR SELF

205. TAKE TIME FOR JESUS

The new year is here. If you are like most people, you have already hit the ground running. The holidays are behind us, and a new year stands before us. Have you set some lofty goals for this year? "I'm going to go to the gym three times a week." "I'm going to take the time to read more." "This year I am going to spend more time writing, golfing, gardening, painting ..." I hope you take the time to do all of those things. But we all still have our "dailies" to take care of. Whether it is school, work, or chores around the house, they are things that just have to be done. It's easy to confuse a lot of activity with the true purpose we all have.

One day, Jesus entered the house of a friend of His named Martha. Martha was busy with the "dailies" of having a houseguest, like making sure the house was picked up, preparing the food, setting the table, and pouring drinks for everyone. Meanwhile, her sister Mary decided to just take a seat at the feet of Jesus and listen. This frustrated Martha enough that she came to Jesus and said, "Lord, don't you care that my sister has left me to do the work by myself? Tell her to help me!" Then Jesus responded ...

"'Martha, Martha,' the Lord answered, 'you are worried and upset about many things, but few things are needed—or indeed only one. Mary has chosen what is better, and it will not be taken away from her'" (Luke 10:41-42).

This year, do not let the things that need to be done overshadow what is most important. Like Mary, let's take the time to sit at the feet of Jesus and just listen. Martha was trying to prepare the perfect meal for Jesus. But what Jesus really wanted was just Martha's presence.

206. FAITH AT THE SPEED OF SOUND

Have you ever flown at a speed of 768 miles per hour? The answer is no for most of us. But some people have. About 768 miles per hour is how fast you need to go to break the sound barrier, depending on weather and altitude. For many years it was believed that the sound barrier could not be broken. During World War II, many aircrafts approached the speed of sound. As they did, the plane would shake and in many cases begin to fall apart. So, it was believed for many years that the speed of sound could not be broken by a manned aircraft. Experiments approached the speed of sound, but they would throttle down when nearing 768 mph. It was described as an invisible wall.

On October 14, 1947, in the Bell X-1 rocket plane, the sound barrier was officially broken by U.S. Air Force Captain Chuck Yeager. After breaking through the sound barrier, the shaking would cease, and there would be smooth flying. By 1959, a plane had been developed that could travel five times faster than the speed of sound.

When we are striving to live by faith, we will often get to 767 miles per hour and then pull back. Our world will start shaking and rattling around us. The timid will throttle down. God wants us to throttle up. When things get scary, it usually means we are close to a breakthrough. This invisible wall keeps us from experiencing even greater blessings that God has for us on the other side. Ask yourself a few questions. What barriers have kept your faith from growing? What fears do you have that keep you from pushing forward? What blessings are waiting for you when you break through the invisible wall that is holding you back?

Keep pushing forward. There is smooth flying just ahead.

"Even though I walk through the darkest valley, I will fear no evil, for you are with me; your rod and your staff, they comfort me"
(Psalm 23:4).

347

207. SEEING YOURSELF THROUGH GOD'S EYES

What do you see when you look in the mirror? When most people look at themselves, they focus on the negative. We see a hairline that is creeping in the wrong direction or color that is fading or a style we would like to change. We look at our face and see wrinkles or acne (depending on our age). All of that is surface stuff. What do you really see when you look in the mirror? Do you see someone you are proud of or someone who has disappointed you? Do you see someone whose best days are ahead of them or someone who is way past their prime? Do you see someone who is too young, too old, not gifted enough, or not knowledgeable enough to be used in God's Kingdom?

When God looks at us, He sees something vastly different than what we see. Some of us have been taught, and some may still believe, that God sees the same negative things we see in ourselves. Not true! When God looks at each of us, He sees His child. He sees the potential of what we could do in His kingdom if we would only surrender to Him. As David was growing up, he was just the little brother who got stuck with jobs his older brothers would rather not do. David was even the last thought of his father when he found out that one of his sons would be the next king. When David volunteered to fight Goliath, even King Saul had zero confidence in his ability to win because he only saw a weak boy. When David went to battle Goliath, he was mocked by Goliath, who called David a stick.

"The Lord does not look at the things people look at. People look at the outward appearance, but the Lord looks at the heart"
(1 Samuel 16:7).

People's view of David and God's view of David are vastly

different. God saw a giant slayer. God saw a King who would rule His people. God saw a man after His own heart. Don't buy into what people see in you. Don't even believe what you see in yourself. Trust only what God sees in you.

208. STANDING OVER A PILE OF ASHES

Last week as fires were burning on the west coast the images were hard to watch. As the winds changed and the fires grew, people were told to leave everything and evacuate. It was heartbreaking to hear the interviews with families as they stood weeping in front of a pile of ashes that used to be their home, not knowing what they were going to do. Fortunately, I have never known that exact situation, but I have known many who have.

Heartbreak comes in many different forms as we live in this fallen world. We have all stood over a pile of ashes, not knowing what we are going to do. Your pile of ashes may have been a broken relationship, the divorce of your parents, or your own divorce. It may have been the loss of a loved one, the loss of a job, the sentence from a judge, or a diagnosis from the doctor. Our pile of ashes is a life that has been devastated. We all ask the same question, "What am I going to do now?"

David stood in front of a pile of ashes. His life had been devastated by his own sin. In Psalm 51, David described himself as having a broken spirit, crushed bones, and overwhelmed with guilt. If you have ever stood over a pile of ashes, listen to the words of David.

"Restore to me the joy of your salvation and grant me a willing spirit, to sustain me" (Psalm 51:12).

In those few words, David asked God for what was really most important in life. God, give me back the joy of having salvation through You. That is the most important blessing in this world. Then God, give me what I will need to get me through the challenges that I am facing. If you find yourself standing over a pile of ashes, remember what is most important. All things in this world are subject to fire. But your relationship with God is everlasting.

209. WOULD YOU RATHER FAIL TRYING OR FAIL WATCHING?

Have you ever heard of a business called Traf-O-Data? My guess is that you have not heard of it. Traf-O-Data was founded in the early 1970s. City engineers would stretch rubber tubes across roads to record the amount of traffic that traveled down that particular road. That data would be manually read and used to adjust traffic lights and improve roads. Traf-O-Data was created to computerize the data received to assist traffic engineers. In 1975, the business was defunct. I guess you could call that a failed business adventure. But here is the interesting part: Traf-O-Data was co-founded by a man named Bill Gates. What could be considered a failure was a vital step in the creation of Microsoft. And the rest is history. Bill Gates is now one of the richest men in the world.

Failure is at the top of the list of fears for most people. The fear of failure is a strong enough force that it keeps people from even attempting to follow their dreams and passions. What if I go all in on my dreams and they crash and burn? What if I follow my passion, and it leads me down a dead-end street? The vulnerability is just too much for some people to risk. So, they spend their life just watching from the bleachers.

You can't win the game from the bleachers. You will never succeed unless you get out on the field and just go for it. God created you with unique gifts and passions for a reason. Don't let opportunity pass you by as you sit on the sidelines with your fears. Yes, you might fail. But that failure may be the very step you need to get you to your next step. And that step may be the one that changes the world. It is better to fail trying than to fail watching.

"… being confident of this, that he who began a good work in you will carry it on to completion until the day of Christ Jesus"
(Philippians 1:6).

210. STRIKE THREE

After watching his heroes play baseball, a young boy made a proclamation, "I will be the greatest baseball player of all time!" So, he picked up a baseball and a bat and went outside to practice. Holding the ball in one hand and the bat in the other, he repeated his commitment, "I will be the greatest baseball player of all time!" He tossed the ball up, gripped the bat, and took a mighty swing. Thud, the ball hit the ground at his feet. Undeterred, he picked up the ball and shouted, "I will be the greatest baseball player of all time!" Once again the tossed the ball in the air and took a swing at it. Thud, the ball hit the ground at his feet. Another swing and a miss. With great determination, he picked up the ball and repeated his mantra, "I will be the greatest baseball player of all time!" Concentrating, he tossed the ball and took another swing. Thud, the ball hit the ground at his feet. Strike three! He dropped the bat and lifted both arms in the air and shouted, "I will be the greatest pitcher of all time!"

"I can do all this through him who gives me strength"
(Philippians 4:13).

This young boy gives us an example of undeterred optimism. We may fall short in one area of life, but that may just open the door for us to excel in another area.

Peter was going to be the greatest fisherman of all time. Instead, he became one of the greatest followers of Jesus that this world has ever seen. Zacchaeus was going to be one of the greatest chief tax collectors of all time. Instead, he became one of the most generous people who ever lived. Paul was determined to stop the spread of Christianity. Instead, he became one of the greatest missionaries of Jesus who has ever lived. If one door has been shut in your face, that is not the end of your story. God will open another door and give you the strength to keep going. Trust in God. With God, strike three never means you are out.

355

keep going. Trust in God. With God, strike three never means you are out.

211. A TEACHER TEACHES

This past week we had to say goodbye to my father-in-law, Hickory Starr. Even though his health was slowly declining, the end came so quickly. My relationship with him started long before either of us ever knew we would be related one day. The first time I remember meeting him was the day I was promoted to my sixth-grade Bible class. We walked into class and written on the chalkboard was "Hickory Starr." One of the kids asked, "What is a Hickory Starr?" I don't recall any particular lessons that were taught that year. The only thing I remember was that he asked a lot of questions. He made us think about the Bible, not just learn the stories. When I returned home for the summer after my first year at college and walked into Bible class, there he was again. All summer long, I sat at the feet of my future father-in-law and studied the Bible. Even at this time, we had no idea that we would someday be related.

The conversations we had over the next 33 years were not all that different from the ones we had in Bible class. He was a teacher. He would always ask questions and share his insights. And that really didn't change when grandkids came into the picture. He was never really a get-down-on-the-floor-and-play grandpa. He was always teaching. He was a living, breathing example of what is written in Deuteronomy 11.

"Teach them to your children, talking about them when you sit at home and when you walk along the road, when you lie down and when you get up" (Deuteronomy 11:19).

About 10 days before he passed, the two of us sat in a hospital room alone for a couple of hours. And to no surprise, he was still teaching. I thank you, Lord, for putting Hickory Starr in my life. He challenged me to consider Your Word like few others ever have. Rest in peace.

212. THE VIEW IS WORTH THE STRUGGLE

Twenty-seven years ago I went on my first Wilderness Trek. Our youth group was attempting to summit Mount Sherman, which has an elevation of 14,043 feet. We started climbing before sunrise. During the hike, I told our guide that I was exhausted, and I was not sure if I could make it. He said something to me that I have never forgotten. He told me if a helicopter dropped us off on the top of the mountain, we would have no appreciation for the view. The joy and the accomplishment would only come after the struggle.

The other day, Krista and I were looking at a picture from our wedding. We were so young and hopeful about our future. Now, thirty-three years later, we are very proud of where we stand. We have two amazing kids who now have families of their own. We have the two best grandchildren in the world. We have each dedicated our lives to blessing others through nursing and ministry. But we didn't get here without a struggle. We have had to overcome many adversities along the way. Going through them together only made us stronger.

We are not promised an easy trail in life. It will have many challenges and setbacks along the way. Jesus didn't have an easy life. His disciples didn't have an easy life. But we live with a promise from God that will help us when we are feeling overwhelmed.

"And God is faithful; he will not let you be tempted beyond what you can bear. But when you are tempted, he will also provide a way out so that you can endure it" (1 Corinthians 10:13).

When you feel like giving up, just remember this promise from God. He will see you through any adversity that you face. And remember, the joy and the accomplishment will only come after the struggle.

213. LEAVING FEAR IN THE CLOSET

Satan has many tools in his toolbelt. One of his favorites is fear. He knows that fear will cause us to doubt God. Fear will lead us to value the opinions of others over the opinion of God. Fear will keep us from reaching out to those in need. Fear will keep us silent when we should speak up. Fear will keep us from making changes that need to be made. When a Christian lives in fear, Satan wins.

In 2001, a movie came out called *Monsters, Inc.* It is an animated kids' movie that deals with the monsters who come out of children's closets at night. The monsters would come out kids' closets and make them scream. Those screams would then be harnessed as the natural resource to power the monster's world. Think electricity. All is well until they encounter a little girl who has no fear at all. She sees the monsters as pets and just laughs at them. This disrupts the entire power system of the monsters' world. It's a great movie, which I recommend for all ages.

Fear only has the power we give it. If we give in to fear, it will paralyze us. We will not enjoy the abundant life and the peace of God that He has promised us. In Isaiah 43:1, the Lord speaks and says, "Do not fear, for I have redeemed you; I have summoned you by name; you are mine." The antidote to fear is the love of God. Fear will subside when we place our hope in the Almighty, all-powerful Creator of all things.

"There is no fear in love. But perfect love drives out fear, because fear has to do with punishment. The one who fears is not made perfect in love" (1 John 4:18).

Spoiler alert! At the end of the movie, the monsters realize that a child's laughter produces more energy than their screams. I guess the spiritual moral of the story is that joy is greater than fear. When fear creeps in, just remember, the One who is in us is greater than the one who is in the closet.

214. TAKING A LEAP OF FAITH

I recently read the story of a man named Lex Gillette. He is from Raleigh, North Carolina. In 2007, he graduated from East Carolina University. He loves to play the piano and sing. But that is not what he is best known for around the world. He is a track and field athlete who has competed in the last five Paralympic Games (2004 in Athens, 2008 in Beijing, 2012 in London, 2016 in Rio de Janeiro, and 2020 in Tokyo). He medaled in all five games in the long jump competition.

So, what is his disability? Lex Gillette is completely blind. Let me describe how the long jump event works for him. He begins by standing at the end of a narrow hundred-meter track. When he is ready, he sprints straight down the track, making sure not to veer to the left or to the right. Then he must time his jump perfectly to soar through the air, and then land in a sand pit he cannot see. On April 23, 2015, he broke the world record for Paralympians by leaping twenty-two feet, two inches.

How is this even possible? As Lex begins his sprint, his trainer stands at the end of the sand pit and yells, "Fly," over and over. Lex will use his trainer's voice as a homing beacon, helping him keep running straight and know when to leap. For Lex to complete the jump, he must not only listen intently to his trainer's voice, but he must also completely trust his trainer.

"So do not fear, for I am with you; do not be dismayed, for I am your God. I will strengthen you and help you; I will uphold you with my righteous right hand" (Isaiah 41:10).

As you walk through the challenges of life, keep Lex in mind. Do not let your personal limitations keep you from doing great things. Do not listen to the naysayers who will try to limit you. Focus solely on the voice of God, your trusted trainer. Running straight toward Him will keep you on the narrow path. And when the time comes, take a leap of faith. The landing will be soft, and you will be welcomed with a loving embrace.

215. A BEAUTIFUL DISTRACTION

As an "upper middle-aged" person, I have a pet peeve that I see every day. I get irritated when I see young people in social settings with their faces buried in their phones. I tried to look up the average time that teens spend on their phones, but the search was useless. The statistics change with every study. The amount of time teens spend on social media is shocking. I just want to grab their phones and shout, "Look up! There is a real world all around you!" My frustration has one big flaw. It's not just the young people who are preoccupied with their phones. Krista and I made the mistake of showing our mothers Facebook. We thought they would enjoy seeing pictures and keeping up with the grandkids. Two problems: First, once grandparents got on Facebook, it marked the beginning of the end of Facebook. Second, Facebook became their only source of news, and that's a problem.

My simple point is this: It is so easy to get distracted that real life can just pass you by. I am not a social media junkie. But I am not innocent. My distractions include professional and college sports, which will have absolutely no impact on my life. I also get distracted by music, television, and old movies. These distractions keep me from focusing on what is real and important.

"But when you pray, go into your room, close the door, and pray to your Father, who is unseen. Then your Father, who sees what is done in secret, will reward you" (Matthew 6:6).

In context, Jesus was telling His listeners not to flaunt their religion in front of others. But the idea of going into your room and closing the door seems to be saying that the one praying needs to focus and have no distractions. Rather than living in such a way that lets the unimportant distract you, why don't we let Jesus be our distraction? He is a beautiful distraction. It will be time well spent.

216. COMMITMENT STARTS IN THE HEART

Many years ago, I was disturbed by a religious show I watched on television. I don't remember what the show was called but, I vividly remember the content. A group of Christian college students spent their spring break going on a mission that they called "Beach Reach." They spent their week of spring break at a popular resort beach where thousands of other college students came to party. The Christian group used their van to drive people home from bars after they got drunk. They spent their days on the beach sharing Jesus with swimmers, surfers, drinkers, and sunbathers.

The moment of the show that stood out to me was when they taught one young man the gospel and immediately baptized him in the ocean. As the film crew was interviewing the teacher, the recently baptized student was in the background, celebrating his commitment by drinking a beer with his friends. They asked the teacher what he thought about the student he had just baptized continuing his drinking habit. The teacher's response disturbed me, challenged me, and eventually taught me a lesson. He said, "He has been changed on the inside. It will take a while for his outside to follow."

That goes against everything I had learned up to that moment. What I had understood about becoming a Christian and living as a Christian was that you had to first clean up your life so that you would then be worthy of becoming a Christian. As the years passed and I studied the life and teaching of Jesus, I discovered my thinking error. Jesus always started with the heart. With the adulterous woman, Jesus saved her from certain death, He forgave her, and then told her to go live a better life. When Jesus met a Samaritan woman who was divorced five times and was currently living with a man, He gave her "living water" before she made one single change in her life. As Jesus was being crucified, a thief hanging next to him was granted access into paradise while being executed for his life of crime.

"And we all, who with unveiled faces contemplate the Lord's glory, are being transformed into his image with ever-increasing glory, which comes from the Lord, who is the Spirit"
(2 Corinthians 3:18).

May our teaching reflect the teaching of Jesus. It starts with the heart. Only then can we marvel at what the Holy Spirit can do to change a life.

217. ANOTHER YEAR OLDER

As a child, I always hated February 28. Why that day specifically? Because it was the day after my birthday. That meant that it was 364 days until my next birthday and ten months until Christmas. It seemed like it would be forever until I could open another present. This past week, I turned fifty-eight years old. Birthdays are not nearly as fun as they used to be. I really wish they wouldn't come as often as they do. When I was younger, I used to sit around with my friends and talk enthusiastically about what's going on in the world of sports, movies, or current events. Now, when I sit around talking with people my age, it sounds more like an organ recital. We talk about which organs in our bodies have stopped working. So, this year on the morning of my birthday, I decided to kick the blues and turn on some '80s music, the soundtrack of my youth. The playlist included a song from my senior year of high school, "Footloose." Perhaps it was because of my birthday, but the lyrics of that song spoke to me in a way that they never had before.

Believe it or not, the voice of Kenny Loggins helped me that morning. Getting older can either get you down or motivate you. I have an angel I have been married to for thirty-six years. I have two amazing children, who now have amazing families of their own. I have two incredible grandchildren with one more on the way. I have a job I love, and I am surrounded by a loving church family. So, I choose not to be depressed because I am getting older. I choose to commit to living in the joy of the Lord with every day He blesses me with.

"My flesh and my heart may fail, but God is the strength of my heart and my portion forever" (Psalm 73:26).

Get ready, world—I'm about to cut footloose!

218. TAKE COURAGE

Fear will have an interesting effect on your life. While fear may keep you from dangerous situations, fear will also keep you from some wonderful opportunities. Fear can be paralyzing. Fear will keep you from pursuing opportunities in life and will keep you from pursuing relationships that may be a blessing. Is fear good or bad? The answer is both. It all depends on who or what you fear and what it does to you.

The gospels of Matthew, Mark, and John all recount a night when the disciples were in a boat in the midst of a powerful storm. Were the disciples afraid? Interestingly, none of the gospels says they were afraid. Until … Jesus came to them walking on the water. It wasn't until they saw Jesus that they became terrified.

"But Jesus immediately said to them: 'Take courage! It is I. Don't be afraid'" (Matthew 14:27).

The disciples had misplaced fear. They should have been scared of the strong winds that could sink their boat. But evidently, they were fine with that. They should have been comforted by the presence of Jesus. But that is when they began to fear. They had it all wrong, just like we do. We are fearful of what is happening on Wall Street. We are fearful of enemies across the seas. We are fearful of a global pandemic. We are fearful of one party or another gaining power in our government. Yet eternal judgment doesn't seem to affect our daily lives at all. Our fear is misplaced.

When you find yourself living in fear, stop and ask yourself, "What is causing my fear?" Then remember that, as Christians, we live with the presence of Jesus in our lives through the gift of the Holy Spirit. Then, take courage!

219. BE YOURSELF

"So God created human beings in his image. In the image of God he created them. He created them male and female"
(Genesis 1:27).

Recently, I read: "God has never looked in your mirror and wished He saw someone else." Could the same be said about each of us? Have you ever looked in your mirror and wished you were seeing someone different? At each step of God's creation, He said the same thing, *"It is good."* We were all created in the image of God. So, of course, when He looks at us, He sees something good even if we can't see it. When we look in the mirror, we often see flaws we would like to change. We wish we were taller or maybe a little shorter. We wish we could lose some weight or be in better shape. We wish our hair was fuller or thinner or a different color. Some people just wish they had some hair. We want a smaller nose or wish our eyes were a different color. Now, look a little deeper in the mirror. Do you wish you were a little more stoic or maybe more emotional? Do you wish you were a little more reserved or maybe more outspoken? Do you wish you were more confident? Do you wish you were more compassionate? Do you wish you were more carefree? Do you wish you were more analytical?

The fact is, we are God's most creative act. If God wanted you to be like other people, He would have made us all the same. God has given each of us different parts of His character. Try to see this in yourself. Then try to see it in other people. Then, just maybe, you will see some good in the people that you are convinced were put on Earth to drive you nuts.

Be yourself. Everyone else is already taken.

220. LOVE DOES

Have you ever been ready to put your head on your pillow only to take a look at your "To-do" list for the day and realize it is more like a "To didn't get it done" list? You woke up that day with motivation and enthusiasm but you ended the day with disappointment wondering why you didn't accomplish your goals? I've often heard the saying "It's the thought that counts." But just thinking about accomplishing your goals doesn't get the job done. Also, I have never been helped or encouraged by someone's thoughts. It is so much easier to love people with our intentions than it is to love them in real life. It's so much easier to make plans than it is to make plans happen. It's so much easier to set goals than it is to accomplish goals. Here is a blunt fact: No one is remembered for what they planned to do.

King David had great plans to build a temple. But God told him he was not the man for the job. His son Solomon would be the one to build the temple. David could have sulked and pouted. But instead, David made it his project to gather all the materials for the construction of the temple. David showed us what the attitude of a man after God's own heart looks like. Even if your plans don't line up with God's plans, you still roll up your sleeves and do what you can.

That's what love looks like. Love is so much more than a feeling. Love is action. Love is showing up even when you don't know what to say. Love is working hard even when you feel underqualified for the task at hand. Love is supporting others and receiving no credit for yourself. Simply put, love doesn't just think about it; love does it!

"Do not merely listen to the word, and so deceive yourselves. Do what it says" (James 1:22).

221. TRAGEDY OR TRIUMPH? YOU DECIDE!

Many people will not recognize the name Dave Dravecky. He was a pitcher who played for the San Diego Padres and the San Francisco Giants in the late '80s. Dave was an All-Star pitcher who won sixty-four games throughout his career and struck out 558 batters. Dave was a committed Christian. He and a few of his teammates became known as the "God Squad" in the locker room because they chose not to engage in the wild life of professional athletes but would instead have Bible studies in their hotel rooms while they were on the road. In October of the 1988 season, a cancerous tumor was found in the shoulder of his pitching arm. He underwent surgery to remove half of his deltoid muscle and freeze his humerus bone in an attempt to eliminate all the cancer cells. Through Dave's faith and determination, he attempted a comeback. After rehabilitation and pitching in the minor leagues, he returned to Major League Baseball on August 10, 1989, to pitch eight innings and win the game 4-3.

"Let your eyes look straight ahead; fix your gaze directly before you. Give careful thought to the paths for your feet and be steadfast in all your ways. Do not turn to the right or the left; keep your foot from evil" (Proverbs 4:25-27).

As Christians living in a fallen world, we can expect hardships and roadblocks. Jesus didn't tell His disciples that this might happen. He said it would happen. When hardships come, Satan will tell you to give up. He will whisper in your ear and tell you it is not worth it to keep trying. When we face challenges in our walk with God, remember what the Proverb teaches us: Focus on your goal, concentrate, endure and avoid evil.

The rest of the Dave Dravecky story can be looked at as tragic or triumph. Five days after his return, he was pitching again. In the sixth inning, as he threw the ball, his humerus bone snapped. Cancer had returned. Eventually, his arm and shoulder had to be amputated. Did Dave give up? No! He has gone on to author several books and travels the world as a motivational speaker, sharing his faith. Don't let this world stop you from your most important purpose. Keep looking forward and take each step by faith.

222. HEART HOARDERS

Hoarders is a reality TV show on the A&E network that is currently in its thirteenth season. It features people who struggle to let go of anything. Their houses become so cluttered with stuff that they approach being unlivable. Hoarding is considered a psychological disorder linked to depression. I don't know that I have ever watched an entire episode. Before it ends I find myself wandering around my house looking for something I need to throw away or a dish that needs washing.

As difficult as it is to watch someone who can't let go of stuff and ends up living in house full of filth, it is harder for me to watch someone who can't let go of things and they end up living in a life full of filth. They keep bad habits in their lives that are detrimental. But they just can't let go. They keep people in their lives who are bad influences and continually bring them down. But they just can't let go. That becomes a life that is spiraling downward. As sad as house hoarders and life hoarders are, there is another type of hoarding that is even worse—heart hoarding. That is a person whose heart is filled with the guilt and shame of past sins. They also hold on to things like bitterness, rage and anger. And they continue to be broken by the things that others have said or done to them.

Stop right now and take inventory of your heart. Is it so cluttered with negativity from the past that there is no room for love and blessings? It may be time for an intervention. On the hoarders show, they bring in an expert who assists the hoarder with cleaning up the mess. They separate out the things that are worth keeping and the things that need to go. If you are a heart hoarder, it is time to bring in the Lord and let Him do the same.

"Therefore, if anyone is in Christ, the new creation has come: The old has gone, the new is here!" (2 Corinthians 5:17).

There is a better life waiting for you. Start with your heart. We will get to the cluttered closets later.

372

223. GET ON YOUR FEET

This year I have been to my fair share of funerals. The first thing that usually happens at a funeral is the reading of the obituary. After hearing several of these, it makes you stop and think, "What will my obituary say?" I hope the headline of my obituary would be that I lived my life as a child of God. Sprinkled in with that, I hope that being a good husband, father and grandfather would be said. And that I spent the last 35 years of my life (hopefully more) serving as a minister trying to spread the light of God's love to others. One thing I hope that is not mentioned is that I was a failed business owner. That's right, at one time I tried to start a business. But it failed to ever get off the ground. I'd rather that fact about my life just fade away. When the business fell apart, I just put that in the "that wasn't God's plan for me" file and moved on to bigger and better things.

Let me give you the resume of a man who had more failings than you have probably ever heard before. This man lost his job so he decided to run for the state legislature. He was defeated. He failed in a business adventure. His sweetheart died. He had a nervous breakdown. He ran for Speaker and was defeated. He ran for Congress and was defeated. He was rejected as land officer. He ran for Senate and was defeated. He was defeated for nomination for Vice President. Again, he was defeated for U.S. Senate. Then in 1860, Abe Lincoln was elected President. We remember Abe Lincoln only as President and the positive things he did while he was in office. The reason we do not dwell on his failings is because he refused to let his missteps define him. He continued to pick himself up and move on to something bigger and better.

"... for though the righteous fall seven times, they rise again"
(Proverbs 24:16).

As Christians, we will stumble and fall. Don't let that define you. Get on your feet and keep moving forward toward bigger and better things.

224. PARENTING

I will never forget the day my Middle School-aged daughter was in my office and found the book, *The Strong-Willed Child* by Dr. James Dobson. She asked, "Dad, did you read this book because of me?" I answered her honestly, "No, I read it because I was a youth minister. I reread it because of you." Now that our kids are grown and have families of their own I can look back with some objective hindsight at the way Krista and I parented.

Here are a few of my conclusions: First, parenting is a rollercoaster. There are days you will feel like the greatest parent on Earth. Then other days, you will feel like you have scarred your child for life. On those days, Krista and I would joke and say, "Well, it will all come out in therapy." My second conclusion is that it is very hard to feel confident in your parenting skills. You can read a hundred books on parenting, and you will find a hundred different methods and theories. You may excel at one but find yourself lacking in ninety-nine. My third conclusion is that the main ingredient needed for parenting is effort. It is exhausting. But you can't give up or get lazy. Dig down and find strength for today. When your head eventually hits the pillow, pray for strength for tomorrow.

As a young parent, I thought the only way we were going to be seen as successful parents was if our son played in the NBA and our daughter was elected President. My definition of success has now changed. The number one goal of parenting is to make sure your kids know that they are loved. They are loved by God. And they are loved by you.

"I pray that out of his glorious riches he may strengthen you with power through his Spirit in your inner being, so that Christ may dwell in your hearts through faith. And I pray that you, being rooted and established in love, may have power, together with all the Lord's holy people, to grasp how wide and long and high and

deep is the love of Christ, and to know this love that surpasses knowledge—that you may be filled to the measure of all the fullness of God" (Ephesians 3:16-19).

The NBA will have plenty of stars, and there will always be someone in the White House. And neither of those will be one of our children. And we're okay with that because we believe God has bigger plans for each of them.

225. YOU NEVER KNOW

About fifteen years ago, my daughter was on a city league basketball team in Granite City, Illinois. On the nights that she had practice, I would sit in the gym and watch. Occasionally, I would pick up a spare basketball and shoot a few free throws on one of the side baskets. On a few occasions, a little girl would come over and take a few shots with me. She was the little sister of one of my daughter's teammates. It took all of this little girl's strength to get the ball up to the basket. I would rebound for her and encourage her to try again. Nothing out of the ordinary, right? Well, this weekend I will be watching that little girl play in the NCAA Final Four. She is the captain of the Iowa Hawkeyes. Her name is Kate Martin. Her teammates nicknamed her "The Glue" because they say she is the one who holds the team together. Looking back, I could have never imagined that scrappy, determined little girl would go on to achieve such great things.

"'For I know the plans I have for you,' declares the Lord, 'plans to prosper you and not to harm you, plans to give you hope and a future'" (Jeremiah 29:11).

When we look at a child, we tend to put limitations on what they could eventually become. On some occasions, we may actually dream big for them. But our big dreams are nowhere near the possibilities God may have for them. Sadly, we do the same thing when we look in the mirror. We put limitations on our own possibilities in life. Read Jeremiah 29:11 again. It's not about our plans; it's about God's plans. And with God's plans, there are no limits. If you want to unlock God's potential, then keep reading in Jeremiah 29.

"Then you will call on me and come and pray to me, and I will listen to you. You will seek me and find me when you seek me with all your heart" (Jeremiah 29:12-13).

Don't limit yourself. Call on God, pray to God, and seek Him with all your heart. Then stand back and watch what God can do. This is very hard for a Sooners fan to say, but "Go Hawkeyes!"

226. TURN THE PAGE

When my son was in high school, we loved watching the television show *24*. The show starred Kiefer Sutherland as an American counterterrorist agent named Jack Bauer. Each season covered twenty-four consecutive hours, using the real-time method of narration. Each episode covered one hour of the day, during which there was a terrorist threat. And each episode ended on a cliffhanger. This was before the day of binge-watching, so we had to wait a week before the seemingly impossible situation was solved. Only for that episode to end on another cliffhanger. It was excruciating, and we loved it.

I have a Bible that has Genesis 6:7 at the bottom of the right-hand page. That verse reads:

"So the Lord said, 'I will wipe from the face of the earth the human race I have created—and with them the animals, the birds and the creatures that move along the ground—for I regret that I have made them.'"

That is the last verse before you turn the page and find verse 8. Just imagine reading your Bible one night before bed and saying, "Okay, one more page," and verse 7 is the last verse you read before closing your Bible, turning out the light, and going to bed. I believe nightmares would follow. Most of us would have to turn the page and keep reading after a cliffhanger like that. Fortunately, verse 8 reads:

"But Noah found favor in the eyes of the Lord."

You know the rest of the story. God saved humanity through one man's family, and here we are today. Can you see your life like a book? Some pages are going to end on an ugly note. At the end of some chapters, it will seem like there is no hope for the future. But with God, good news is on the next page. With God, there is always the hope of salvation and eternal life.

"The Lord is not slow in keeping his promise, as some understand slowness. Instead he is patient with you, not wanting anyone to perish, but everyone to come to repentance" (2 Peter 3:9).

If you are at the bottom of a page in your life and the outlook is bleak, just keep reading. Turn to God and find the hope that is on the next page.

227. THE MAIN THING

So far, 2021 has been a whirlwind for the Treat family. It started with the passing of my father. Exactly one month later, my sister-in-law passed away. Then we helped packing and moving my mother-in-law. We are in the home stretch of planning our son's wedding, which includes getting suits for the groomsmen, making arrangements for the rehearsal dinner, and travel plans. We are also trying to spend as much time as possible with our new grandson. Add to that, we are at the tail end of a global pandemic (hopefully). And, by the way, we both have full-time jobs. When we became empty-nesters, we both wondered what we are going to do with all our free time. Now we are wondering when we get to have all that free time.

I remember the days of having two kids at home and our week was filled with school activities, sports practices and games, band concerts, and youth group. We thought life could not be busier. But we were wrong. I don't look to the retirement years with any amount of optimism because some of the retired people I know are some of the busiest people on Earth.

The point is that we will always have an excuse to put God on the backburner. We say with our mouths that God is the most important. But our actions say a different message. We use the excuse that the immediate trumps the important. But that is just us trying to justify our actions.

"But seek first his kingdom and his righteousness, and all these things will be given to you as well. Therefore do not worry about tomorrow, for tomorrow will worry about itself. Each day has enough trouble of its own" (Matthew 6:33-34).

I have heard it said that if your schedule is too busy for God, then God did not make your schedule. I've also heard that if the devil can't make you bad, he will make you busy. Yes, this world can be a whirlwind at times. But don't let the busyness of the moment steal what is most important. Always remember, "The main thing is to keep the main thing the main thing!"

228. LIVING DEBT FREE

Last week in our Sunday morning Bible class, we studied the Ten Commandments. I described the Ten Commandments to be like a mirror rather than a checklist. What does a mirror do? A mirror cannot make you beautiful. A mirror simply reveals what needs to be cleaned up or fixed. One realization we all have when we look into the mirror is that we are not perfect. Looking into a mirror can cause a number or different reactions. Some will see their flaws and work to correct them. Others will see their flaws and decide to never look in the mirror again.

The Bible tells us about an extraordinary practice in ancient Israel called the Year of Jubilee, which happened every fifty years. The Year of Jubilee involved a year of release from indebtedness and all types of bondage. All prisoners and captives were set free, all slaves were released, all debts were forgiven, and all property was returned to its original owners. One of the benefits of the Jubilee was that all people could take a deep breath and rest.

> *"When you were dead in your sins and in the uncircumcision of your flesh, God made you alive with Christ. He forgave us all our sins, having canceled the charge of our legal indebtedness, which stood against us and condemned us; he has taken it away, nailing it to the cross" (Colossians 2:13-14).*

When we stand at the foot of the cross, we all realize that we are all flawed. The cross reveals we are all far from perfect. Much like looking in the mirror, we can react differently. Some choose to turn away and live with their imperfections. But for those who submit to the cross, it is much like the Year of Jubilee. We are released from our bondage. We are no longer slaves to sin. All our debts are forgiven. And we can take a deep breath and rest. The difference for us is that the Year of Jubilee doesn't just happen every fifty years. It can happen at any time. The blood that Jesus shed on the cross is ready to forgive you at any moment. So, accept His invitation to submit. Then relax, take a deep breath, and be assured that you are now living debt free.

229. AMAZING GRACE

Captain John Newton was a slave trader in the mid 1700s. On his voyages, his ship carried goods to Africa and traded them for slaves to be brought back to North America. In 1748, John Newton awoke to find his ship caught in a severe storm. He began to pray for God's mercy. The storm subsided, and he started reading his Bible and other Christian literature. By the time he reached his home shore, John Newton was a true believer in God and committed his life to being a Christian. What followed may be surprising to you. The ship was loaded again, and Captain John Newton continued to be a slave trader. Later, when he no longer served as Captain, he continued to invest his money in the slave-trading business.

As time went on and his faith grew deeper, he began to see that the evils of the slave-trading business and his commitment to God did not mesh. Not only did Newton denounce the slave trade, but he also worked to have it completely abolished. Later in his life, John Newton became a minister and a songwriter. His most famous hymn that we still sing today is "Amazing Grace."

"For now we see only a reflection as in a mirror; then we shall see face to face. Now I know in part; then I shall know fully, even as I am fully known" (1 Corinthians 13:12).

God's work is not complete in us when we commit our lives to Him. Actually, that is only the beginning. As our faith grows, we will continue to discover things in our lives that do not mesh with the commitment we have made. That is simply called growth. We are not who we used to be. And we are still not what we are going to be. So, give yourself some grace when you look back at the person you used to be. But don't become stagnant. Continue growing closer to God, and He will reveal the things in your life you need to change. Accepting the gift of amazing grace from God does not mean that you have crossed the finish line. It is only the first step in becoming more like Jesus and less like the world.

230. FAMILY REUNION

As the sun rose on Sunday morning, a few ladies were on their way to the tomb of Jesus. They were carrying spices to anoint the dead body of Jesus, who had been crucified three days earlier. As they discussed who would roll the stone away from the entrance of the tomb, they were met by an angel.

"The angel said to the women, 'Do not be afraid, for I know that you are looking for Jesus, who was crucified. He is not here; he has risen, just as he said'" (Matthew 28:5-6).

For us today, this is the most important moment in history. The death, burial, and resurrection of Jesus opened the door for our eternal life. If we put our faith in Jesus by making Him the Lord of our lives, we will spend our eternity in His presence along with all of those who believe.

Two days ago, Krista and I, along with the rest of our family, were in the cemetery laying her mother to rest. Over the past four years, we have buried all four of our parents. Also during this time, Krista's older sister died. Without a doubt, this has been a difficult season of life for us. This would be devastating were it not for the empty tomb of Jesus. Because of the resurrection of Jesus, we know that the grave is only a step into eternity. So, we live with the assurance that there is a great family reunion in our future.

The heart problems and the diseases that took our family members' earthly lives will be no more. The next time we see them, we will all have new bodies that will not age and will not suffer. We will smile, laugh, and sing together in the presence of the One who saved us. It will not only be a family reunion with those who were closest to us in this life, but our family reunion will include all of God's family from the past, present, and future. Would you like to reunite your loved ones who have died in the Lord? Would you like to meet some of the men and women we have read about in the Bible? Follow God today so we can be together tomorrow.

231. MY FAILURE WILL NOT DEFINE ME

Maybe you have heard about this man. He attempted to earn his PhD in literature at Lincoln College in Oxford, but he flunked out. He wrote a book titled, *And to Think I Saw it on Mulberry Street*," which was rejected by twenty-eight separate publishers. But he kept on writing. Today he has sold more than 700 million books. His name is Theodor Giesel. But you probably know him as Dr. Seuss.

Failures are a part of life. I just looked up the best career batting average ever in pro baseball. Ty Cobb's batting average was .366. That means that more than 63 percent of the time he batted, he failed to get a hit. The most accurate three-point shooter in NBA history is Steve Kerr. During his career he made 45.4 percent of his three-point attempts. That means he missed more than half of the shots he took. What these athletes know is that failure will come. But failure does not define true success.

What do you think your percentage is on resisting temptation? One thing I know for sure, it is not 100 percent. So, we all have failed. Here is some good news: God only uses failures in His Kingdom. The Bible is full of great failures. When you fail, you have to answer two questions. First, what did you learn from your mistake? Second, what are you going to do now?

"My flesh and my heart may fail, but God is the strength of my heart and my portion forever" (Psalm 73:26).

Don't let your failures define you and your future. Trust in God to give you the strength to rise again. God does great things through failures. Strive to become the greatest failure ever.

232. YOUR TESTIMONY HAS POWER

I love to hear a great testimony of how God has dramatically changed a life. It is so powerful to hear the story of someone who was living in the grip of addiction and then one day they were introduced to God. After giving their life to God, He changed their life completely. Their addiction was broken and they are now living for Him. What an amazing testimony of the power of God.

One of the greatest stories I have ever heard happened several years ago. A youth minister friend and I were preparing for a class that we were going to teach at a camp. Our class was titled, "Free in Christ." We went behind the bars of a maximum-security prison to meet an inmate who was converted while he was incarcerated. We never found out what crime he had committed, but it was enough to send him to prison for twenty-five years. Not only did he become a Christian, but he wrote several books while in his prison cell that are now teaching others about the grace of God. The thing I remember most was him saying, "I am now free." Even though he had several more years to serve behind bars, in his heart he was free. What a testimony!

My guess is that your testimony is not near as dramatic as his. If your testimony is similar to mine it sounds something like this: I was raised in a Christian home and taken to church every Sunday. When the time came that my parents felt I was old enough I was baptized. Yes, I have sinned. But on the surface, my life after baptism is not much different than my life before baptism. That's a good story, but it doesn't have the powerful shock value of the drug addicted gang member who is now a believer.

It doesn't seem to be as powerful, but it should. Both extremes tell the same story. The story is that God can take a sinner and make them

His child. You are not defined by who you were, no matter how good or how bad. You are defined by God. And He wants nothing more than to call you His child!

"Yet to all who did receive him, to those who believed in his name, he gave the right to become children of God" (John 1:12).

233. COMFORTABLY NUMB

Repetition is comfortable; change is scary. We know this to be true in our lives. When we know what the day is going to hold, no surprises coming our way, no problem. We can relax, we've been there before. However, when we are stepping into the unknown, like a new job, a new relationship, or new commitments, we become nervous, anxious, and uptight. So, it is easier to just stay in our own lane day after day, week after week, and year after year.

In the Bible there's a place called the Pool of Bethesda. The spring was believed to be stirred by angels every so often, and when stirred, those who managed to jump in the pool would be healed. Every day, a large number of disabled people would lie next to the pool, getting as close to the edge as possible so they wouldn't miss their shot at being healed. One day, Jesus walked up to the pool and met a disabled man who had been lying by the pool for 38 years.

"When Jesus saw him lying there and learned that he had been in this condition for a long time, he asked him, 'Do you want to get well?'" (John 5:6).

What may sound like a stupid question really has a lot of bite. This man was at the place of healing. He knew the potential of the water. And who in their right mind would want to remain disabled? Yet he refused to answer Jesus's simple question. He only made excuses as to why his life has remained the same for almost four decades.

I believe this describes a large number of "church-goers." We become comfortable with our average Christian lives and our daily struggles. And just like the disabled man, we are so close to a radical upgrade to our lives, but we remain on the edge of the pool. Jesus is inviting us to take a leap of faith and jump into the pool. Put your total faith in Him and experience all He has to offer. But so many have found a comfortable place by the edge of the pool, making excuses. Jesus has a question for you today: "Do you want to get well?"

234. FINDING HOME

Krista and I spent this week in Malibu, California, at the Pepperdine lectureships. This is only the second time I have ever been to California. And I have to tell you, I could get used to this. We had a little free time on Tuesday, so we took off for a drive up the coast. It was a beautiful day. We got an upgrade on our rental car so I opened up the sunroof, put on my Ray Ban sunglasses, and hit the gas. We were on the Pacific Coast Highway with the Pacific Ocean on our left and the Santa Monica Mountains on our right. There was a cool breeze blowing the ocean air into the car. I felt like a real celebrity. Like I said, I could get used to this. But here is the strange thing; I began to miss Marshall, Texas. I just didn't feel right in California.

Being on the coast is not all that it is cracked up to be. When it came time to fill up the gas tank, we had to pay almost $6 a gallon. Even driving in the car, I got a sunburn on one side of my face and on one arm. When we took a walk down the beach, we had to walk over some rocks. I took a bad tumble and bruised my backside. I started looking forward to Saturday when we would return to our own house, and I could sleep in my own bed.

There is something to be said about the comforts of home. When you are someplace else, things just aren't quite right. It dawned on me that Marshall, Texas, is not my home either. As nice as it is, I'm not always comfortable there either. The Apostle Paul explained it best.

"But our citizenship is in heaven. And we eagerly await a Savior from there, the Lord Jesus Christ, who, by the power that enables him to bring everything under his control, will transform our lowly bodies so that they will be like his glorious body"
(Philippians 3:20-21).

I hope I never get too comfortable in this world. As nice as

California, Texas, and even Oklahoma are, they are not my home. I am a citizen of heaven. That's where I will finally be comfortable. That's my home.

235. NO FEAR

When I was a youth minister in the '90s, the slogan "No Fear" started popping up on T-shirts. It started with the big athletes, then the skater kids, then it seemed that everyone was wearing them. My friends and I just had to laugh for two reasons. First, all teens have fears. The reason most of them were wearing the "No Fear" shirt was the fear of not fitting in. The second reason this was funny to us was because if you lived with no fear, you would not live long. Fear is one of those neutral things. When fear is working correctly, it can save your life and save your soul. When fear is misused, it can stifle your life and keep you from being all God has designed you to be.

I have a new fear that was just triggered recently. I never thought I had a fear of heights. The other day, I saw that iconic picture of those steelworkers eating lunch on the beam of a high-rise building being constructed in New York. My stomach just flipped. They were just eating lunch and laughing, 840 feet above the ground with absolutely no safety ropes attached. So, I guess I have a fear of heights. But is that a bad thing? I don't need to be on a beam 69 floors above the ground. I believe that is fear working properly. I will gladly give fear that power in my life. However, if I allow fear to keep me from sharing the gospel with others, that is giving fear too much power. Giving fear too much power can keep you from setting goals and reaching for them. Allowing fear to reign in your life will keep you from some great blessings God has in store for you. So, how do we find the right balance? Consider this passage of scripture.

"For God has not given us a spirit of fear, but of power and of love and of a sound mind" (2 Timothy 1:7).

Paul is saying we should never let fear hinder us from a holy life and sharing the gospel with others. So, in that case, "No Fear" is the right motto. But when it comes to walking the high beams, I'm going to use my sound mind and stay on the ground.

236. YOU HAVE A STORY TO TELL

John 9 tells the story of a man who was born blind. He spent his evenings at home, living with his parents. He spent his days begging in the streets because there was nothing else he could do. But everything changed the day Jesus and His disciples walked by. The man could hear the disciples asking Jesus about the theology behind why the man was blind. But Jesus refused to engage in the theology of his blindness. Instead, Jesus spit on the ground, made some mud, placed it on his eyes, and told him to go down to the pool and wash it off. And in that instant, the man could see for the first time.

The Pharisees were brought in to investigate the situation. They pressed the man and his parents about how this drastic change occurred. The parents, who were afraid of the Pharisees, simply said, "Our son is a grown man, let him tell his story." The Pharisees, who were not fans of Jesus, basically said to the man, "Tell us the truth. We don't believe Jesus healed you, because He is a sinner." Listen to the man's response.

"He replied, 'Whether he is a sinner or not, I don't know. One thing I do know. I was blind but now I see!'" (John 9:25).

There are two ways to tell stories about ourselves. Our stories can stay focused on us, presenting us in the best light. Or our stories can put the focus on God by simply stating the difference He has made in our lives. Your testimony has great power. You don't have to have a powerful "Prodigal Son" story. The power of your story is found in the difference that God has made in your life and how He has saved you. So, share your story with others. But remember that you are not main character. We all have at least a little mud in our eyes. Put the focus on the One who took away the mud and gave us perfect vision.

237. SECOND BEST

Settling for second best—it's a trick as old as time, literally. Adam and Eve were in the garden, enjoying the best that God had to offer. Enter Satan. With a clean piece of fruit and a half-truth wrapped around a lie, they settled for second best. Esau did the same thing. Esau was the firstborn, and he had it all. He was set for life. But Jacob tempted him with a steaming pot of stew, and Esau sold out. He settled for a temporary full belly over a lifetime of blessings.

When it comes down to it, Satan is really a one-trick pony. He gets us to settle for the temporary satisfaction while we give up an eternity of heavenly blessings. Ask a kid if he would rather have a candy bar today or a new car when he is sixteen. He will settle for the candy bar every time. Ask a sixteen-year-old if he would rather have a new car or a retirement plan. He will take the car every time. We adults call that immaturity. But we are guilty of the same thing. Would you rather have a little cash today or a reputation of integrity? Would you rather have a little pleasure for a moment or a marriage of purity? The stakes are higher, but the temptation is all the same.

"Therefore we do not lose heart. Though outwardly we are wasting away, yet inwardly we are being renewed day by day. For our light and momentary troubles are achieving for us an eternal glory that far outweighs them all. So we fix our eyes not on what is seen, but on what is unseen, since what is seen is temporary, but what is unseen is eternal" (2 Corinthians 4:16-18).

It comes down to focus. Don't let Satan blur your vision with temporary treasures that are here today and gone tomorrow. Fix your eyes on eternal blessings, real blessings. Don't settle for second best.

238. GAME FACE

"It's time to put on your game face!" I must have heard that phrase a thousand times. Growing up playing sports, I knew the meaning behind this phrase. We would be in the locker room about to run onto the court or field and the coach would tell us, "It's time to put on your game face." That meant to look confident, bordering on arrogant, to try to intimidate our opponents. But here is the truth. Many times, I was not confident. There were times I knew we were outmatched by our opponents. There were times I was nursing an injury that would keep me from being at my best. But still, I tried to put on my "game face."

You may have never been in a locker room, but as Christians, we know what it means to put on our game face. For instance, you are having a heated argument on the way to worship. But before you get out of the car, time to put on your game face. Or you are saddened by a sudden loss or a tragic situation in your life, but as soon as you pull into the church parking lot, game face. For some reason, Christians have been taught not to show their real emotions. Even though you are hurting inside, when someone asks how you are doing, you respond with the standard answer, "I'm fine."

"The righteous cry out, and the Lord hears them; he delivers them from all their troubles. The Lord is close to the brokenhearted and saves those who are crushed in spirit" (Psalm 34:17-18).

The church is called a family for a reason. You can be real with your family. If you are hurting or upset, share that with your brothers and sisters in Christ. We are here to pray with you and bear each other's burdens. No life is perfect. Come be a part of this imperfect family.

239. ONE THING LEADS TO ANOTHER

It was an unusually warm day in early December in Glenpool, Oklahoma. Krista was at work and would not be home until after dark. I was home alone and decided to put up the Christmas lights on our new house. I imagined how happy she would be when she turned the corner and saw our home all lit up. So, I grabbed the lights and a ladder and got to work. It was taking longer than I thought, because about every five feet, I had to climb down and move the ladder. Then, I decided to climb onto the roof, thinking it would make the process much faster. I had to step on the top rung of the ladder to reach the roof. As I pressed up to the roof, the ladder toppled over. In my younger days, I would have just jumped off the roof. But I knew my knees and ankles could not handle the drop. So, there I was, stuck on my roof with the Christmas lights dangling and my cell phone inside the house. About 90 minutes later, as it was getting dark, a mother and her daughter were walking their dog down our sidewalk. I shouted at them to come help me. They stood the ladder back up, and I was able to make it back on solid ground.

Experts estimate we make 35,000 decisions a day. Most of those decisions seem very unimportant. But every decision we make sets the course for the next decision. One bad decision will lead you down the road with the potential of making more bad decisions with greater consequences. And before you know it, you find yourself in a place you never could have imagined. On the other hand, one good decision will lead you down the road with the potential of making more good decisions, which may lead to greater blessings. That makes each of your 35,000 decisions very important.

"Trust in the Lord with all your heart and lean not on your own understanding; in all your ways submit to him, and he will make your paths straight" (Proverbs 3:5-6).

One careless decision of putting up Christmas lights when no one else was home led me down a road that left me on my roof for an hour and a half. One careless decision in your life can lead you down a road to a dark place. So, trust God and submit to Him. That will put you on a path that will lead you straight to heaven.

240. KEEP PRESSING ON

"Those who cannot remember the past are condemned to repeat it." That is a quote from George Santayana, which has been requoted and misquoted hundreds of times. While there is some truth to that statement, it is not biblical. The truth in that quote is that we need to learn from the past. We need to know what steps were taken that led us to bad situations or bad decisions. And also, we need to know what steps were taken that led us to good situations and good decisions. But here is the problem with dwelling on the past. Satan will use it against you. Our enemy will use the past to puff us up or leave us stuck in a rut. If we continually dwell on our past successes, we will become prideful and arrogant. On the other hand, if we continually dwell on our past failings, we will become depressed and allow the mistakes of yesterday define our tomorrows.

The Apostle Paul had the right perspective on yesterday, today, and tomorrow.

"Not that I have already obtained all this, or have already arrived at my goal, but I press on to take hold of that for which Christ Jesus took hold of me. Brothers and sisters, I do not consider myself yet to have taken hold of it. But one thing I do: Forgetting what is behind and straining toward what is ahead, I press on toward the goal to win the prize for which God has called me heavenward in Christ Jesus" (Philippians 3:12-14).

If you look at Paul's past, he had many regrettable things on his resume. But after his conversion, he became a great servant in the Kingdom of God. Satan could have used either of those things against him. So, to avoid Satan's trap, Paul chose to focus on the future. Like all of us, your past will be chock-full of many failures and many successes. Don't let yesterday get in the way of your today or your tomorrows. Keep pressing on!

241. ASTRONAUTS, NINJAS, AND FOOTBALL PLAYERS

Take a room full of kindergarten students and ask them what they want to be when they grow up, and you will hear a variety of wild answers. How fun would this world be if every kindergartener's dream came true? There would be a lot more people up in space, we would have an abundance of Presidents, there would be cowboys everywhere, more football players than we could ever imagine, and ninjas would patrol the streets. Why doesn't this happen? The practical answer is reality. But the true answer is that adults squash their imagination, tone down their dreams, and guide them down a more reasonable path.

Jesus often spoke to audiences full of religious leaders. These men had memorized books of the Bible. They probably expected Jesus to stop and commend them on their religious commitments and the degrees they had earned. Instead, Jesus pointed to the children and told them that if they wanted to find real faith, they would need to follow the example of these children. They would need to trade in their weathered, complicated faith and regain a childlike sense of wonder. Why? Because nothing is impossible to kids. They only believe they can't when the grownups tell them they can't.

When our heads tell our hearts that our dreams are too big or that we should grow up and be more reasonable with our faith, we just need to stop, go to the park, and watch kids play. Last Friday night, we went to the park, and little Taya Anderson proclaimed she was Spiderman and proceeded to climb to the very top of a large rope web. Is she Spiderman? I'm not going to tell her otherwise. All I know is, she was standing at the top of the web. Children are the ones Jesus sent to be our guides because faith isn't figuring out what we're able to do; faith is deciding what we're going to do even when we think we can't.

"Jesus replied, 'What is impossible with man is possible with God'"
(Luke 18:27).

242. ORDEAL OR ADVENTURE?

In the fall of 1998, I was a youth minister in Bartlesville, Oklahoma. In our congregation, we had many St. Louis Cardinals fans. If you recall, 1998 was when Mark McGwire was chasing the homerun record. I thought it would be a great event to take a group to a game. Yes, it was a seven-hour drive, and we would have to stay overnight, but I thought I might get a few to go. So, I bought fifteen tickets. Those went quick. So, I bought fifteen more. Those went quick. When we left Bartlesville, we had forty people going with the hope of seeing Mark McGwire hit at least one homerun.

It was a hot Saturday afternoon when Mark McGwire came to bat in the bottom of the first inning. After a questionable called third strike, Mark turned and said a "no-no" to the umpire and was thrown out of the game. Thirty-nine people turned to look at me as if I caused this or that I could do something about it. We were forced to watch eight more innings of "McGwireless" baseball in the heat.

Disappointed, we headed to our vans for a long ride home. One of our vans started and then stalled in the parking lot. I got out to see what the problem was because that's what men do. All I could report back was that something had fallen off and something else was leaking. We sent thirty people home, and ten of us had to walk five miles to the garage while they worked on our van. Needless to say, we made it home around four in the morning. When the ten people looked at me, all I could say was, "Well, I promised you an adventure!"

That's life in a nutshell. Our best-laid plans can change in a heartbeat. You can do one of two things. You can grumble and complain that life is not fair. Or you can look at your new situation as an unexpected adventure. It boils down to this: Do you live with hope or fear? When the world throws a curveball at you, and you live in fear, you will instantly think of all the bad things that can happen. Or you can live with hope. When the curveball comes, you can see it as an adventure with things to see and lessons to learn. (We walked through parts of St. Louis that a tour guide will never show you.)

The world has thrown us a big curveball with this pandemic. Are you living in fear or living with hope?

"Have I not commanded you? Be strong and courageous. Do not be afraid; do not be discouraged, for the Lord your God will be with you wherever you go" (Joshua 1:9).

243. LET'S MAKE GOD SMILE!

When you try to picture humility, what comes to mind? The picture I get is usually some type of pushover who gives in to everything. Or I see someone who is a paid servant who always answers, "Yes, sir" or "No, sir." It is a little easier to picture the opposite of humility. One antonym of humility is arrogance. When I picture arrogance, I see someone who can't stop looking at themselves in the mirror. Or someone who is so into themselves, they can't or won't see other people. Paul gives us a good definition of humility in his letter to the Philippians.

"Do nothing out of selfish ambition or vain conceit. Rather, in humility value others above yourselves" (Philippians 2:3).

Humility doesn't insist we hide or make ourselves look small. Humble people aren't concerned with seeming less important. As a matter of fact, they just don't think about themselves much at all. They consider others. Considering others means thinking about them, praying for them, doing unselfish acts of love with no expectation of reciprocation.

Jesus was the ultimate example of humility. His entire agenda was for the betterment of others. Every healing, every miracle, every word He said was for lifting others up. Philippians 2 also says that Jesus humbled himself by becoming obedient to death—even death on a cross. Why did Jesus die on the cross? So we could find salvation through Him. That's humility.

God delights in humble people because they continue the work of Jesus. Humble people pray for God to open their eyes to the pain of people around them. They give in secret without a second thought. They don't keep track of all the good they've done. It's these kinds of people who make God smile.

244. WHAT'S IN A NAME?

This week at our JOY (Just Older Youth) group luncheon, I took a moment to brag on my Oklahoma City Thunder basketball team, which made it to the finals. The Thunder used to be the Seattle Super Sonics. They changed their name to Thunder when they moved, as an obvious reference to the weather. It is interesting how teams choose their names. The Thunder are playing the Indiana Pacers, who got their name from the pace car used in the Indianapolis 500. A few NBA team names are pretty obvious like the Miami Heat, Phoenix Suns, Denver Nuggets (because of the gold rush), Detroit Pistons (the Motor City and parts of an engine), Orlando Magic (Walt Disney's Magic Kingdom), Houston Rockets (the home of NASA) and the Philadelphia 76ers (the Declaration of Independence was signed in Philadelphia in 1976). Some are a little more obscure, like the Los Angeles Lakers. There are no lakes in the area. But the team was originally in Minnesota, the land of 10,000 lakes. And then there are the Memphis Grizzlies. Memphis is not known for their grizzly bear population. But the name was given to the team when they were located in Vancouver. But the most nonsensical name in the NBA is the Utah Jazz. That makes no sense unless you know that they used to be located in New Orleans. The point is that names have meanings.

"The disciples were called Christians first at Antioch" (Acts 11:26).

When the word Christian was first used, it was meant to be an insult. Believers in Christ were looked down on in society. Throughout time, in various places, being known as a Christian put a target on one's back. Many have been persecuted for wearing the name Christian. As believers today, we are blessed to wear the name Christian. Yes, Jesus Christ died for all people, but only those who believe in Him and follow His commands can be known as Christians.

During my life as an athlete, I have been a Townsend Tiger, a Del City Eagle, a York College Panther, and a Wayland Baptist University Pioneer. But only one name really matters: Christian. That is the only name that will get me to heaven.

245. JUST KEEP WALKING WITH GOD

If you haven't noticed, I have been limping around for the last couple of weeks. While doing a service project at camp a couple of weeks ago, a large bank of lockers fell on my leg. After two different sets of X-rays, I found out there were no breaks or fractures in my leg. After an MRI, I found out that there were no tears in muscles or ligaments. The problem is a lot of soft tissue damage and some pretty severe skin damage. The result is a bunch of pain, and, you guessed it, a limp. I have prayed and prayed for healing. I believe it is happening, just not as rapidly as I wish. I am beginning to identify with the words of David.

"Have mercy on me, Lord, for I am faint; heal me, Lord, for my bones are in agony" (Psalm 6:2).

The lesson I am learning is that healing takes time. The injury was immediate. But the healing process will be a journey. What is true about our physical healing can also be said about our spiritual healing. The forgiveness of God is immediate and complete. But for us, the process of healing can take time. Even though we are forgiven, we may still carry around the guilt and shame we feel from our sin. God promises forgiveness to all of those who turn to Him. But meanwhile, we still are walking through life with a "spiritual limp." The only cure is to keep growing closer to God. The more we walk with God, the more our limp fades away. Someday, this injury of mine will be a distant memory. But until then, I will continue the therapy that has been prescribed to me with the belief that tomorrow will be better than today.

246. WHO AM I?

There is only one truth. But throughout our days, we hear lots of different stories. As a parent, you will hear many conflicting stories. Our children tell stories from the time they are toddlers, just to get themselves out of trouble, to the time when they are teenagers, and the stakes are raised significantly. I remember lying in bed one night after a long evening of trying to find the truth in what our teenage son was telling us. I looked at Krista and said, "I'm tired of having to be a detective." The same is true when we watch the news. You could spend an hour watching Fox News and the next hour watching CNN, and it will leave you with the same question: "What is the truth?"

Let's turn the tables for a minute. What do you believe about yourself? You grew up believing what your parents say about you. Hopefully, good things. But in some cases, parents say hurtful things to their children. As you get a little older, you begin to believe what your friends say about you. Again, friends' opinions can be beneficial or detrimental to your self-concept. We will even listen to what strangers believe about us. People who do not know us can have amazing power over how we see ourselves.

So, which story should I believe? What is the truth? When you look in the mirror, what do you believe? So often, the opinion of others is how we measure our self-worth. Those opinions play in our minds, like tapes we can't turn off or erase. We may want to believe differently from what others say, but those tapes are embedded. So, what do I really believe about myself?

"Then King David went in and sat before the Lord, and he said: 'Who am I, Lord God, and what is my family, that you have brought me this far?'" (1 Chronicles 17:16).

Here is the true answer to this question. You have to go to the source of ultimate truth to understand who you are. If you wonder how your Creator feels about you, just read Ephesians 1. Here are some "truths" you will find there: You are holy; you are blessed; you are chosen; you are loved; you are redeemed; you are included; you are sealed with the promise of the Holy Spirit. YOU ARE A CHILD OF GOD!

So which story should I believe? I choose to believe the story of the One who created me.

247. JUST FIVE SECONDS

A couple of days ago, I was talking to my wife, and I said, "If I could only go back in time and change five seconds of my life, everything would be different." I would like to go back about four weeks ago when that bank of lockers fell on my leg. If I could change those five seconds, I would not be in so much pain at the moment. If I could change those five seconds, I would have avoided a hospital visit, along with six doctor's appointments (and counting). If I could change those five seconds I would not be having sleepless nights, and I would not be walking with a limp. Krista just looked at me and said, "A lot of people would like to go back in time and change five seconds of their life." We were both right. Sometimes, all it takes is a five-second decision to ruin a life.

In the same way, just a 5-second decision can change your life in a positive way. The moment you decide to commit your life to God can not only change your life, but it can also change your eternity. Decisions alter the course of your life. But your decision to follow Jesus can not only give you forgiveness for all of your sins, but it can also open the door for eternal life in heaven.

One more thought about five seconds. Actually, this will take a little less than five seconds. One day, the skies will open up, and our earthly lives will cease to exist.

"Listen, I tell you a mystery: We will not all sleep, but we will all be changed—in a flash, in the twinkling of an eye, at the last trumpet. For the trumpet will sound, the dead will be raised imperishable, and we will be changed" (1 Corinthians 15:51-52).

Such a short amount of time can make a world of difference. Make the most of every five seconds you are given.

248. TEXT MESSAGES

I have an evolving relationship with texting. When I first began to receive texts, I hated them. When my kids texted me, I would immediately call them back. It drove them crazy but I didn't want to type when I could just talk. As time has passed, it is now the best way to reach me. I can't always take a phone call, I will eventually get to my emails, and I seem to recall a thing called a "letter" that would come in the mail, but I haven't seen one of those in years. However, when I get a text, I will read and usually respond immediately.

In the book of Proverbs, Solomon shared the wisdom God blessed him with in short bursts, much like a text message you might receive on your phone. Solomon was the king of texting long before the phone was invented. Here are some of the "texts" Solomon sent:

"The mouths of fools are their undoing, and their lips are a snare to their very lives" (Proverbs 18:7).

"Walk with the wise and become wise, for a companion of fools suffers harm" (Proverbs 13:20).

"A gentle answer turns away wrath, but a harsh word stirs up anger" (Proverbs 15:1).

"Lazy hands make for poverty, but diligent hands bring wealth. He who gathers crops in summer is a prudent son, but he who sleeps during harvest is a disgraceful son" (Proverbs 10:4-5).

"There is a way that appears to be right, but in the end it leads to death" (Proverbs 14:12).

"When pride comes, then comes disgrace, but with humility comes wisdom"(Proverbs 11:2).

Fools give full vent to their rage, but the wise bring calm in the end"
(Proverbs 29:11).

"As iron sharpens iron, so one person sharpens another"
(Proverbs 27:17).

(Rich and poor have this in common: The Lord is the Maker of them
all" (Proverbs 22:2).

So much wisdom in so few words.

249. CHECK UNDER THE HOOD

We've all been there. The car we're driving starts sputtering, overheating, stalling, or completely dies. So, we do what we have to do —take it to a mechanic. We explain the problem to him and leave it in his capable hands. Imagine the next day you go to pick up your car. As you drive away, it immediately stalls out. You go back to the mechanic for an explanation. He says, "Yeah, it looked pretty bad, so I had it washed and waxed. I thought that made it look a lot better." Frustrated, you remind him of the problems and ask him to fix them. You return the next day to pick up your ca,r and it won't even start. The explanation from the mechanic this time was, "I gave it a new paint job and a sunroof. Looks great, huh?" Now you are furious as you remind him of the problems and demand that they be addressed. A week goes by, and your car is ready. Again, it will not start. His explanation this time. "It didn't seem to be running well, so I put some new tires on it. I think you'll be happy. They are top of the line!"

Sound stupid? Not so fast. Have you ever felt like your life is sputtering? Or you're having emotional problems? Or maybe you have just shut down completely? Our typical solution is to just smile our way through it. Just fake it till we make it. That is our way of just washing and waxing our problems. We haven't fixed anything. Or next, we try to buy things to change our attitude. We buy new clothes or golf clubs or jewelry. That's our version of a new paint job and a sunroof. We try to make the outside look prettier and happier. Still, we haven't fixed the problem. Then we try to adjust our lifestyle. We start new habits and break old habits. We change our actions, hoping that will change our attitudes. That is our version of buying new tires. But that still does not fix the root problem.

"Create in me a pure heart, O God, and renew a steadfast spirit within me" (Psalm 51:10).

All we wanted from the mechanic is to lift the hood and fix the real problem. To fix our lives, we must go to the heart of the problem. The problem is not appearance or lifestyle; it is a heart problem. If life is not all it should be, start by checking 'under the hood.' Get your heart right. Then you will be ready for some new paint and tires.

250. ARE WE LIVING IN FEAR?

I was born in 1967. Which means my childhood was spent living in the '70s. Looking back, I love that because my childhood was spent in a time where parents lived without a great deal of fear. After dinner I would often ask my parents, "Can I go play?" The response I remember most was, "Yes, but be home when the streetlights come on." So out the door I would go. No cell phone. No restrictions. No fear.

Then June 1, 1980, happened. It was a dark day. Not because I was entering my teenage years. But that was the day that CNN launched its twenty-four-hour news network. Before this, we heard the national news one time a day and the local news twice a day. In our town (Del City, Oklahoma), the newspaper came out once a week. If you were starved for more, you could get the *Daily Oklahoman*. The news was just a report of what was happening at the time without commentary or opinions. But all of that changed on June 1, 1980. A twenty-four-hour news network meant reporters had to dig for news and strive for ratings. What was the best formula they found to get people to tune in? FEAR! Trouble anywhere in the world was reported, and we were told how that affected us. Crime anywhere in the US was reported, and we were told that it could be happening in our neighborhood. By the way, CNN is not the only one guilty of this; they were just the first.

Looking back forty years later, I can see that innocence and freedom were slowly being replaced by fear and protection. Ignorance is not a good thing. We should be informed. But God's creation was never meant to live in constant fear.

"For God has not given us a spirit of fear, but of power and of love and of a sound mind" (2 Timothy 1:7).

I don't blame Ted Turner for all the problems in the world. But we have life stolen from us when we let fear rule our lives more than faith and love. We need to quit letting fear call the shots in our lives. Live boldly every day!

251. HE'S MY GRANDSON

I was blessed to have my grandson Judah at our house for a few days during the week of VBS. Krista had to work, so it was just Judah and Pop Pop on Monday and Tuesday. On Tuesday, we made a trip to Walmart. As we entered the store, a kind lady said, "Oh, what a cute boy." I responded, "Thanks, he's my grandson." So, for the next twenty minutes, Judah continued to repeat, "He's my grandson. He's my grandson." It was cute for a minute. But after about the fiftieth time of "He's my grandson," I began to long for the day when he could express some original thoughts, and I could hear what's really going on in that head of his.

At that age, kids are a lot like parrots. They catch on to a phrase and just repeat it over and over. It's sad when people go through life and never grow out of the parrot stage. Whether it is peer pressure, shyness ,or fear, they just go through life saying and doing what everybody else is saying and doing.

God made each of us to be special. There is no other you out there. I was making this point to the kids at VBS during our game time. Two classes in a row had sets of twins, which actually helped my point. I looked at them and said, "Even you two are different from each other."

"Yet you, Lord, are our Father. We are the clay, you are the potter; we are all the work of your hand" (Isaiah 64:8).

We are all clay in the hands of the potter. And God does not make the same pot twice. God made each of us not only to look different from everyone else but also to think differently from everyone else. Why? Because the world doesn't need a copy of someone else. The world needs you.

252. BAGGAGE

Almost thirty years ago, Krista and I were leaving on our honeymoon. We were going to spend a week in Cancun, Mexico. Neither of us had ever been out of the country. So, neither of us really knew what to expect. While I was packing, I wanted to make sure that I had the right clothes for every activity for every day. I needed to put clothes together that matched and looked cool. I needed the right shoes for every occasion. I needed to have every toiletry item imaginable. (Who knows if they have hair gel in Mexico?) I needed some books to read while we relaxed on the beach. I assumed that Krista was going through the same anxiety.

Needless to say, we over-packed. This became evident when we left our car behind at the airport, and it was just us and our baggage. Being a brand-new husband, I wanted to be a gentleman and help her with her bags, but I was having enough trouble with my own. We both struggled until we were able to check our bags. All was good until we got to Cancun and had to pick up our bags and make our way to the hotel.

We were exhausted and hurting when we finally reached the front desk. We checked in, got our key, and loaded up for the long walk to our room. At this time, a very small, older hotel employee asked, "Can I carry your bags to your room?" At first, we resisted. Finally, we said sure and waited for him to get a cart or something. He proceeded to pick up every bag by himself. He carried them to our room with a smile on his face. As he placed them in our room, he simply said, "Welcome to Cancun." I was amazed and embarrassed.

What a metaphor that is to our Christian life. We go through life carrying all the things we need along with all the things we believe we can't live without and other things that we just can't let go of. We struggle with every step, not knowing how long we can continue.

"Come to me, all you who are weary and burdened, and I will give you rest" (Matthew 11:28).

If you feel you have more than you can carry, accept the invitation of Jesus. Allow Him to carry the load. That is what He came here to do!

253. JUST PASSING IT ON

Last week I spoke the final words to my mother that I will ever get to say to her. She was lying in a bed in Hospice care, and I knew her time was short. So, I leaned down, kissed her forehead, and said, "Thank you for my faith." I don't believe that I would have a relationship with God had it not been for my mother. Thinking back on my childhood, I cannot remember a Sunday that we did not attend worship services. My dad worked nights, so it was up to Mom to wake us up and get three children dressed and sitting in Bible class. I remember many Sundays that I fought her every step of the way. But every Sunday, she persevered. And it didn't end there. Not only did she make sure we learned about faith, she lived it every day.

"But as for you, continue in what you have learned and have become convinced of, because you know those from whom you learned it, and how from infancy you have known the Holy Scriptures, which are able to make you wise for salvation through faith in Christ Jesus" (2 Timothy 3:14-15).

I have always said the goal of parenting is to plant the seed of faith in your children and move the ball a little farther down the field. To take what you were given and improve on it so the next generation can do the same. My mother did exactly that. And Mom, I hope I have made you proud. I have a strong Christian marriage, and I have served as a minister for thirty-four years. Krista and I have raised two children who are faithful believers and have married wonderful Christians. Our son is a youth minister and is teaching the next generation about living faithfully. Our daughter is a Bible class teacher and is raising her two boys in a faithful household. So many lives have been affected because of your faithfulness. Thank you, Mom!

254. LET ME CHECK MY CALENDAR

Does anyone remember the Palm Pilot? It was a big thing in the late 1990s and early 2000s. The Palm Pilot was a handheld PDA (personal digital assistant). If you had to schedule a meeting, you would get out your Palm Pilot and use your stylus to put that meeting on your calendar. That way, when someone asked you to meet with them, you could say, "Hold on. Let me check my calendar." Then you could pull out your very own personal digital assistant to see if you were available. You could also use your stylus on your little screen to write down notes that you could save and check later. And then—BONUS—you could also save people's contact information.

When I got my first Palm Pilot, I thought I was so important. I would carry it with me always and try to find opportunities to say, "Let me check with my personal digital assistant to see if I'm available." Now fast forward twenty-plus years. Everything that Palm Pilot did is now just a couple of seldom-used apps on my phone.

Do you think Jesus could have used a Palm Pilot? He was a busy man with many important things to do. But one thing Jesus taught us is that He was never too busy to be interrupted. When a little child or a person in need came to Him, Jesus never turned to His disciples and asked them to find a slot later in the day when He wasn't booked. When Jesus was on His way to heal an important man's daughter, and a bleeding woman touched His garment, He didn't respond by saying, "I'm busy at the moment; check with me tomorrow." When Jesus saw a man in a sycamore tree, He didn't check His calendar to see if He had any time available next week. Jesus's earthly life was full of interruptions, and that was just fine with Him.

"'What do you want me to do for you?' Jesus asked him"
(Mark 10:51).

Jesus was always ready at the drop of a hat to care, love, encourage, heal, teach, or just spend time with others. How do you want to be remembered? For how busy you were—or how available you were?

426

255. A SUCCESSFUL FAILURE

Recently I read a book titled *Losing My Voice to Find It* by Mark Stuart. It is the autobiography of a man who was a rock star but literally lost his voice. Mark Stuart was the founder and lead singer of the group Audio Adrenaline. I started listening to their music in the mid-nineties. I had the privilege of meeting Mark one time. I took my youth group to see them in concert. Before the music started, the youth ministers were called into a back room of the arena. Mark walked in, shook our hands, and stood up on a chair to speak to us. He said, "I don't take for granted that God has given me the opportunity to stand in front of 10,000 teenagers tonight. Most of them came for the music, but we came to give them a message. That message is to put their hope in Jesus Christ." He then led us in a prayer and blessed us for the work we were doing.

Audio Adrenaline was a big deal. They won two Grammy awards and multiple Dove awards. For more than a decade, they headlined arena tours around the world. At the peak of their success, Mark lost his voice. Not just for a night, but permanently. But that is not the end of his story. Mark is the son of a preacher/missionary. His dad had a love for the people of Haiti, and that love was passed down to Mark. After losing his voice he focused his attention on the lost children of Haiti. He founded the "Hands and Feet Project," which has raised millions of dollars for orphans in Haiti. When hurricanes and earthquakes devastated Haiti, Mark was there. He became the connection on the ground for CNN, MSNBC, and the BBC.

"And we know that in all things God works for the good of those who love him, who have been called according to his purpose"
(Romans 8:28).

I have started one business in my life. When I resigned from youth ministry, Krista and I developed a seminar called "The Journey

Home." It was a weekend seminar to be held in churches, designed to enhance communication within the family unit. We presented the seminar three times to great success. But the business failed. Had the business not failed, I don't believe I would have ever become a preacher. I believe that is why I loved Mark's book so much. Are you a failure because you are a rock star and lost your voice, or your business failed? The world may see it that way. But when you see it through God's eyes, it looks different. With God, a failure is just a step to get you where He needs you the most.

256. RESUMES

The Apostle Paul was a great man. I think we can all agree on that. In Philippians 3, Paul sets down his usual gracious, humble self and does a bit of bragging.

"If someone else thinks they have reasons to put confidence in the flesh, I have more: circumcised on the eighth day, of the people of Israel, of the tribe of Benjamin, a Hebrew of Hebrews; in regard to the law, a Pharisee; as for zeal, persecuting the church; as for righteousness based on the law, faultless" (Philippians 3:4-6).

That may not sound so impressive to us. But let me assure you, that is a packed resume. It would be like someone today saying, "I am among the greatest who has ever lived. I was born into a wealthy, respected family. My parents raised me right. I have more college degrees and titles than I care to mention, and I have the wealth and success to prove it. But am I a good man? Just ask anyone. There is not a single person who has anything bad to say about me. I am a leader in business and a leader in the church."

It would be an honor to know someone like that. But as Paul continues writing, he turns an unexpected corner.

"But whatever were gains to me I now consider loss for the sake of Christ. What is more, I consider everything a loss because of the surpassing worth of knowing Christ Jesus my Lord, for whose sake I have lost all things. I consider them garbage, that I may gain Christ" (Philippians 3:7-8).

Paul is saying that the greatest things we can do in our lifetime are garbage (his words) in comparison to simply knowing Jesus. Is Paul saying that being a successful person is not important? Not at all. Paul put years of time and effort into becoming a successful, respected person. But he is saying to keep it in perspective. If you become President, CEO, doctor, or emperor but miss out on knowing Jesus, you have missed what really matters.

257. THE NEXT CHAPTER

This week I got to say "hello" and "goodbye" to a whole bunch of college students. On Wednesday, Travis and I set up a booth on the ETBU campus and met with dozens of incoming students to our community. That same night at our Wednesday evening service, we wished several of our young adults the best as we sent them away to college. Do you remember that time in your life? Maybe it was college, leaving for the military, or maybe it was just leaving home to get your own apartment. It is that time when you are literally starting a new chapter in your life. It doesn't just happen when we turn eighteen. It also happens when we accept a new job or leave an old job. It happens when we say, "I do." It happens when we retire. One chapter of our lives ends, and another begins.

The thing about new chapters is that we never know what is about to happen. We may think we know, but life will always present us with many twists and turns we did not see coming. For some, that is exciting. For others, a new chapter in life will fill you with anxiety. How can you know that this new chapter in life will be okay? David wrote a Psalm that will ease your mind as you turn the page and begin the next chapter in your life.

"The Lord says, 'I will make you wise. I will show you where to go. I will guide you and watch over you'" (Psalm 32:8).

"Wicked people have many troubles. But the Lord's love surrounds those who trust him" (Psalm 32:10).

Don't begin a new chapter in your life without trusting the Lord and following His lead. Then we have the assurance that the next chapter in our life will be okay!

258 DON'T BE DEFINED BY YESTERDAY

"That's not who I am, it is just something I did." That sounds like either a lame excuse or a justification for some bad behavior. But let's look at it from another perspective. While at camp with the teens last summer, we went to see a movie on Saturday night. As we were leaving the theater into a dark parking lot, I was searching for our van. I was not looking down, and I stepped off of a curb. The next thing I know I am bumbling and stumbling on the pavement. I don't know what hurt worse, my pride or my knees, wrist, and shoulder. Even though my pride took a big hit, I got right back up and continued walking. A few times during the week the teens reminded me of my fall, but they didn't have to—the bruised knees and sore wrist were all the reminder I needed. So, here's the deal. Yes, I'm the guy who fell. But no, I'm not the guy who falls. I may fall again someday. But one fall in the past or a fall I may have in the future does not define me.

I wish we could all apply that lesson to our walk with God. We have all bumbled and stumbled over some sins in the past. But we do not have to let that define us. Others may even remind us of our past sins, but they don't have to. We have the pain and the scars to remind us. We could all learn a lesson from Paul.

> *"Brothers and sisters, I do not consider myself yet to have taken hold of it. But one thing I do: Forgetting what is behind and straining toward what is ahead, I press on toward the goal to win the prize for which God has called me heavenward in Christ Jesus"* (Philippians 3:13-14).

At one time in Paul's life, Christians were his sworn enemy. He was solely focused on having all believers in Christ arrested and killed. But

Paul refused to let that define him. His new focus was to serve God and spread the word about Jesus. Paul understood that he is not defined by yesterday. He is defined by who he is today and what he is striving for tomorrow. So, like Paul, I'm still up and walking forward. I'm just extra aware of curbs that may trip me up.

259. THE VIEW FROM THE TOP

My son just got back from spending a week in the mountains of Colorado with his girlfriend and her family. While there, he spent some quality family time and helped out with some chores around the cabin. Brandyn and Emily were able to sneak away a few days and do some hiking. They sent me a picture of them standing on the summit of a mountain with a sign in their hands. The sign read, "Mt. Sherman —Elevation 14,036." It took a few minutes for me to remember that Mount Sherman was the first mountain in Colorado that I ever summited. I texted them back and told them that I stood exactly where they were twenty-four years earlier. That climb happened with my youth group from Bartlesville, Oklahoma, on our first Wilderness Trek.

I now remember the day vividly. We began hiking before the sun came up. Along the way several of the teens decided that they could not make it to the top. I spent the hike encouraging, challenging, and pushing them up the mountain. When we got to the final push to the summit around noon, I was spent. It took the encouragement of my intern and other sponsors to get me to the top. I will never forget standing on the top of that mountain. It was breathtaking. Pictures do not do justice to feeling like you are standing on top of the world. Here are a few things I learned that day. First, the climb to the summit is incredibly hard. Second, the summit comes just after you feel like you can't go another step. And third, the view is worth the struggle.

The mountains are a great spiritual teaching tool. Our walk with Christ is not an easy road to take. Many times along the way, you will feel like giving up. The blessings of God seem to arrive immediately following a difficult time of testing. And once we receive the blessings from God, we realize that the struggle was worth it. That is true in our earthly lives, and I know it will be true in our eternal lives.

*"So let's not get tired of doing what is good. At just the right time
we will reap a harvest of blessing if we don't give up"*
(Galatians 6:9).

So, hang in there. Remember that something breathtaking is only a few steps away.

260. HAVE YOU EVER SEEN A BIRD MOW THE LAWN?

Okay, I realize how stupid this question sounds. But I promise it will make sense. Don't spend any time trying to figure out the physics of a bird being able to start and push a mower. And don't delve too deeply into the animal kingdom to find out which birds eat grass and how much can they eat. The answer to the question is much simpler than all that.

Have you ever seen a bird mow the lawn? Many people from the Boston area can tell you yes. My favorite basketball player of all time is Larry Bird. He was a very simple lower-class boy from the small town of French Lick, Indiana. He just happened to have the drive and an amazing talent to play basketball. After college, he was drafted by the Boston Celtics. To buy a mansion in a gated community was not in his nature. So, he bought a house in a Boston suburb that was very middle class. It seemed ridiculous to him to hire someone to mow his yard. He was raised to take care of the things he had. So, when the Boston Celtics had a home game on Sunday, Larry would spend Saturday taking care of his yard. As he cut his grass, hundreds of people would gather just to watch and take pictures. They could not believe that the MVP of the NBA would do something as common as mowing the yard. Larry Bird considered it an honor to be a homeowner and took pride in making his yard look nice.

"Humble yourselves before the Lord, and he will lift you up"
(James 4:10).

Here's the point: You and I were lowly sinners when the King of Kings called us to be a part of His kingdom. Is there any service in this kingdom that is beneath us? If God calls us to service in any capacity in His kingdom, we should humbly and enthusiastically get to work!

261. MIRROR, MIRROR ON THE WALL

Take a look in the mirror. What do you see? For me, I see a guy who still has a full head of hair. A little gray is sneaking in, but it still covers my head. I see eyes that are still blue, even though they look tired. I see a few wrinkles and a couple of age spots, but I feel like I have earned every one of them. Now look a little deeper in the mirror. What do you really see? For me, I see a guy who has a lot to be proud of but with a number or regrets. I see a guy who is committed to God and trying to live right but has fallen short.

"So God created mankind in his own image, in the image of God he created them; male and female he created them"
(Genesis 1:27).

When God made you, He gave you individual attention. You are unique. There is no other who is just like you. But in each of us, He added one special ingredient. God added His image to each of us. The fallen world we live in has tried to taint and tarnish that image, but it is still there. Somewhere deep within you lies the very image of God. God loves you, and He has put in you the ability to love Him and to love others. That leads us to part two of this exercise.

Take a look around. What do you see? Daily you will see all sorts of people. Some are lovable. Some are not so lovable. When you run across those who are not so lovable, just remember:God made them with the same care and love that He made you. They were also made in the image of God. Keeping that in mind makes it harder to hate or discriminate against others. When those negative feelings toward others creep in, just head back to the mirror and take a good deep look. God loves you, and God loves them. Try to do the same.

262. TO MY FELLOW WORRYWARTS

I'm worried. I'm worried about this global pandemic. I'm worried how this pandemic will affect the future of the church. I'm worried how this pandemic will affect the life of my baby grandson. I'm also worried that my neighbor is secretly listening to my conversations. I'm worried that the moles in my yard are destroying the foundation of my house. I'm worried that all the single socks I've lost through the years have gathered together and are coming to get me. I'm worried that I didn't actually pass my kindergarten class and I'm going to have to go back and repeat it. Well, I'm just worried.

Worry is a life stealer. If I spend today worrying about tomorrow, what have I accomplished today? Worry will not only occupy your mind, but it can also destroy your health. Can you imagine God worrying about anything? When Jesus was in the flesh, did you ever see Him worrying? By the way, Jesus had a lot of things He could have been worried about. Not only did Jesus refuse to worry, He had a lot to say to us worrywarts. Remember these "red letter" words from the sermon on the mount:

"Therefore I tell you, do not worry about your life, what you will eat or drink; or about your body, what you will wear. Is not life more than food, and the body more than clothes? Look at the birds of the air; they do not sow or reap or store away in barns, and yet your heavenly Father feeds them. Are you not much more valuable than they? Can any one of you by worrying add a single hour to your life? And why do you worry about clothes? See how the flowers of the field grow. They do not labor or spin. Yet I tell you that not even Solomon in all his splendor was dressed like one of these. If that is how God clothes the grass of the field, which is

here today and tomorrow is thrown into the fire, will he not much more clothe you—you of little faith?" (Matthew 6:25-30).

Why do you think Jesus told us to look at the birds and the flowers? I believe that He asked us to focus on things we can actually see rather than spending our time and energy focused on things that may or may not ever be a problem. I found this quote that puts worry in perspective: "Worry is worshiping the problem."

How would your life change if you turned from worry and turned to worship? Take the time you spend worrying and use it thank God for His blessings and His promises. That would improve my life dramatically. Besides, I'm not even sure if my kindergarten teacher is still alive.

263. THE COMPARISON GAME

While I was in college, I went back to my original home of Muskogee, Oklahoma, for a family event. While I was there, one of my cousins said to me, "Every time I see a college basketball game come on TV, I watch to see if you are playing." Yes it was true that I was on scholarship playing college basketball. However, York College was never going to show up on ESPN. While I was proud that I was playing college basketball, the comment made me realize that there were thousands of players who were so much better than me. No matter who you are, or what you do, or how good you are, the comparison game is always dangerous. It will do one of two things. It can make you feel bad about yourself because you just don't measure up to the others. Or it will make you arrogant, thinking how much better you are than the others. Neither of which will improve your mental health.

The comparison game is not good for our spiritual health either. If we compare ourselves to all the "perfect" people at church, it is easy to get discouraged, thinking we will never measure up and wondering how God could ever love us. However, if we look around at others and think we are so much better than all of them, it will fill us with the wrong kind of pride that doesn't please God. The only spiritual comparison we need to make is to compare ourselves to Jesus. Then we realize He is perfect, and all of us fall short. But here is a verse that can give us security and make us feel better about ourselves.

"No, in all these things we are more than conquerors through him who loved us" (Romans 8:37).

Through Christ, we are all victorious. So, stop comparing yourself to others and go be the best you as possible.

264. HERE'S MUD IN YOUR EYE

One day, Jesus and His disciples encountered a man who had been blind from birth. After a brief discussion of why this man was born blind, Jesus proclaimed, "I am the light of the world." Jesus then proceeded to heal the man of his blindness. Notice the method of healing that Jesus chose to use.

"After saying this, he spit on the ground, made some mud with the saliva, and put it on the man's eyes" (John 9:6).

We know that Jesus was able to heal just by speaking. Other times, Jesus chose to heal by touch. But this time, Jesus chose to spit in the dirt, scoop up the mud, and rub it on the man's face. Sounds gross, but it gets worse. Jesus instructed the man to walk through town with the mud on his face to wash it off in the pool of Siloam. Only then would he receive healing. Why would Jesus opt for this method of healing? I have a theory.

Last week my daughter sent us a picture of our two-year-old grandson named Jordan. He had been playing in the park, and his face and hands were covered in mud. Everyone else noticed the mud, but Jordan could have cared less. He was just a kid with a heart full of joy. There is a reason that Jesus said in Matthew 18:3, *"Truly I tell you, unless you change and become like little children, you will never enter the kingdom of heaven."* Children value the joy in their hearts over the opinions of others. The man walking through the crowd with mud on his face was not worried about what others thought of his appearance. He was full of joy, believing Jesus had cured him of his ailment. So, who cares if you have mud in your eye as long as you have the joy of the Lord in your heart?

265. BE REAL

It's that time of year again. That time of year when, for one night, we put on a costume and pretend to be something we are not. For kids, this can be a lot of fun. They get to play dress up and pretend to be a superhero or a cartoon character they love. For one night, they get to be Spiderman, Buzz Lightyear, or a princess, and they are rewarded with a big bag of candy. We take a lot of pictures and let them enjoy the night. Some adults are not happy letting the children have all the fun. However, adults tend to choose their costumes a little differently than the kids. Adults usually go with something really scary, someone in the news, or a celebrity.

That's all good and fun as long as we keep it to one night. We have a problem when we wake up every morning and put on a costume. Then we go through the day pretending to be something we are not. As adults, we can get so good at it, we can fool a lot of people. And at times, we begin to believe our own lie.

"Woe to you, teachers of the law and Pharisees, you hypocrites! You are like whitewashed tombs, which look beautiful on the outside but on the inside are full of the bones of the dead and everything unclean. In the same way, on the outside you appear to people as righteous but on the inside you are full of hypocrisy and wickedness" (Matthew 23:27-28).

The only people Jesus took issue with were those who were pretending to be something they were not. He had harsh words for the ones who were faking it. But you see Jesus showing compassion and speaking kindly to people who were sinners and had really messed up in life. What is the difference? It's not the failings; it's the honesty. One of my favorite quotes from Abraham Lincoln is, "You can fool some of the people all of the time, and you can fool all of the people some of the time, but you cannot fool all of the people all of the time." If I could be so bold as to add one line to his quote, "You can't fool God any of the time."

So, be real with God and with everyone around you. Your honesty will be appreciated and rewarded.

266. A WORK IN PROGRESS

Over the past several months, I have loved taking a few minutes of our morning worship and sharing a little "sermonette" for the little children. We have read books, broken sticks, sung songs, discussed scripture, and had a water pitcher that seemed to never run out of water. I have loved the way they listen and participate. However, we have had a couple of moments when one or more of the children were having a bad morning. A sibling has been hit, tears have been shed, harsh words have been said, and some have just wandered off. After one of these incidents, I have never thought that any of these children were bad kids. They were just having a bad moment. I know that they all have a lot of room to grow. And God, with our help, will continue to grow them into wonderful members of God's family. We can all understand that children are a work in progress.

"... being confident of this, that he who began a good work in you will carry it on to completion until the day of Christ Jesus"
(Philippians 1:6).

Can we give the same grace we extend to our children to others? Dr. Phil has said, "When someone shows you who they are, believe them." I believe that to a certain extent. But it doesn't tell the entire story. There are too many examples in the Bible that teach us otherwise.

Paul used to be a man who persecuted Christians. But did that define his entire life? Peter used to be a man who spoke up to quickly, could not control his actions, and denied Christ. But did that define his entire life? I could go on and on, but I think you get the point. When we know someone's past, see someone acting up, or just being plain old evil, that may define them in the moment. But that does not define their entire life. God is still working on them. Instead of focusing on who they were or who they are, we need to focus on what they can become through the power of God.

One last thought: When you look in the mirror, you know exactly who you have been and who you are today. But always remember that God is not finished with you yet. If you allow God to do some work on you, He will shape you into a beautiful masterpiece.

267. JUST TRAVELING THROUGH

I have been on Wilderness Trek multiple times. On Wilderness Trek, the group begins at the company's headquarters, where we load up our backpacks with food, clothing, cooking supplies, our sleeping bag, and a tent. Then it is off to low camp, where we leave behind all of life's luxuries that we have become accustomed to. The next five days are spent hiking, rappelling, attempting to summit a mountain, and smelling bad. I'm sure there were many rules we had to follow, but I only remember one. Our guide told us, "While we are out here, leave nothing but footprints and take nothing but pictures." What he was saying is that we are not the owners of this mountain; we are only traveling through. So, while we are here, we must be good stewards and try to leave it better than we found it.

Among the many life lessons learned on trek, this one may be the most profound. We are not residents of this world; we are just passing through. While we are here, God has blessed us with many beautiful things and wonderful people. We will also face many challenging moments to overcome and difficult people who will test us. But one thing is certain, we can't take anything with us when we leave. So, enjoy the journey, soak in the beauty, and make the most of every opportunity to love those around you. But remember not to get distracted by the things of this world. They are not ours for the taking.

"What is your life? You are a mist that appears for a little while and then vanishes" (James 4:14).

One last thought. Our guide told us to leave nothing but footprints. When we leave this world, we will leave our footprints behind. Make sure the footprint you leave behind will be one of love and joy. Leave this world better than you found it.

268. FIND YOUR SWEET SPOT

Have you ever heard the phrase "your sweet spot"? Every golfer knows what it means to hit your sweet spot. It happens when your swing is just right, and you hit the ball on the exact spot on the club that the designers intended. The result? It seems like it takes no effort, and the ball goes high, long, and straight down the fairway, exactly where you planned. Every baseball player understands their sweet spot. When you hit the ball perfectly on the barrel of the bat, and it soars toward the fence. That happened a lot for me this past softball season. Not as a batter. I was the pitcher. I saw a lot of guys hit the sweet spot.

Do you know that you have a "sweet spot" in life? Some are living in it every day, some are still searching for it, and some have given up hope of ever finding it. Your designer took the time to make you unique and give you a sweet spot.

"The Spirit has given each of us a special way of serving others"
(1 Corinthians 12:7).

God didn't skip you or forget about you. God has given you a uniquely special gift to be used in His Kingdom. That is your sweet spot. If you would rather go to the dentist than stand up and preach, then preaching is not your sweet spot. If you would rather swim in the sewer than lead a song, then song leading is not your sweet spot. But keep searching for your sweet spot. God has never added anyone to the church just to sit on a pew. You are a part of the body, and you have a function that is necessary for the body to be made whole. The Apostle Paul told the young minister Timothy, in 2 Timothy 1:6, *"For this reason I remind you to kindle afresh the gift of God."* The church needs you to find your sweet spot. We are incomplete without you.

269. AND THEY LIVED HAPPILY EVER AFTER

Could you open a book, read one chapter in the middle, and fully understand the entire book? The answer is no. All you would have is a brief glimpse at a moment in the story. You would not have the entire story. You would not know all the things that led up to that moment. And you obviously would not know how the story ends. The same could be said about our lives. One brief moment does not tell the entire story. Could you imagine the misunderstanding you would have if you just flipped through the Bible and read a page here and a page there?

If you just read 1 Samuel 11, you could conclude that David was womanizing king who used his power for his own selfish desires. You would miss the fact that he was chosen by God to be a king and would forever be known as a man after God's own heart.

If you just read Exodus 2, you would see Moses as a murdering coward who ran to the desert to hide from Pharaoh. You would not see Moses standing before Pharaoh demanding that he release the Israelites. You would not see Moses standing before God and receiving the Ten Commandments. You would miss God using this man to lead His people to the promised land.

If you just read Genesis 37 and 39, you would see Joseph as a hated brother who was sold into slavery and a falsely accused man condemned to prison. You would miss him becoming the second-most-powerful man in Egypt.

If you just read Matthew 26, you would see Peter as a weeping, broken man who denied even knowing Jesus. You would miss him becoming a great preacher and missionary.

The point is that one chapter does not define your life. All of us have some good chapters and some bad chapters in our past. And we will most likely have some good and bad chapters in our future. But one chapter does not tell the whole story. Don't let one chapter define your life. Realize that today, you are in the middle of one of your chapters. God is still writing your story. Hold on to hope. God loves to write stories with a happy ending.

"… being confident of this, that he who began a good work in you will carry it on to completion until the day of Christ Jesus"
(Philippians 1:6).

270. A LEGACY OF LOVE

Everyone in this world is known for something. At a minimum, we are known as being a member of a family. We are a son or daughter, brother or sister, father or mother. But outside of that, how are you known? We are known as being an employee or a boss. We are known for our opinions. We are known for our accomplishments. And sadly, we are sometimes known by our failings.

All those things are important. But what you are known for will directly affect how you will be remembered. Will I be remembered as a devoted husband? Will I be remembered as a loving father? Will I be remembered as a dedicated minister? Will I be remembered as a committed Christian? Will I be remembered as a faithful friend? Will I be remembered as someone who was kind to strangers? Will I be remembered as someone who was a friend to the friendless? Will I be remembered as someone who put others first? What will my legacy be?

The legacy you leave behind will not be from one single thing you do in your lifetime. Your legacy will be formed by the character you display over time. There is only one formula for leaving a positive legacy. It all boils down to the way you love.

The Apostle Paul put it this way:

"Do everything in love" (1 Corinthians 16:14).

Jesus said it this way:

"By this everyone will know that you are my disciples, if you love one another" (John 13:35).

John, the disciple whom Jesus loved, had this to say:

"Dear friends, since God so loved us, we also ought to love one another" (1 John 4:11).

How do you want to be remembered? Do you want to be remembered well? Leave a legacy of love.

SCRIPTURE REFERENCES

- Genesis 1:27—pages 367 and 438
- Genesis 6:7-8—page 379
- Genesis 12:1—page 222
- Exodus 16:4—page 86
- Deuteronomy 6:4-7—page 290
- Deuteronomy 11:19—page 356
- Deuteronomy 31:8—page 35
- Joshua 1:9—page 407
- Joshua 24:15—pages 8 and 9
- 1 Samuel 16:7—page 348
- 1 Samuel 17:8-11—page 41
- 1 Samuel 17:47—page 119
- 2 Samuel 16:7—page 163
- 1 Kings 19:11-12—page 149
- 1 Chronicles 17:16—page 412
- Nehemiah 4:16-17—page 114
- Esther 4:14—page 245
- Psalm 6:2—pages 55 and 411
- Psalm 7:17—page 192
- Psalm 9:1—page 192
- Psalm 23:4—page 347
- Psalm 25:4-5—page 21
- Psalm 32:8—page 431
- Psalm 32:10—page 431
- Psalm 34:17-18—page 400
- Psalm 34:18—page 93
- Psalm 46:10—page 143
- Psalm 51:10—page 417
- Psalm 51:12—page 350
- Psalm 70:5—page 211

- Romans 14:19—page 333
- Romans 15:7—pages 15 and 253
- 1 Corinthians 2:9—page 70
- 1 Corinthians 6:19—pages 16 and 81
- 1 Corinthians 10:13—page 357
- 1 Corinthians 11:1—page 169
- 1 Corinthians 12:7—page 448
- 1 Corinthians 13:1-3—page 177
- 1 Corinthians 13:4-8—page 263
- 1 Corinthians 13:11—page 311
- 1 Corinthians 13:12—page 385
- 1 Corinthians 13:13—page 252
- 1 Corinthians 15:51-52—page 414
- 1 Corinthians 15:52—page 89
- 1 Corinthians 15:57—page 19
- 1 Corinthians 15:57-58—page 89-90
- 1 Corinthians 16:14—page 451
- 2 Corinthians 1:3-4—page 72
- 2 Corinthians 3:18—page 364
- 2 Corinthians 4:8-9—page 162
- 2 Corinthians 4:15—page 3
- 2 Corinthians 4:16—page 272
- 2 Corinthians 4:16-18—page 399
- 2 Corinthians 4:18—page 181
- 2 Corinthians 5:17—pages 16 and 371
- 2 Corinthians 5:20—page 244
- 2 Corinthians 5:21—page 15
- Galatians 1:10—page 142
- Galatians 4:7—page 15
- Galatians 5:1—page 15
- Galatians 5:14—page 231
- Galatians 5:22-23—page 288
- Galatians 6:9—page 435
- Ephesians 1:3—page 16
- Ephesians 1:4—page 16
- Ephesians 1:7—page 16

- Ephesians 2:4-5—pages 62 and 145
- Ephesians 2:8-9—pages 11, 60, and 129
- Ephesians 2:8-10—page 46
- Ephesians 2:10—page 16
- Ephesians 2:19-20—page 326
- Ephesians 3:16-19—pages 375-376
- Ephesians 3:20—page 274
- Ephesians 3:20-21—page 201
- Ephesians 3:21—page 327
- Ephesians 4:2—page 234
- Ephesians 4:29—pages 232 and 239
- Ephesians 4:32—page 276
- Ephesians 5:1-2—page 303
- Ephesians 5:25-27—page 67
- Philippians 1:6—pages 352, 445, and 449
- Philippians 1:27—page 332
- Philippians 2:3—page 408
- Philippians 2:3-4—page 294
- Philippians 3:4-6—page 429
- Philippians 3:7-8—page 429
- Philippians 3:12-14—page 403
- Philippians 3:13-14—page 432
- Philippians 3:20—page 16
- Philippians 3:20-21—page 394
- Philippians 4:4—pages 185 and 287
- Philippians 4:7-8a—page 132
- Philippians 4:13—page 354
- Philippians 4:19—page 189
- Colossians 1:17—page 83
- Colossians 2:13-14—page 383
- Colossians 3:12—page 227
- Colossians 3:12-14—page 53
- Colossians 3:14—page 333
- Colossians 3:17—page 174
- 1 Thessalonians 5:11—pages 265 and 285
- 1 Thessalonians 5:11-13—page 267

- 1 Timothy 1:16—page 204
- 2 Timothy 1:6—page 448
- 2 Timothy 1:7—pages 396 and 419
- 2 Timothy 1:9—page xvii
- 2 Timothy 3:14-15—page 424
- 2 Timothy 4:7-8—pages 179-180
- Titus 2:11—page 75
- Hebrews 4:13
- Hebrews 6:19-20—page 79
- Hebrews 8:12—page 57
- Hebrews 10:23-25—page 187
- Hebrews 10:24-25—page 4
- Hebrews 10:36—page 190
- Hebrews 11:1—page 112
- Hebrews 12:2—page 169
- James 1:17—page 34
- James 1:22—page 368
- James 2:5—page 126
- James 2:14—page 115
- James 2:26—page 115
- James 3:3-5—page 289
- James 4:10—page 437
- James 4:14—page 447
- James 5:16—page 320
- 1 Peter 1:3—page 140
- 1 Peter 2:11—page 49
- 1 Peter 4:8—page 48
- 1 Peter 4:10—page 213
- 2 Peter 3:8-9—page 26
- 2 Peter 3:9—page 380
- 1 John 1:9—page 18
- 1 John 2:1-2—page 31
- 1 John 2:17—pages 112 and 334
- 1 John 3:1—pages 20, 43, and 51
- 1 John 3:23—page 236
- 1 John 4:11—page 452

- 1 John 4:11-12—pages 247 and 336
- 1 John 4:18—pages 220 and 358
- 2 John 1:6—page 151
- Revelation 21:3—page 299
- Revelation 21:4—pages 94 and 299

ACKNOWLEDGMENTS

Thank you, first and foremost to my wife, Krista. You have seen the best and worst of me and continue to love me anyway. I know that I would not be the man of God I am today if not for your consistent grace and mercy. You are a woman after God's own heart.

Brandyn and Tori, the greatest son and daughter a father could hope for. You have given me a lifetime of illustrations and have even allowed me to share a few of them. Watching each of you love God and love others is a joy.

Mom, who is no longer with us. Thank you for planting the seed of faith deep within my heart.

Kent Treat and Melissa Pierce, my older brother and sister. You have each blazed the trail in front of me by showing the value of faith, family, and commitment.

Clark Avenue Church of Christ in Granite City, Illinois. During our nine years together you showered me with love and encouragement as I learned how to preach. Thank you for being a key part of raising and shaping my children.

Eastern Hills Church of Christ in Marshall, Texas, my current church family. You have made a difference in my life as we strive together to make a difference in this world.

Marla Caton, Kristy Puesta and Davlyn Hollingshead. It is a pleasure to serve on staff with you as a part of the Eastern Hills family.

ABOUT THE AUTHOR

Phillip Treat was born in Muskogee, Oklahoma, a true Okie from Muskogee. At the age of three, he moved to Del City, Oklahoma, where he graduated from Del City High School. Phillip played basketball for York College and Wayland Baptist University, where he graduated with a BS in psychology in 1989. Later that year, he married Krista Starr. Phillip spent 14 years as a youth minister in Denison, Texas, Ada, Oklahoma, and Bartlesville, Oklahoma. Since then, he has served as a preaching minister in Granite City, Illinois, Jenks, Oklahoma, and currently in Marshall, Texas. Phillip and Krista have two children. Their son Brandyn is married to Emily. Their daughter Tori is married to Ross Saffell. Phillip and Krista are the proud grandparents of two grandsons named Judah and Jordan, and one granddaughter named Joanna Grace.

You can contact Phillip at Phillip.Treat@EHCOC.org